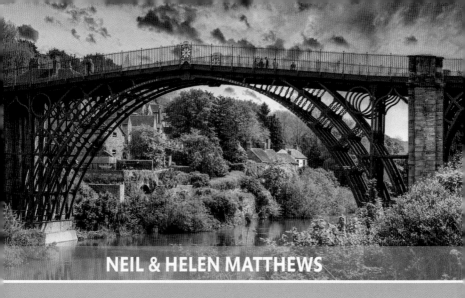

NEIL & HELEN MATTHEWS

HERITAGE WEEKENDS

52 BREAKS EXPLORING BRITAIN'S PAST

Bradt GUIDES

Bradt Guides Ltd, UK
Globe Pequot Press Inc, USA

COVID-19

Please note that research for this guide was carried out during the Covid-19 pandemic. Because of the impact of the crisis on tourism, some businesses or services listed in the text may no longer operate. We will post any information we have about these on ⟠bradtguides.com/updates. And we'd of course be grateful for any updates you can send us during your own travels, which we will add to that page for the benefit of future travellers.

First edition published July 2022
Bradt Guides Ltd
31a High Street, Chesham, Buckinghamshire, HP5 1BW, England
www.bradtguides.com
Print edition published in the USA by The Globe Pequot Press Inc,
PO Box 480, Guilford, Connecticut 06437-0480

Text copyright © 2022 Bradt Guides Ltd
Map copyright © 2022 Bradt Guides Ltd; includes map data © OpenStreetMap contributors
Photographs copyright © 2022 Individual photographers (see below)
Project Manager: Anna Moores
Editor: Samantha Cook
Cover research: Ian Spick, Bradt Guides

ISBN: 9781784778439

British Library Cataloguing in Publication Data
A catalogue record for this book is available from the British Library

Photographs © individual photographers credited beside images & also those picture libraries credited as follows: Alamy.com (A); awl-images.com (AWL); Dreamstime.com (DT); Shutterstock.com (S); Superstock.com (SS)
Front cover TOP: Ring of Brodgar, Orkney (Danita Delimont Stock/AWL); BELOW: Beatles statue, Liverpool (cowardlion/S)
Back cover Beaumaris Castle, Anglesey (Tomas Marek/S)
Title page Shropshire's Ironbridge Gorge (Davelees/S)

Map David McCutcheon FBCart.S

Typeset and designed by Ian Spick, Bradt Guides
Production managed by Page Bros Ltd; printed in the UK
Digital conversion by www.dataworks.co.in

ABOUT THE AUTHORS

Heritage Weekends is **Helen and Neil Matthews'** second book for Bradt, following *Slow Travel: The Chilterns and the Thames Valley* in 2019. Both have written history books based on their PhD theses: Pen & Sword published Helen's *The Legitimacy of Bastards: The Place of Illegitimate Children in Later Medieval England* (2019) and Neil's *Victorians and Edwardians Abroad: the Beginning of the Modern Holiday* (2016).

ACKNOWLEDGEMENTS

Researching and writing a guidebook during a pandemic and its aftermath is not something we'd like to repeat. Nonetheless it's been a positive reaffirmation of the extraordinary heritage that everyone in these islands shares. We'd like to thank the team at Bradt for turning our words into a beautiful final product.

For help, advice and encouragement of various types, thanks also to Mike Bagshaw, Laura Bogard, John Brazier, Peter Burley, Lynsey Clague, Iwan ap Dafydd, Adam Davis, Richard Davis, Katie Featherstone, Darren Flint, Donald Greig, Gemma Hall, Kirsten Hamilton, Tim Hannigan, Vicky Inglis, John J Johnston, Suzanne King, Marie Kreft, Tim Locke, Anna McNally, Laurence Mitchell, Helen Moat, Derfel Owen, Alexandra Richards, Rebecca Rideal, Fiona Ryland, Mark Rowe, Kate Simon, Jill Starley-Grainer, Matthew Sweet and Antonia Windsor.

We dedicate this book to everyone in our heritage industry, whatever their role, as well as the archivists, archaeologists, historians, researchers and teachers who help us all to understand and appreciate Britain's past.

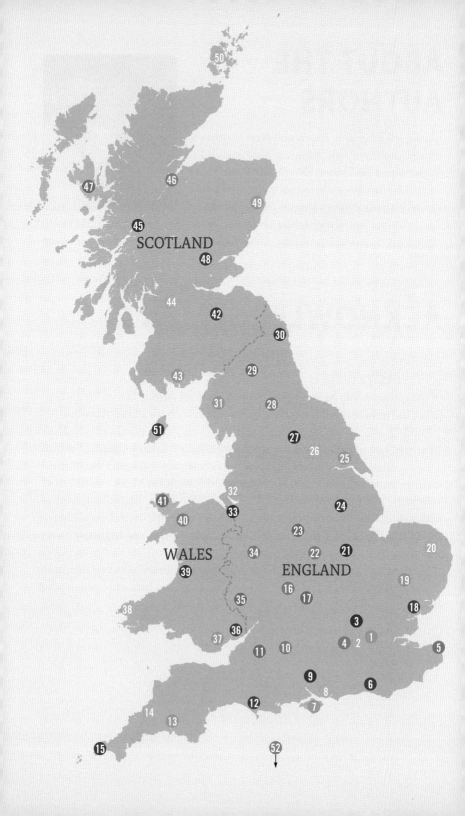

CONTENTS

FEEDBACK REQUEST

At Bradt Guides we're aware that guidebooks start to go out of date on the day they're published – and that you, our readers, are out there in the field doing research of your own. So why not tell us about your experiences? Contact us on ✉ info@bradtguides.com. We will forward emails to the author who may post updates on the Bradt website at �⟨ bradtguides.com/updates. Alternatively, you can add a review of the book to Amazon, or share your adventures with us on social media: 🖪 BradtGuides 🐦 BradtGuides & DrNeilMatthews & HMatthews67 📷 BradtGuides & nmatthews68 & hsmatthews17.

↑ Time to spare on our Avebury weekend? Visit Cherhill White Horse, (page 59). (stocker1970/S) → Museum of Island Life, Skye (page 237). (stocker1970/S)

INTRODUCTION

History and heritage – traditions, objects and creations that have passed down to us through the centuries – are an integral part of British life. History is a staple of publishing, TV, films and the stage (who'd have thought we'd have a hit musical celebrating the lives of Henry VIII's six wives?) Millions of us visit our wealth of historical sites each year, and over five million have joined heritage organisations that preserve, excavate, explain and promote those sites. Our past is one of our greatest passions, and a major attraction for visitors from all over the world.

That passion also generates controversy: whether it's the regular reviews of the history curriculum for schools, recent debates about the significance of statues or the prominence of the Black Lives Matter movement. A simple truth underlies these and other debates: history is always contested. Our understanding of the past evolves all the time, in the light of new evidence, new interpretations and new theories. History isn't here to make us feel good about ourselves, although what we find may move or inspire us. We can hear the voices of one section of humanity without silencing others.

Heritage Weekends includes itineraries for a wide range of historical sites and stories, to help you explore for yourself and draw your own conclusions. Roaming round England, Wales, Scotland and two dependencies, we've picked out 52 locations where you can enjoy getting closer to our natural, architectural, industrial or cultural heritage. Some are off the mainstream tourism track, neglected or underrated places that deserve more attention. Others are famous, but you may see them in a new light.

It's time to visit some of the most important, beautiful, diverse, fascinating and eccentric examples of British heritage; from mines to mansions and everything in between. Whether you're planning a long-distance break or exploring your own backyard, pack your Jane Austen bonnet, make sure the kids have brought their Viking swords – and join us for this magical history tour.

USING THIS GUIDE

Heritage Weekends comprises 52 ideas for weekends with historical and heritage themes. Each entry comprises a brief overview; a summary of the **star attractions**; and the **essentials** on how to get there, **where to stay** and **where to eat**, with further ideas for trips and activities if you have **time to spare**. The longer entries suggest two-day **itineraries** and some have boxes that **focus on** one particular aspect of the location or the wider context. The itineraries are only suggestions! You may prefer to spend more time at specific attractions and less time at others, according to your interests. While we have not highlighted them specifically, plenty of vegetarian, vegan, plant-based and gluten-free eating options are available.

The steep stairs and uneven paths which characterise many heritage sites can present a challenge for **accessibility.** Fortunately, many sites now prioritise access for everyone, with lifts, handrails, braille guides and notices, accessible visitor centres, handling collections and sensory experiences. The recent transformation project at Dorset Museum (page 67) is an excellent example of what's possible. Check the relevant websites for details of facilities at individual attractions before visiting.

Note that a number of historic houses in this guidebook offer unique accommodation within the main property, or on the estate, while many visitor attractions that we mention run their own cafés, tea rooms or restaurants.

↑ Castell Coch, near Cardiff (page 178). (Pepgooner/S)

We don't have space to list every one of these accommodation and eating options, but they're often a wonderful way to add an extra historic touch to your weekend.

Many sites and properties are managed by, or affiliated to, one or more national or UK-wide heritage organisations. To minimise duplication, we use their initial abbreviations in the text and we've listed their websites here:

Art Fund (AF) ⌘ artfund.org

CADW (CW) ⌘ cadw.gov.wales

English Heritage (EH)
⌘ english-heritage.org.uk

Historic Houses (HH) ⌘ historichouses.org

Historic Scotland (HS)
⌘ historicenvironment.scot

Jersey Heritage (JH) ⌘ jerseyheritage.org

Landmark Trust (LT) ⌘ landmarktrust.org.uk

Manx National Heritage (MNH)
⌘ manxnationalheritage.im

National Trust (NT) ⌘ nationaltrust.org.uk

National Trust for Scotland (NTS) ⌘ nts.org.uk

Royal Horticultural Society (RHS) ⌘ rhs.org.uk

Joining one or more of these heritage bodies may mean you can visit free or at a reduced cost, or gain access to special events or facilities, at some attractions. The

↑ Verulamium Museum, St Albans (page 15). (SS)

standard entrance ticket for various museums, galleries and exhibition centres doubles as an annual pass, while entry to some others is free; this is often the case if educational institutions or local authorities run them. Please check the relevant websites before you visit.

For transport, we've tried wherever we can to suggest public transport alternatives. In many cases, taking the train may be the best option. As with the heritage organisations above, we use the train companies' initials in the text and we've listed their websites here:

Avanti West Coast (AV) ✎ avantiwestcoast.co.uk
Chiltern (CH) ✎ chilternrailways.co.uk
East Midland (EM)
✎ eastmidlandsrailways.co.uk
Great Western (GWR) ✎ gwr.com
Greater Anglia (GA) ✎ greateranglia.co.uk
London North Eastern (LNER) ✎ lner.co.uk
Northern (NR) ✎ northernrailway.co.uk
ScotRail (SC) ✎ scotrail.co.uk

Southeastern (SE) ✎ southeasternrailway.co.uk
Southern (SR) ✎ southernrailway.com
South Western (SW)
✎ southwesternrailway.com
Thameslink (TH) ✎ thameslinkrailway.com
TransPennine Express (TP) ✎ tpexpress.co.uk
Transport for Wales (TW) ✎ tfwrail.wales
West Midlands (WM)
✎ westmidlandsrailway.co.uk

A NOTE ON TIME PERIODS

This book covers a reasonably wide range in terms of locations and types of heritage. Defining time periods can be contentious. For this book we've used the following definitions:

NEOLITHIC AGE c4000BC–c2500BC
BRONZE AGE c2500BC–c800BC
IRON AGE c800BC–AD43
ROMAN From the Roman invasion of AD43 to the late 5th century
EARLY MEDIEVAL From the late 5th century to the end of the 10th century
MEDIEVAL The 11th, 12th and 13th centuries
LATE MEDIEVAL The 14th and 15th centuries
TUDOR 1485–1603, the dynasty which began with Henry VII and ended with Elizabeth I
STUART 1603–1714, starting with the accession of James I (who was already James VI of Scotland) and concluding with the accession of George I

GEORGIAN 1714–1837, covering the reigns of Georges I–IV and William IV
REGENCY 1800–37, reflecting the political position between 1811 and 1820 when George, Prince of Wales, governed as Regent, and also a longer period generally described as the 'Regency era' for its developments in architecture, literature, fashion and other areas
VICTORIAN 1837–1901, the reign of Queen Victoria
EDWARDIAN 1901–14, encompassing the reign of Edward VII (1901–10) and the run-up to World War I (1914–18)

INTERWAR 1918–39, between the end of World War I and the outbreak of World War II

WORLD WAR II 1939–45

POSTWAR From 1945 to the present

Each entry shows, in the top right-hand corner of the page, the main time period(s) to which that entry relates. These are only indications, however, and inevitably you may find sites of interest covering a variety of periods. The boundaries, for instance, between early medieval, medieval and late medieval history are sometimes hard to place! If you want to focus on specific eras, the *Index of Periods of History* (page 272) may be useful.

FOCUS ON...

ENGLAND

⌃ Silbury Hill, Avebury. (Kevin Standage/S)

1 LONDON

BEYOND THE BRITISH MUSEUM

I n the heart of Bloomsbury, London's British Museum was the world's first free national public museum when it opened in 1759, and it now attracts six million visitors a year. It's a marvel: two million years of human history, eight million artefacts. In the capital's galaxy of museums and exhibitions, it's a huge, blazing sun. Here's a counterintuitive idea, though. Go beyond the sun; try exploring some of the other stars and planets. There are plenty of excellent, and much smaller, museums close to the British Museum to entertain, amaze, amuse and inform you, covering everything from the dodo to postage stamp design.

THE ITINERARY

DAY 1 Start your museum tour on Euston Road with the **Wellcome Collection** (AF ⚲ wellcomecollection.org), part of the Wellcome Trust global charitable foundation. Its inspiration is the collection of a million objects, including 125,000 medical items, which Sir Henry Wellcome (1853–1936) collected during his life and career in pharmaceuticals. One permanent exhibition, *Being Human*, features 50 artworks and objects on the themes of genetics, minds and bodies, infection and environmental collapse; everything from portable gene sequencers to an astronaut carrying their belongings in a backpack. The other permanent exhibition, *Medicine Man*, showcases items from Wellcome's personal collection – a remarkable range, from prosthetic limbs to the 18th- and 19th-century diagnostic dolls that Chinese women used when consulting doctors. 'Interventions' (comments on specific items) by artists and writers address the collection's colonial context, an admirable way to maintain its relevance.

A short walk away, on University Street, four skeletons gaze down at you from a balcony, while a fifth dangles by its finger bones: an orangutan, a chimpanzee, a human, a gorilla and (dangling) a gibbon. They welcome you to the **Grant Museum of Zoology and Comparative Anatomy** (AF ⚲ ucl.ac.uk/culture/grant-museum-zoology). The Grant has served since 1827 as a teaching collection – originally for the University of London, now for University College London (UCL) – and opened to the public in 1996. It derives its name and much of its collection from Robert Grant (1793–1874), England's first professor of zoology and comparative anatomy. The 68,000 specimens, of which only a fraction is on display, come in a variety of forms: fluid-preserved, pinned entomology, taxidermy, freeze-dried and skeletal. The more poignant examples include extinct species such as quagga – a sub-species of zebra – and dodo. Captions explain among other things that a brain coral is not, in fact, a brain and that the flying lizards on display don't fly (they glide from tree to tree by flaring their ribs into 'wings'). The Micrarium displays some of the museum's smaller exhibits on a wall of microscope slides. It's all wonderful, and much of it is weird: one exhibit, a glass jar full of specimens of the European mole *talpa europaea*, even has its own Twitter account (@GlassJarOfMoles).

SOMETHING OLD, SOMETHING BLUE: LONDON'S BLUE PLAQUES

As you wander between London's museums, you'll come across some of the capital's 950+ **blue plaques** commemorating significant individuals, groups or events and their London connections. The scheme started in 1866 and relies on private donations and proposals from the public. Plaque locations near the British Museum include Great Russell Street, home to architect John Nash, creator of Regent Street and Regent's Park; Gower Street, marking the house in which artists of the Pre-Raphaelite Brotherhood met; and Gordon Square, home to Virginia Woolf, Clive Bell and other members of the Bloomsbury Circle of artists, writers and thinkers who, in Dorothy Parker's words, 'lived in squares, painted in circles and loved in triangles'. See ⊘ english-heritage.org.uk/visit/blue-plaques for further information.

Around the corner on UCL's campus in Malet Street is the **Petrie Museum of Egyptian Archaeology** (⊘ ucl.ac.uk/culture/petrie-museum). It's named after the archaeologist Flinders Petrie (1853–1942), who held England's first chair in Egyptology here and whose personal collection of antiquities forms part of the museum's 80,000 artefacts. Arguably, though, it should be the *Edwards* Museum: the bequest of the writer, traveller and Egyptologist Amelia Edwards (1831–92) enabled the founding both of UCL's Egyptology department and the museum. The collection covers Egypt and the Sudan, and the curators have managed to display a staggering number of items in just two rooms: tools, weapons, jewellery, inscriptions and much else. The Tarkhan dress, from a 1st Dynasty tomb c2800BC, is a highlight; it may be the world's oldest dress. Much of the collection sheds light on Ancient Egyptian beliefs about death and the afterlife. Take a moment to look at the mummy cases, on the outside of which their wealthy owners would have formulae, and symbols such as scarab beetles, inscribed to secure eternal life; and the *shabti*, small figures placed within tombs to perform tasks for the dead.

DAY 2 Just off Gray's Inn Road, **The Postal Museum** (AF ⊘ postalmuseum.org) delves into the history of Britain's postal system. There's a wealth of information on everything from post workers' uniforms to the 17th-century merchants who set up a private Penny Post system, and some strange stories: the 1816 mail coach which fought off an attack by an escaped lion, for example, or the suffragettes who posted themselves to 10 Downing Street. Across the road from the main museum, Mail Rail enables you to ride on the underground network which distributed post across London for much of the 20th century (look out for the dartboard on one platform, and the 'graveyard' of discontinued trains in a siding). Using interactive models, you can try your hand at steering a miniature train, managing the signalling or sorting post inside a travelling post office. The main exhibition area houses some early postboxes – did you know they were once green? – as well as the coaches, motorbikes, cars and vans which have delivered post down the ages. You can even design your own stamp.

A few minutes away, in Lincoln's Inn Fields, **Sir John Soane's Museum** (AF ⊘ soane.org) provides an astounding contrast. This was the home, museum and library of one of Britain's most famous architects, Sir John Soane (1753–1837), who had a private Act of Parliament passed to leave the building to the nation after his death, to be maintained as it was during his lifetime. You will discover Soane's ingenious use of light and various architectural tricks designed to create theatrical spaces for his collection – antiquities, furniture, sculpture, architectural models, paintings. Look upwards in the Breakfast Room to see the shallow dome, concealed skylights and more than 100 mirrors. In the Dome Area, skylights of yellow glass illuminate classical fragments, vases and casts to evoke the ruins of ancient Rome. The same central light bleeds down into the crypt and sepulchral

ESSENTIALS

GETTING THERE & AROUND All the museums listed in this chapter are within an easy walk or a couple of underground stops from the mainline stations at King's Cross, Euston or Marylebone. Holborn and Russell Square tube stations on the Piccadilly line are convenient for several locations (including the British Museum) and accessible directly from London Heathrow. See ⊘ tfl.gov.uk for more.

STAYING **Montague on the Gardens** (⊘ montaguehotel.com) is a Georgian townhouse with an enviable location moments from the British Museum, while the **Thanet Hotel** (⊘ thanethotel.co.uk) is a family-run alternative in nearby Bedford Place. Budget options include the **Morgan Hotel** (⊘ morganhotel.co.uk) on Bloomsbury Street, the **Euston Square Hotel** (⊘ euston-square-hotel.com) on North Gower Street and the **Staunton Hotel** (⊘ stauntonhotel.co.uk) on Gower Street.

EATING For lunch, try **Caffè Tropea** (⊘ caffetropea.co.uk) in Russell Square. **La Fromagerie** (⊘ lafromagerie.co.uk) is one of several cafés and restaurants on Lamb's Conduit Street, between the Postal Museum and Sir John Soane's Museum; if you can't get enough of cheese, you'll enjoy the raclette and cheeseboards (non-cheese options are available).

TIME TO SPARE? *Of course* you'll still visit the **British Museum** (⊘ britishmuseum. org). Our favourite places include the Egyptian sculpture gallery (Room 4) covering three millennia of pharaonic history, with star exhibits such as the Rosetta Stone and the statue

chamber, which contains the sarcophagus of King Seti I and its hieroglyphs that explain how the soul travels through the underworld. The Picture Room, featuring masterpieces by Canaletto, Hogarth and others, uses pairs of timber-hinged 'movable planes' that open up, enabling the room to display three times as many pictures as a normal room of that size.

A mile west, via Oxford Street, the **Cartoon Museum** (AF ⌀ cartoonmuseum.org) promotes cartoons and comic art, whether created for entertainment, political communication, satire or other purposes. Your favourite cartoon strip is almost certainly here, whether it's the adventures of Dennis the Menace in the *Beano*, Britain's longest running children's comic, or Desperate Dan in *The Dandy*. The caricaturists and satirists of bygone ages are well represented: *Temperance Enjoying a Frugal Meal* (1792), by James Gillray, depicts a British monarch (George III) eating a boiled egg. Recent special exhibitions have focused on cartoon depictions of US presidents, the graphic novel series *V for Vendetta* and legendary cartoon characters Judge Dredd and Luther Arkwright.

of Ramesses II; and the clocks and watches gallery (Rooms 38–39) which traces the history of timepieces, with hundreds of working exhibits ticking, striking and chiming the hours. A few minutes away on Euston Road, the **British Library** (⌀ bl.uk) runs an inspiring programme of exhibitions and events. Its Treasures gallery showcases Magna Carta, the works of Shakespeare and other beautiful, exciting and important books, maps and manuscripts. Also on Euston Road, as a change from museums, **St Pancras Church** (⌀ stpancraschurch.org) is worth a diversion, both for the Acropolis-inspired caryatids above the north and south entrances and for the art exhibitions in the crypt. Several other museums within ten to 12 minutes of the British Museum are well worth visiting. To the northeast in Brunswick Square, the **Foundling Museum** (AF ⌀ foundlingmuseum.org. uk) celebrates the work of the Foundling Hospital (founded 1741), the UK's first children's charity, which cared for babies at risk of abandonment for more than two centuries. The **Charles Dickens Museum** (AF ⌀ dickensmuseum.com) is based in 48 Doughty Street, the house where the novelist completed *The Pickwick Papers* and *Oliver Twist*, wrote the whole of *Nicholas Nickleby* and worked on *Barnaby Rudge*, all in less than three years. Just off Tottenham Court Road, **Pollock's Toy Museum** (⌀ pollockstoymuseum.co.uk) houses a global collection of toys, doll's houses, puppets, games and more. The star exhibits are the exquisite handmade Victorian toy theatres, which were East End toy-shop owner Benjamin Pollock's speciality. The **Bow Street Police Museum** (AF ⌀ bowstreetpolicemuseum.org. uk), which opened in 2021, tells the story of London's early law enforcers, the Bow Street Runners, and the creation of the Metropolitan Police. The site was both a police station and a magistrates' court, which has seen famous and infamous defendants including Oscar Wilde, the Pankhurst sisters, the Kray twins and Chile's General Pinochet.

2 TWICKENHAM

HISTORIC HOUSE HEAVEN

Not so long ago Twickenham, nine miles west of Heathrow on London's western edge, was a rural retreat. There have been human settlements by the Thames here since the early Neolithic period. The medieval and early modern periods saw farming, fishing and boatbuilding flourish, while in Georgian times Twickenham's reputation as a scenic retreat was attracting eminent figures such as Sir Joshua Reynolds and Alexander Pope. A railway station opened in 1848 and further development followed. Although modern Twickenham is the largest town in the London borough of Richmond upon Thames, its rural origins still show, and an Act of Parliament protects the view from Richmond Hill. In and around Twickenham stands a handful of outstanding and remarkably varied historic houses: a Neoclassical villa with an Oriental flavour; a ducal power base; an artist's retreat; a Gothic Revival fantasy; and a grand Stuart-era property.

THE ITINERARY

DAY 1 Four miles north of central Twickenham, the original **Osterley Park** (AF, NT, RHS) was a 16th-century creation; the Child family acquired it in 1713. Three generations of the family were Directors, and one Child was a Chairman, of the East India Company (EIC). The fortune they amassed enabled them to commission Robert Adam (1728–92) to remodel the house on Neoclassical lines, demonstrating their educated status. For the entrance, Adam's visit to Italy in 1758 inspired the dramatic double portico which links the wings of the U-shaped red-brick building. Inside the sober grey and white entrance hall, statues of Roman gods await in alcoves: Hercules holds the golden apples he seized from the edge of the world while Apollo, god of poetry and music, leans on a lyre. Further classical references abound in the library, the drawing room and on the Great Staircase. For late 18th-century visitors, the highlight might have been the Etruscan Dressing Room with decorations on the walls, ceiling and matching chimney board in the style of Greek and Etruscan vases, following the popularity of Josiah Wedgwood's work. Throughout the house, the Child family's acquisitions – which no doubt their EIC connections helped them to bring here – catch the eye. Many come from the Far East, such as the Chinese black and gold lacquered chairs in the South Corridor, or the mother-of-pearl models of pagodas and imperial junks in the Long Gallery. The gardens and parkland, including the semi-circular Garden House, make a refreshing contrast. To the west, the Great Meadow provides a reminder of tranquil days past, with lady's bedstraw and knapweeds flourishing.

Robert Adam's services were also in demand three miles southeast of Osterley at **Syon House** (HH, RHS ⏀ syonpark.co.uk), where the 1st Duke and Duchess of Northumberland commissioned him to rework the building's interiors. The impact of Adam and the skilled craftsmen he employed is clear from the sequence of state rooms. Subdued colour palettes in the Great Hall and the Dining Room alternate with more lavish presentation in the Ante Room, the Red Drawing Room

← Osterley Park. (The National Trust Photolibrary/A)

and the Long Gallery. Not everything is as it seems. While a bronze sculpture *The Dying Gaul* faces a statue of Apollo in the apse of the Great Hall, other statues in that space may have mismatched ears or hands. Some items came incomplete from the Continent, to get round local laws forbidding the shipping of complete statues, with parts added later. The glorious cerise Spitalfields silk wall hangings in the Red Drawing Room were rewoven in the 1820s and reversed and rehung later. And look out, in the Long Gallery, for the false bookcase which conceals an exit to the south lawn. The purpose of the roundels of the Percy family lineage (see also *Alnwick & Warkworth*, page 151) was clear: to impress visitors with the owners' pedigree, power and prestige.

A friend of Joseph Mallord William Turner (1775–1851) recalled Turner's wish that 'if he could have his life again, he would have been an architect'. The artist designed Sandycombe Lodge in central Twickenham, now known as **Turner's House** (⊘ turnershouse.org), for himself and his father, and they lived here between 1813 and 1826. This was a rural retreat, a place where the artist could walk, sketch, fish and entertain friends while his father performed the household chores. The Trust which acquired the house has restored it close to its original condition. The bricked-in windows at the front of the handsome exterior hint at the fact that Turner changed his mind frequently as building proceeded. He had help from friends such as Sir John Soane (page 6) – they were professors together at the Royal Academy – and the arches in the small entrance hall and cross-corridor are very Soane-like touches. Two rooms flank the central drawing room, one being the dining room where you can turn the key in the 'speaking clock' for spoken performances of reminiscences from Turner's friends. The two upstairs bedrooms appear modest after such a grand entrance, but a digital telescope in the main bedroom recreates the view as it was in his day, as far as the Thames. The second bedroom houses displays of some of Turner's etchings, along with changing exhibitions which help to build a picture of the great man and of those who lived here after him.

DAY 2 If Turner's House was a retreat, **Strawberry Hill House** (AF, EH ⊘ strawberryhillhouse.org.uk), a mile away, was a case of reinvention. It was the creation of Horace Walpole (1717–97), son of a prime minister and also an antiquarian, collector and author of *The Castle of Otranto* (1764), the first Gothic novel. With help from friends, Walpole spent many years building a house whose style anticipated the Gothic Revival movement and inspired the term 'Strawberry Hill Gothic'. The turreted white exterior gives a hint of the theatricality inside. Walpole wanted the visitor's experience of the house to represent a type of journey, ascending from darkness to light. The entrance hall, with its stone-coloured *trompe l'oeil* tracery on the walls and painted glass lantern with a single candle

↑ The Great Conservatory, Syon House. (Paula French/S) → Strawberry Hill House. (HM)

inside, evokes what Walpole called 'gloomth'. From here you climb to a sequence of ever more dazzling rooms, from the white library to the deep purple of the Holbein Chamber (which holds replicas of 33 copies of portraits by that artist) and the extravagant red and gold of the fan-vaulted Gallery and the Round Drawing Room. Individual elements of room designs borrow from St Paul's and Rouen cathedrals, the Palace of Westminster and the Uffizi Palace in Florence, among other places. Gothic arches run like a golden thread through the house, along with Walpole's collections of coins, medals, pictures and historical memorabilia, and his obsession with his ancestors' role in the Crusades (the suit of armour on the staircase; the painting on the library ceiling; the recurring Saracen's head motif).

In the suburban district of Ham across the river, the splendid **Ham House and Garden** (NT) stands as a monument to the 17th-century high life. The Murrays, later the Dukes and Duchesses of Lauderdale, received Ham from Charles I. After the latter's execution, the family stayed on good terms with Cromwell and in secret

ESSENTIALS

GETTING THERE & AROUND From London Heathrow, various stops on the Piccadilly tube line are convenient for Osterley Park (Osterley), Syon House (Boston Manor, then the E8 bus) or central Twickenham (Hounslow Central, then the 281 bus). Check Transport for London (⊘ tfl.gov.uk) for details. Twickenham has three rail stations: Twickenham itself, St Margarets to the north and Strawberry Hill to the south. From central London, a District line branch stops at Kew Gardens and terminates at Richmond, and several trains per hour run at weekends (SW) between London Waterloo, St Margarets, Twickenham and Strawberry Hill. The nearest main road for Osterley and Syon Park is the A4. The grounds of Marble Hill House (see opposite) lead to the river and **Hammertons Ferry** (⊘ hammertonsferry.com) can take you across the river to Ham.

STAYING The **Alexander Pope Hotel** (⊘ alexanderpope.co.uk) is a short walk from Strawberry Hill House. In neighbouring Richmond upon Thames, **Richmond Hill Hotel** (⊘ richmondhill-hotel.co.uk) blends modern comfort with Georgian style notes such as freestanding roll-top baths.

EATING **Ristorante del Posto** (⊘ delposto.co.uk) on St Margarets Road serves an excellent spaghetti with swordfish, and the ricotta mousse with pistachio is unmissable. The highlight at **Le Salon Privé** (⊘ lesalonprive.net) on Crown Road is cod brandade parcel with carrot puree and lemon sauce. Twickenham's Church Street is home to many cafés.

TIME TO SPARE? Across the Thames from Syon House lie the beautiful and historic **Royal Botanic Gardens, Kew** (⊘ kew.org). A short walk south from Turner's House brings

contact with the exiled Prince Charles, returning to favour when the latter became Charles II. The Lauderdales ensured that Ham became one of Stuart England's grandest homes. Plaster figures on either side of the Great Hall's mantelpiece represent William and Katherine Murray, the first owners, in the guises of Mars and Minerva, the gods of war and wisdom. The black-and-white marble floor is the original. Other Stuart-era features survive: the rare Parisian furniture with dolphin decoration in the North Drawing Room; the original parquet floor, marble fireplace and plaster ceiling in the Queen's Bedchamber; and the Green Closet, housing William's collection of miniatures and small oil paintings. The formal walled gardens are just as fascinating, retaining the spirit of the original. The lawns burst into life each spring with crocuses, tulips, muscari and wild flowers, while the Cherry Garden contains clipped box-hedged compartments full of lavender, with a statue of Bacchus at the centre – the only original piece of garden sculpture to survive at Ham.

you to **Marble Hill House** (AF, EH), a Palladian villa built for George II's mistress in 66 acres of riverside parkland. Ten minutes' walk from Marble Hill House along the riverside, the **Orleans House Gallery** (⊘ orleanshousegallery.org) promotes contemporary artists and holds the Richmond Borough Art Collection, including about 500 local views. Its owners built the remarkable Baroque Octagon Room to entertain royalty; George I, George II and the latter's wife Queen Caroline all visited. Around the corner from Strawberry Hill House, **Pope's Grotto** (⊘ popesgrotto.org.uk) is the extraordinary last surviving aspect of Alexander Pope's villa, into which he incorporated minerals from around the world. Close to Ham House, **Richmond Park** (⊘ royalparks.org.uk) has seven centuries of royal connections; Charles I brought his court here to escape a London plague and introduced the red and fallow deer that still roam freely. Finally, Twickenham Stadium hosts England's rugby union teams and the **World Rugby Museum** (⊘ worldrugbymuseum.com).

↑ Royal Botanic Gardens, Kew. (PhilMacDPhoto/S)

3 ST ALBANS

ROMANS & ROSES

The city of St Albans, around 20 miles north of London, has had several names over the last few millennia. As the Iron Age settlement Verlamion, it was a trading hub for the Celtic Catuvellauni tribe. After the Roman invasion of Britain in AD43 it became Verulamium. The Catuvellauni chose to co-operate with the invaders, so the settlement received 'Latin rights' and grew significantly, with Roman building works including a unique theatre and paved roads, notably Watling Street. By the 4th century AD, the town had gained a new name, St Albans, to mark Alban's martyrdom at Roman hands as punishment for helping a Christian priest (later called Amphibalus) to escape persecution. Over a thousand years later, St Albans witnessed two battles in the Wars of the Roses. By walking around the historic centre, you can trace both the Romans' influence and key locations for the Roses battles.

THE ITINERARY

DAY 1 On St Albans' western side, the **Roman Theatre** (⊘ gorhamburyestate. co.uk) is unique in Britain as a Roman theatre with a stage, instead of the more

↑ Roman Theatre. (Nicola Pulham/S)

familiar amphitheatres of the time. As it developed between the 2nd and 4th centuries, its capacity grew to around 2,000 spectators. Excavations found traces of shops, a shrine and a villa around the theatre. You can find out more about local life in Roman times at the nearby **Verulamium Museum** (⊘ stalbansmuseums. org.uk): a thorough, and impressive, attempt to evoke Roman life, with sections on different subjects such as merchants and markets or death and burials. In the latter, an actor on video plays 'Posthumus', a man whose skeleton was among the many archaeological discoveries, explaining what we can deduce about his life while the skeleton sits, without comment, below the screen. The combination of captioned exhibits, information screens and models in recreations of typical villa rooms works well, with some surprising nuggets of trivia (this is the place to find out how to cook boiled ostrich). Three highlights stand out. The first, the Sandridge Hoard, is a spectacular collection of 159 gold coins, dating to the early 5th century, which was found near the road from Verulamium to Colchester. Most local people of that time would never have owned one gold coin; it seems likely these were the property of an exceptionally wealthy citizen who may have buried them to avoid the risks of robbery on the road. The second is the fine collection of well-preserved wall and ceiling paintings, their rich colours and designs imitating marble, and the mosaics that graced dining and reception rooms as well as bath suites. Tesserae (small cubes) of cut stone or tile and sometimes glass combine in shades of white, blue, brown and grey to beautiful effect. Our favourite is the 'sea god' mosaic featuring Oceanus or Cernunnos (cAD160–190), with protruding horns which may or may not be lobster claws. The third highlight, a short walk from the museum building, is the Hypocaust – an early underfloor heating system which allowed hot air to circulate beneath the floor and through the walls. This hypocaust and the mosaic which covered it are over 1,800 years old, and they may have been part of the reception and meeting rooms of a large town house.

DAY 2 Legend has it that **St Albans Cathedral** (⌂ stalbanscathedral.org) stands on the ground where the Romans executed Alban and where his grave lay. The first church on this site was probably a simple structure, before King Offa of Mercia founded a monastery here in AD793. By 1115 the Normans had rebuilt the abbey church in Romanesque style, and it became England's leading Benedictine abbey for much of the Middle Ages, with many pilgrims visiting the shrines of Alban

↑ St Albans Cathedral. (Pajor Pawel/S)

THE WARS OF THE ROSES

The mid-15th century unrest in England was neither a dispute between Yorkshire and Lancashire, nor anything much to do with roses. (Shakespeare has a lot to answer for.) The Wars of the Roses originated in the unpopular rule of Richard II and struggles between descendants of his uncles, the Dukes of York and Lancaster. Henry Bolingbroke, the son of John of Gaunt, Duke of Lancaster, deposed Richard in 1399 and became Henry IV. His son Henry V died young. Henry V's infant son Henry VI grew up to be pious but weak, with more interest in founding educational establishments than governing (see *Windsor & Eton*, page 20) and prone to favouritism. This alienated some powerful magnates including Richard, Duke of York, who was descended on his paternal and maternal sides from Edward III (Richard II's grandfather). When Henry VI had a breakdown in 1453, York became Protector of England, taking partisan lines in some local disputes; in the north, he supported his Neville in-laws over their neighbours, the Percys. When Henry recovered, he resumed control and summoned the Yorkist leaders to appear before a great council. However, the Yorkists took up arms, marched south and defeated a royalist force at the first Battle of St Albans in May 1455, replacing Henry VI with a Yorkist protectorate. An uneasy peace lasted for four years until hostility broke out again, orchestrated by Henry's formidable wife, Margaret of Anjou. The Yorkist leaders fled abroad, returning in September 1460 with Richard, Duke of York hoping to claim the throne. He was killed at Wakefield that December, and the victorious Lancastrian army marched south towards London, defeating the Yorkists at the second Battle of St Albans in February 1461 (page 18). Richard's son Edward fought back with the help of his cousin Richard Neville, Earl of Warwick (aka 'Warwick the Kingmaker'), defeating the Lancastrians at Towton and becoming Edward IV. Eight years later, Warwick changed sides. His rebellion briefly restored Henry VI to the throne again, but Edward prevailed with victories at Barnet and Tewkesbury in 1471. Edward's death in 1483 left a minor, Edward V, as his successor. The latter's uncle Richard, Duke of Gloucester, claimed the throne as Richard III, but his death at Bosworth in 1485 ushered in the Tudors and ended the Wars of the Roses.

For more on the Battle of Bosworth see page 111. See also *The Nevilles of Raby* (page 138) and *The Percys: Conflicts & Shifting Allegiances* (page 151).

and Amphibalus. After dissolution in 1539 and years of decline, restoration work began under George Gilbert Scott (1811–78) and the church became the cathedral for the new diocese of St Albans. Today the cathedral, witness to centuries of faith, provides a marvellous series of spaces for contemplation. Most of St Alban's shrine, like other parts of the building, is a reconstruction, but the wooden watching loft through which officials monitored it is a 15th-century original; it may be the only surviving example of its type in England. You will also see a reconstruction

of the splendid white shrine of St Amphibalus near the Lady Chapel. Despite the loss of some detail over time, the 13th-century wall paintings in the nave remain vibrant; they were limewashed before being rediscovered six centuries later. Subjects include St Christopher, Thomas Becket and the parting of Alban and Amphibalus. A mixture of architectural styles is evident in various places such as the south transept, where Saxon stone pillars and Roman tiles co-exist in harmony along with a pair of enormous doors that once stood at the main entrance. Look out, too, for the statue of Nicholas Breakspear who, as Adrian IV, remains the only English Pope in history (1154–59). The cathedral also contains several reminders of the Wars of the Roses: red and white roses in the tower ceiling panels; carvings of Yorkist symbols on a screen between the High Altar and St Alban's shrine; and the chapel containing the tomb of Humphrey, Duke of Gloucester (d1447), son of Henry IV, brother of Henry V and uncle of Henry VI.

By leaving the cathedral and walking via the old Abbey Gatehouse towards Fishpool Street, you can find some of the key locations for the second Battle of St Albans (1461; page 17). The walk comprises two loops, each taking around an hour: the first from Fishpool Street round Branch Road, Folly Lane and Catherine Street to the top of St Peters Street, and the second from there along Harpenden Road to Beech Road, Seymour Road and Sandridge Lane. The first retraces the

↑ Beech Bottom Dyke. (HM)

movements of the Lancastrians as they tried to find a way past Yorkist defences. Obstacles included the Tonman Ditch, replaced centuries later by what is now Victoria Park. It was at this end of St Peters Street that the Lancastrians broke through. On the second loop, the Harpenden Road-Beech Road junction marks the point where Yorkists deployed to defend possible attacks from the north. The defences incorporated the Beech Bottom Dyke, a late Iron Age earthwork with steep banks on either side which, even after 2,000 years, remains formidable. This area was open heath and scrub at the time of the battle. Events reached a climax on the site of the playing field on Sandridge Road, where the Yorkists eventually retreated. An avenue of cherry trees, red and white blossom alternating, commemorates the battle.

Day 2 walk adapted from Burley, Elliott and Watson, The Battles of St Albans *(Barnsley: Pen & Sword, 2007). Thanks to Dr Peter Burley for taking us around the route.*

ESSENTIALS

GETTING THERE St Albans City station is 20 minutes from London St Pancras by train (TH) and St Albans Abbey station is linked with London via Watford Junction (⊘ abbeyline. org.uk). The main road links are the M1 (J6), A1(M) and M25 (J21A and 22). Parking is a challenge, so it's often simplest to find a car park in the town centre and explore on foot.

STAYING In Fishpool Street, **St Michael's Manor Hotel** (⊘ stmichaelsmanor.com) has 30 bedrooms within five acres of country gardens, complete with its own lake. Just over a mile outside the city, **Sopwell House Hotel** (⊘ sopwellhouse.co.uk), a splendid Georgian spa hotel, has historical links to Anne Boleyn and Lord Mountbatten.

EATING For a quick stop, have tea in the old courtroom in **St Albans Museum** (see below). **Lussmanns** (⊘ lussmanns.com), near the cathedral, champions sustainable food; the North African spiced cod cheeks and the lamb and date ragout are excellent. Make sure to visit at least one of the city's 100-odd pubs; St Albans is the home of the Campaign for Real Ale.

TIME TO SPARE? The highlight of **St Albans Museum** on St Peter's Street (⊘ stalbansmuseums.org.uk) is its courtroom, one of the few remaining pre-Victorian examples in Britain; at the time of writing, the cells from which the accused went up to stand in the dock are undergoing restoration. Seven miles east of the city, **Hatfield House** (⊘ hatfield-house.co.uk), a splendid Jacobean home to the Earls and Marquesses of Salisbury, has been a filming location for *Sherlock Holmes*, *The King's Speech*, *Rebecca*, *Bridgerton* and many other productions.

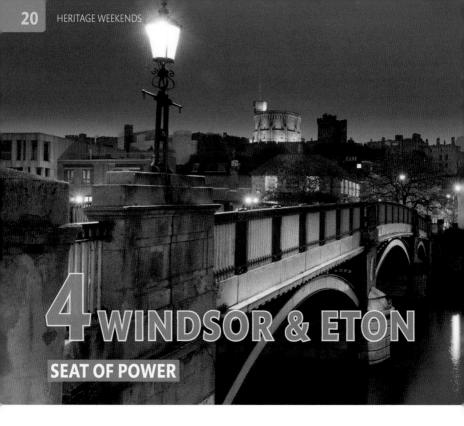

4 WINDSOR & ETON

SEAT OF POWER

The historic market town of Windsor, on the banks of the Thames, has been a seat of British power for close to a millennium. There may have been a significant settlement before William I chose to construct a castle here – Peascod Street is probably of Saxon origin – but William's decision has shaped Windsor ever since. Not content with having the world's most famous castle, Windsor is also neighbour to Eton, home of the world's most famous school (don't let the word 'College' in its name mislead you). Both college and castle embody privilege and power: how to retain and display the former, and how to train for the latter.

THE ITINERARY

DAY 1 From central Windsor, cross the **Windsor Town Bridge** to find yourself in Eton. On its narrow High Street, red-brick buildings alternate with pastel façades, antique shops, gentlemen's outfitters and antiquarian bookshops; Union flags and hanging baskets complete the cheerful scene. A display on the other side of the bridge will help you find the main sights on the **Eton Walkway** which loops round the High Street. The most striking is Antony Gormley's *Edge II* statue on Common House Lane – a man halfway up a building, body parallel to the road. Eton life revolves around **Eton College** (⊘ etoncollege.com), which has educated 20 British prime ministers and many other notables. Henry VI established the

↑ Windsor Town Bridge. (Ollie Taylor/S)

college in 1440 for the free education of 70 poor boys who would then go on to King's College, Cambridge (founded in the following year). Henry's statue stands in the courtyard, where organised tours begin. Walk on his right-hand side as per tradition, so that your heart is closer to him and your sword arm is free. The college chapel features post-war stained-glass windows designed by John Piper (1903–92), which illustrate four parables and four miracles; and Flemish wall paintings, which were hidden by whitewash for centuries, telling of the miracles of the Virgin Mary. Look out, in the Upper School and the College Hall, for boys' names carved into the wood panelling by the pupils themselves, including a young Percy Bysshe Shelley. As a sad counterpoint, memorials in the chapel antechamber and around the cloisters remember many Old Etonians who died in battle. As Thomas Gray, an Old Etonian, put it in his *Elegy Written in a Country Churchyard*: 'The paths of glory lead but to the grave.'

DAY 2 Some of Windsor's most interesting sights are on a small scale. Queen Charlotte Street claims, at 17yds, to be the shortest street in Britain, and you squeeze through medieval cobbled streets to reach Church Street Gardens, the town's smallest public space. Nearby Drury House, now a restaurant, was once the abode of Nell Gwyn, with a tunnel through to the castle for secret liaisons with her

↑ Eton College. (travellight/S)

↑ Windsor Castle. (nitsawan katerattanakul/S)

lover, Charles II. That merry monarch was one of three who have, arguably, had the greatest influence on the development of **Windsor Castle** (⌀ royalcollection. org.uk) over 950 years. William the Conqueror chose the site and built the original castle, Edward III rebuilt it in Gothic style and Charles redeveloped it as a Baroque palace and a response to his cousin Louis XIV's pet projects of the Louvre and Versailles. Today, as the world's oldest and largest inhabited castle, Windsor can seem every bit as overwhelming as those French masterpieces. As you go through the State and Semi-State Apartments (the latter open in autumn and winter), you're only seeing a fraction of the rooms; there are 951 in the Upper Ward alone. So take your time and focus on a few marvels. Look down, in the Waterloo Chamber, at the largest seamless carpet in existence (probably). Check out the massive marble bust of Nelson in the Queen's Guard Chamber, or the life-size tiger's head of gold with rock crystal teeth in the Grand Vestibule. Look up, in St George's Chapel, to admire the magnificent fan-vaulted ceiling at the east end, with the insignia of the Knights of the Garter. Our favourite item is **Queen Mary's Dolls' House**, which is not a toy but a fully furnished architectural

ESSENTIALS

GETTING THERE Regular trains from London (all GWR) take less than an hour, from Paddington to Windsor & Eton Central or from Waterloo to Windsor & Eton Riverside, with both Windsor stations being less than ten minutes' walk to the castle. Windsor is 12 miles from London Heathrow (with direct bus links) and is well connected by the motorway network (M4 J6, M3 J3, M25 J13 or M40 J4).

STAYING On Eton's High Street, **Gilbey's** restaurant (⌀ gilbeygroup.com) offers a luxury studio suite and three townhouse bedrooms. The **Castle Hotel** (⌀ castlehotelwindsor. com) offers four-star luxury across the road, as the name suggests, from Windsor Castle.

EATING For a coffee stop, the **Enigma Café** (⌀ enigma-coffeeshop.business.site) on Eton's High Street has an excellent range of homemade cakes. More substantial fare is available a few doors down at **Gilbey's** (see above). For lunch in Windsor we recommend the **Two Brewers** pub (⌀ twobrewerswindsor.co.uk) in Park Street, or the French cuisine of **A la Russe** (⌀ alarusse.co.uk) near the castle. Five miles northwest, in the 16th-century village of Bray, lie two three-Michelin-starred restaurants: the **Waterside Inn** (⌀ waterside-inn.co.uk) and Heston Blumenthal's **Fat Duck** (⌀ thefatduck.co.uk).

TIME TO SPARE? Eton College opens the **Museum of Antiquities**, **Museum of Eton Life** and **Natural History Museum** (⌀ collections.etoncollege.com) on Sunday afternoons. On Windsor's eastern edge, **Windsor Great Park** (⌀ windsorgreatpark.co.uk)

model of the ideal of an early 20th-century English gentleman's house. Originally a gift for the wife of George V, the house was shown at the 1924 British Empire Exhibition before finding a permanent home at Windsor. Its miniature library includes tiny bound volumes by over 170 authors, while the rest of the house and its basement garage showcases miniatures of great British brands of the time, from Huntley & Palmers biscuits to Rolls-Royce cars. It all exudes exquisite nostalgia in miniature for a lost world.

There is more to Windsor than the castle. On the high street, a short walk from Castle Hill, **Windsor Guildhall** is a stripling of a mere three centuries. Its splendid appearance owes much to four pillars which the town burghers insisted were necessary for weight-supporting purposes. According to a local story Christopher Wren, who oversaw the building's completion, advised against this arrangement, but the pillars went up anyway, leaving a gap at the top. The Guildhall now houses **Windsor Museum** (⌖ windsormuseum.org.uk), with exhibits going all the way back to the Stone Age. There are royal artefacts here, too; the 'silhouette jug' with profiles of Elizabeth II and Prince Philip is the most striking example.

includes a section of stone ruins from Leptis Magna (now part of modern Libya). The park is also home to **Frogmore House** (⌖ rct.uk), a private retreat for the Royal Family that is open to visitors for a few days each year. Four miles southeast along the Thames is **Runnymede** (NT), site of the 1215 sealing of Magna Carta, while seven miles west of Windsor, **Dorney Court** (AF, HH ⌖ dorneycourt.co.uk) is a splendidly eccentric Grade I-listed Tudor manor house, where the first pineapple grown in England was (according to stories) presented to Charles II.

↑ Leptis Magna ruins in Windsor Great Park. (Ion Mes/S)

5 THANET

SHELLS & SHELTERS

Thanet, in northeastern Kent, was once an island, separated from the mainland of southeastern England by the Wantsum Channel until the channel silted up. The last ship sailed through in 1672 and Thanet is now a peninsula, with flat marshland where the channel used to be. There were major Stone Age settlements on Thanet, the Romans landed at least one invasion force here and later, according to Bede, the Jutes Hengist and Horsa helped Vortigern, the British king, to repel other tribes, for which he rewarded them with the Isle. St Augustine landed here in AD597 on a mission from Rome to propagate Christianity, founding a cathedral and abbey in Canterbury. More recent invasions have taken different forms: Thanet was a popular Victorian day-trip destination for London holidaymakers. The area has strong associations with some great creative figures of the past, from Charles Dickens in Broadstairs to JMW Turner in Margate and Augustus Pugin in Ramsgate. Thanet also celebrates the subterranean with a beautiful shell grotto, chalk caves with a chequered past, a curious crustacean exhibition and wartime tunnels that saved thousands of lives.

↑ 'Mrs Booth', near the Turner Contemporary Gallery. (Tourism, Thanet District Council)

THE ITINERARY

DAY 1 Start in the seaside town of Margate, on Grotto Hill, with a lady in a shell suit: not a 1980s fashion disaster, but a clever artwork which has created the lady and her outfit from shells. This greets you at the **Shell Grotto** (⌀ shellgrotto. co.uk), which has been open to the public since 1838. The origins of this curious space are a mystery. It is unlikely to have been a wealthy landowner's frivolous indulgence, as it was not on the grounds of a large estate, and nobody has found any documents predating its discovery in 1835. So it may have been a temple, a secret meeting place for a club or society, a long-lost folly or an elaborate joke. Even the circumstances of the grotto's discovery are the subject of conflicting stories. We do know that it's just over 100ft long, with a chalk stairway leading down via a winding passage to a dome and rotunda space and an altar chamber. There are 4.6 million shells, with cockles, whelks, mussels and oysters combining into patterns which may be symbolic or purely artistic. Use your imagination – or the conjectures and illustrations from a 1954 pamphlet which tried to crack the enigma – and you may see a turtle, a serpent and a skeleton, or the gods Bacchus and Ganesha. Whatever the truth of the grotto's creation, it is a beautiful site. In nearby Northdown Road, the **Margate Caves** (⌀ margatecaves.co.uk; see ad,

↑ Margate Caves. (Simon Richmond)

inside back cover) were 18th-century chalk mines before a house was constructed on the site. The caves' (re-)discovery a century later may have been thanks to a busy gardener, or local rabbits. Enterprising later owners promoted 'Vortigern's Caves' as a tourist attraction and reimagined them as a base for local smugglers. Some of the colourful wall paintings depicting crocodiles, elephants, boars and hippopotami are creative rather than authentic, but there are also 'ghost' paintings, the remnants of much older artwork… including a skull. The space is taller and much longer, at 309ft, than the Shell Grotto, but it has its own atmosphere.

Back towards the seafront, the **Margate Museum** (⊘ visitthanet.co.uk), in Market Place in the Old Town, houses a series of displays in the old police station and magistrates' court. One covers the history of nearby **Dreamland** (⊘ dreamland.co.uk), Britain's oldest surviving amusement park, and other seaside entertainments (keep your eyes peeled for a tiny carriage from a flea circus), while a maritime room is full of models of the steamers that used to bring trippers from London Bridge. The stars of the display upstairs are a prehistoric skeleton, whom the museum staff christened Cecil, and a collection of dolls used to illustrate treatments at the Royal Sea Bathing Hospital during the 19th century. Around the corner in Broad Street, the **Crab Museum** (⊘ crabmuseum.org) explores, with a large dose of humour, the lifecycle of crabs and their importance to a biodiverse ecosystem. The star exhibit, a diorama of a fictional 1926 English village of Crabton-on-Tyne, features various types of crab wearing miniature items of human clothing; if you've ever wondered what a crab looks like with a VOTES FOR WOMEN ribbon, the answer is here. In the toilet is a bonus 'Carb Museum' of carbohydrates 'devised by one of our directors, who is severely dyslexic'. Finish the day down on the harbour with another shell lady; a bronze sculpture of Sophia Booth, Turner's Margate landlady and later his partner. The young Turner went to school in Margate and, in later life, over 100 of his paintings featured views of the harbour. The **Turner Contemporary** gallery (⊘ turnercontemporary.org) stands on the site of Sophia Booth's house.

DAY 2 Three miles southeast of Margate, Broadstairs was already a popular resort by 1892, when George and Weedon Grossmith's *The Diary of a Nobody,* in which the central character Mr Pooter takes his holiday in 'good old Broadstairs', was published. In 1914, while recovering from illness, John Buchan wrote here, working a fictionalised Broadstairs into the climax of *The Thirty-Nine Steps.* The most famous literary visitor, however, was Charles Dickens (1812–70), who spent time in the town on numerous occasions over 20 years. He stayed at Fort House, once a coastal observation station, while writing *David Copperfield*; the building, now inappropriately called Bleak House, continues to loom over Broadstairs' main beach, Viking Bay. Further along the seafront, while staying in Albion Street,

Dickens observed Mary Pearson Strong taking great exception to donkeys in front of her home. The pair became friends and the writer based his character Betsey Trotwood and her home on Miss Strong and her cottage; today it is home to the **Dickens House Museum** (⊘ visitbroadstairs.co.uk) in which you can view early editions of Dickens' novels and some of his letters about Broadstairs. The other main point of interest in Broadstairs stands tall opposite the railway station: the **Crampton Tower Museum** (⊘ cramptontower.co.uk), housed in the tower that formed part of the town's first public water supply system. The main focus of this transport museum is the life and works of local man Thomas Crampton (1816–88), best known for designing the Crampton locomotive and for laying, in 1851, the first successful cable for a submarine telegraph between Dover and Calais. There are informative displays on the evolution of coaches, mail coaches, trams and buses, and several excellent model railways.

Four miles south of Margate, Ramsgate was a medieval farming and fishing hamlet before developing as a port and later, like Margate and Broadstairs, a tourist resort. Thanks to George IV, the harbour here is the only one in mainland Britain to have the designation of Royal Harbour. Perhaps because of its proximity to continental Europe, Ramsgate has a significant record as a military base. Troops were quartered here during the Napoleonic Wars, RAF Manston played a role in World War II and the harbour was the main assembly point for the fleet of small craft that evacuated British forces from Dunkirk in 1940. On 24 August of that year, more than 500 German bombs dropped on the town, and the **Ramsgate Tunnels** (⊘ ramsgatetunnels.org) – which you can explore via guided tours – saved countless lives, on that day and throughout the war. The tunnels extended for over three miles, with 11 entrances at strategic points within five minutes' walk of most areas. The installation of chemical toilets, bunk beds, seating, lighting and a PA system enabled locals to use the tunnels for shelter, to move around town during an air raid or even to take up residence underground if they had lost their homes. The tunnels and the dramatic stories of those who built and used them represent the best of British stoicism. A mile southwest, slightly back from the seafront, stands a more personal construction, the **Shrine of St Augustine and National Pugin Centre** (⊘ augustine-pugin.org.uk). The shrine was the creation of Augustus Pugin (1812–52), the architect who led the Gothic Revival movement and designed much of the new Palace of Westminster. In the wake of laws ending discrimination against Catholics, Pugin – himself a Catholic – wanted to create a tribute to St Augustine, who landed near here. The interior uses sandstone from Whitby and combines encaustic (hot wax) floor tiles, typical Gothic Revival pointed arches and beautiful stained-glass windows to great effect. Look for Pugin's initials in the Chantry Chapel; he and other family members are buried in the vault beneath.

ESSENTIALS

GETTING THERE Thanet is just over an hour from London St Pancras (SE) on a high-speed rail link, with easy connections of five to ten minutes between Margate, Ramsgate and Broadstairs. The main routes by road use the M25 to get around London, then the M2.

STAYING Margate's **Walpole Bay Hotel** (⊘ walpolebayhotel.co.uk) offers a glimpse of interwar holidays with its Otis trellis gated lift from 1927 and an exhibition of local fossils and artefacts from the hotel's 100-year history. Next door to the Shrine of St Augustine in Ramsgate, you can stay in **The Grange** (LT), which Pugin built as a family home, with its own private chapel and a tower from which he could observe local ships. The Georgian **Royal Albion Hotel** in Broadstairs (⊘ albionbroadstairs.co.uk) has excellent views of Viking Bay; Charles Dickens stayed here.

EATING If you like your food with a sea view, there's plenty of choice, from **Margate Coffee Shed** (⊘ margatecoffeeshed.co.uk) on the seafront to Ramsgate's Grade II-listed **Royal Victoria Pavilion** (⊘ jdwetherspoon.com), whose design derives inspiration from Robert Adam orangeries and the Little Theatre at Versailles, or **Archive** (⊘ archivehomestore.co.uk), which serves fresh quiche down by Ramsgate harbour. **Scissortail** (⊘ scissortail.co.uk) in Margate's Old Town makes excellent espresso brownies. Broadstairs has its share of good places to eat: try **Sardinia** (⊘ sardiniarestaurant.co.uk) on Albion Street.

TIME TO SPARE? A short walk up the road from the Shell Grotto, Margate's **Tudor House** (⊘ visitthanet.co.uk) will celebrate its 500th anniversary in 2025; look for the frieze that suggests that a Prince of Wales once stayed here. On Margate's waterfront, **Turner Contemporary** (⊘ turnercontemporary.org) offers superb views of the land, sea, skies and light that inspired the artist, as well as showing work by some of his modern-day successors, while **Dreamland** (⊘ dreamland.co.uk) provides a nostalgic trip back to the amusement parks of old. Ramsgate's Church Hill is home to two quirky attractions, the **Micro Museum** (⊘ themicromuseum.org), which explores the history of computing, and **This Museum is Not Obsolete** (⊘ this-museum-is-not-obsolete. com), celebrating experimental and – despite the wonderful name – obsolete scientific and musical technology. Pugin's house **The Grange** (see above) is open for timed, guided tours. Just outside central Ramsgate, on the site of what was an RAF station until 1996, the **RAF Manston History Museum** (⊘ rafmanston.co.uk) showcases a marvellous array of aircraft and other exhibits including, for your inner 007, a selection of ejector seats. The neighbouring **Spitfire & Hurricane Memorial Museum** (⊘ spitfiremuseum. org.uk) focuses on these legendary aircraft and gives you the chance to take off, fly and land a Spitfire, via a simulator.

6 BRIGHTON & HOVE

BY GEORGE

The East Sussex city of Brighton and Hove was in Anglo-Saxon times the fishing village of Bristelmestune, later Brighthelmstone. Today its nicknames include 'Doctor Brighton', a reference to its 18th-century success in attracting visitors who believed in the health-giving properties of seawater, thanks to the writings of Dr Richard Russell; and 'London-by-the-sea', recognising its popularity as a day-trip destination from the capital and a desirable place to live for London commuters. Films such as *Brighton Rock* and *Quadrophenia* portray the city's seamy side (this was a popular place for 'dirty weekends'), but tolerance and wry humour are also part of Brighton's character. There's a large LGBTQ population here, while BBC Radio's commentary on the local football team's narrow failure to win the FA Cup in 1983 inspired the best-ever fanzine title, *And Smith Must Score*. The city owes its most famous landmark, the Royal Pavilion, to the enthusiasms of George, Prince of Wales (1762–1830), later Prince Regent and George IV. The fashionable crowd followed him here, with many living in the neighbouring village of Hove where residential developments such as Brunswick Square gave the great and the good a refined base away from 'popular' Brighton. Hove still sets itself a little apart; when someone asked Laurence Olivier if he lived in Brighton, the story goes that he replied, 'Hove, actually', a phrase that persists to this day.

THE ITINERARY

DAY 1 The **Royal Pavilion** (AF ⏣ brightonmuseums.org.uk) is one man's extravagant lifestyle writ large. Prince George first came to Brighton in 1783, on medical advice that the air and seawater would ameliorate his gout. He rented a small lodging house three years later and converted it to a modest Neoclassical structure with a central domed rotunda surrounded by Ionic columns; this was known as the Marine Pavilion. A new stable block in the Indian style was added two decades later. Between 1815 and 1823, by which time George was Regent and then King, John Nash (1752–1835) picked up the Oriental theme and constructed an exterior of minarets, domes and pinnacles. This exterior, and the lavish interiors created at the same time, now live again thanks to extensive restoration. George's passion for Orientalism and for excess is everywhere: the one-ton chandelier in the Banqueting Room hanging from a silver dragon's claws; the palm tree columns and carved dolphin furniture in the Banqueting Room Gallery; the lotus chandeliers in the Music Room, with more carved dragons supporting the window draperies; and the paintings of Chinese scenes in the Yellow Bow Rooms, in which George's brothers the Dukes of York and Clarence stayed. The kitchen, with its high lantern ceilings and installations, including five spits, enabled entertaining on a massive scale. A menu from an 1817 banquet for Grand Duke Nicholas of Russia includes eight soups, eight types of fish, 40 entrées, eight roasts and 32 desserts.

The Pavilion gardens today host the **Brighton Museum & Art Gallery** (AF ⏣ brightonmuseums.org.uk) which outgrew the Pavilion rooms in which it started

← The Royal Pavilion. (Stanley Loong/S)

and acquired its own building in 1873. The art and design section and the Ancient Egypt exhibition both impress. The 'Images of Brighton' gallery remembers, among other people and events, influential residents such as Dr Russell and the pitched battles between the Mods and Rockers of the 1950s. 'Queer the Pier', a community-curated celebration of writers, artists, performers, activists and ordinary people, examines Brighton's attraction for the LGBTQ community. The highlight of the museum may be Willett's Popular Pottery, a collection of 2,000 ceramic items from the Georgian and Victorian eras belonging to Henry Willett, a local brewer. Willett organised his collection into social themes, from agriculture and drama to royalty and military heroes, from 'domestic incidents' to 'conviviality and teetotalism'. Some exhibits are political, even satirical, while others are commemorative; the display as a whole is fascinating.

DAY 2 Today's a seafront day. Wander down to the Grade II-listed **Brighton Palace Pier** (⊘ brightonpier.co.uk), which retains the balustrades, two entrance kiosks and its basic structure from its construction in 1899. There are hints of Brighton's maritime heritage in the nearby **Fishing Quarter** (⊘ seafrontheritage.co.uk), between the Pavilion and the remains of the West Pier. The Quarter is a legacy of the 1990s when Brightonian Andy Durr campaigned with local fishermen to promote the city's working heritage – before the Georgian era, Brighton had been well known for its herring and mackerel catches. The volunteer-run **Fishing Museum** uses film, photographs, paintings and artefacts to give a sense of working and social life by the sea for past generations: the West Pier, Punch and Judy shows, the lifeboatmen,

↑ Brighton Palace Pier. (Delia_Suvari/S)

the fish market. The largest exhibit, a 27ft clinker-built punt boat with the legend 'SUSSEX MAID' on its side, sits proud at the centre. Public notices track the days of the Brighton Swimming Club, which combined swimming tuition with aquatic entertainment events. A programme for 19 September 1862 promised the spectacle of the one-legged 'Captain' John Henry Camp 'perform[ing] the difficult task of undressing himself while in the water, smoking a pipe the whole time.'

Walking along the seafront for a mile or so brings you to the point at which eastern Hove meets western Brighton, where you'll find the Brunswick district. During the 1820s this part of town turned into a smart, cream-stuccoed neighbourhood, with new houses following the craze for balconies and bay or bow windows. In Brunswick Square, join a special tour of the **Regency Town House** (⊘ rth.org.uk) at No. 13, along with the basement at No. 10. Volunteers are restoring the four-storey No. 13, to help us understand the Georgians' obsessions with health, high style and harmony between people and nature. They believed that deep mauve, the original colour of the dining room walls, was an aid to digestion, and that using a painted oak finish on the library walls suggested the owner's intellectual qualities. Floor-to-ceiling windows in the drawing room, along with large gilt mirrors, ensured that residents enjoyed views both of the square and of the sea.

ESSENTIALS

GETTING THERE Trains from London's Victoria, Blackfriars or London Bridge take around an hour (SR, TH or Gatwick Express ⊘ gatwickexpress.com). National Express (⊘ nationalexpress.com) runs coaches from various UK locations. The most direct road from the north is the M23/A23, joining from the M25 J7.

STAYING Right on the seafront, the ornate **Grand Brighton** (⊘ grandbrighton.co.uk) has been welcoming guests since 1864; ABBA stayed here after winning Eurovision in 1974. For a boutique option, try **The Charm Brighton** (⊘ thecharmbrighton.co.uk) in Kemptown, which offers spa treatments.

EATING In the Royal Pavilion's shadow, **Al Duomo** (⊘ alduomo.co.uk) is popular with families for its wood-fired pizza oven; we loved the culurgiones stuffed with cheese, potato and a hint of mint. In the Fishing Quarter, stop by **Brighton Smokehouse** (⊘ brighton-smokehouse.business.site) for a delicious hot mackerel ciabatta.

TIME TO SPARE? The model trains, dolls, puppets and much else in the **Brighton Toy and Model Museum** in Trafalgar Street (⊘ brightontoymuseum.co.uk) give a powerful hit of nostalgia, as do the Victorian natural history displays in the **Booth Museum** on Dyke Road and the local history exhibits in the **Hove Museum & Art Gallery** on New Church Road (both ⊘ brightonmuseums.org.uk).

7 ISLE OF WIGHT

VICTORIA'S HOME

A young Arthur Conan Doyle, visiting from Southsea on the mainland, described the Isle of Wight in glowing terms: 'There are moors and fells as bleak as those of Cumberland or the West Riding; chalk downs which recall Kent and Sussex; wooded undulating plains like those of Hampshire; and great stretches of rich arable land as fertile and cultivated as any in Leicestershire.' Something about this island in the English Channel, just off the Hampshire coast, encourages writers to use it as a symbol of the mainland; Julian Barnes set his satirical novel *England, England* here. Plenty of domestic tourists have enjoyed themselves on the Isle; there were ten pleasure piers at one stage, and the pier at Ryde on the northeast coast is the oldest, and second longest, in the country. The Isle of Wight's annual rock festival has run since 1970, while the small northern town of Cowes hosts a world-famous regatta each August. For heritage lovers there's plenty to enjoy. The itinerary below focuses on the north and east, featuring a stately home and a castle which, in their times, have housed two monarchs with contrasting experiences of the island.

THE ITINERARY

DAY 1 Start in East Cowes, near the northernmost tip of the island, at **Osborne House** (EH). Prince Albert designed this summer house and rural retreat in the style of an Italian Renaissance palazzo; Thomas Cubitt, whose firm constructed the façade at Buckingham Palace in 1847, completed Osborne between 1845 and 1851. After Victoria died here in 1901, her son Edward VII presented Osborne to the state and it later opened to the public. Over a century after its last use as her residence, the house stands as a majestic, sometimes intimate tribute to the Queen. The royal couple used Osborne for business as well as relaxation; the Privy Council met here several times a year and Victoria received ministers in the Audience Room, which is notable for a glass and ormolu chandelier depicting convolvulus in a basket. From here you move into the principal rooms: the dining room, drawing room and billiard room. The drawing room in particular might be a surprise if you're accustomed to thinking of Victoria as an elderly woman who was 'not amused'. The yellow damask satin curtains lend a cheerful touch along with idealised statues of the royal couple's children and miniature copies of Italian Old Master paintings. Victoria received foreign royalty here and would often retire to this room after dinner to play cards or to sing and play the piano. Around the corner is the most elaborate billiards table you are likely to see, with legs enamelled to represent marble and frieze panels which Albert designed. The men would play billiards after dinner, out of Victoria's line of sight, standing as royal protocol demanded (unless the Queen allowed them to sit), apart from those occasions when Her Majesty played billiards herself. Upstairs, Victoria's bedroom contains a door which appears to be part of a mahogany wardrobe, but it is in reality the entrance to her lavatory. The matching desks in the sitting

← Osborne House. (English Heritage)

Queen Victoria's Bedroom (English Heritage)

room are a touching reminder of the closeness with which Victoria and Albert worked together on royal business, when they weren't talking with their children or pasting prints of places they had visited into albums. (Albert was not the most conventional father. Go up via the upper terrace of Osborne's gardens to find the Swiss Cottage, where the children grew flowers, fruit and vegetables in their own individual plots, selling the produce to Albert at commercial rates as part of their education. There's a small model fort nearby which Albert also used, for similar educational purposes.) In later life, Victoria's favourite prime minister, Benjamin Disraeli, of whom there is a small portrait in the sitting room, created her Empress of India. That new title is reflected in the Durbar Wing, built in 1890–91 to evoke a land she ruled, but never visited. The corridor here showcases portraits of various Indian subjects, including some of the Queen's servants; this leads to the Durbar Room, which fuses notions of a medieval great hall (a screens passage and minstrels' gallery at one end, with a servery beyond) and a heady mix of north Indian architectural styles – specifically Moghul architecture from the 16th and 17th centuries. It took more than 500 hours to create the peacock that preens over the chimneypiece, and the deep coffers of the ceiling echo designs from medieval Indian temple structures. Completing the imperial effect is a collection of gifts from India to the Empress for her Golden and Diamond Jubilees, including caskets which contained addresses from her Indian subjects. The room is a powerful reminder that, no matter how much Victoria, Albert and the children loved Osborne as a place to relax, there was still an Empire to run.

DAY 2 Six miles south of Osborne, near the centre of the island, stands a castle with another famous royal resident, though the circumstances were less happy and the stay was shorter. **Carisbrooke Castle** (EH), once the site of a Saxon enclosure, became a castle soon after the 1066 invasion and another Norman motte and bailey castle after that. All those builders recognised the same basic fact that the hilltop location is excellent as a defensive position. Carisbrooke adapted over the years in the face of possible French and Spanish invasions and, in the 1590s, was wholly refortified as an artillery fortress. Since the English Civil War it has been less a military presence and more of a ceremonial or symbolic place, the residence of the island's governors including Princess Beatrice, Queen Victoria's daughter. Among the earliest owners were the de Redvers family who held Carisbrooke for almost two centuries until 1293. The last owner, Countess Isabella de Fortibus, was responsible for many changes to the structure; some of these survive to this day, including the rectangular stone tower within the gatehouse, and the Great Hall and St Peter's Chapel, which now house a museum. The layout incorporates a shell keep (a stone wall around the top of the motte, with buildings within, rather than a tower); walk along the parapet on top of part of the curtain wall

↑ Carisbrooke Castle. (English Heritage)

and up to the keep for sweeping views of the surrounding countryside. There have been donkeys at Carisbrooke since at least the 17th century, turning the treadwheel to obtain water from the 160ft-deep well. Once piped water became available, in the 20th century, the wheel and its operators became part of the visitor attraction. There are short demonstrations; one of the women looking after the two donkeys we saw commented that the donkeys only walk for two rotations 'so it's just good exercise for them.' Another 17th-century visitor was rather more famous for staying here, but not for the reasons he might have wished. By late 1647 Charles I, who had escaped from effective house arrest at Hampton Court Palace, wanted to use the Isle of Wight as a base from which to negotiate with the Parliamentarians. Charles put himself under the protection of the island's governor, whom he mistakenly thought was a secret Royalist; instead the governor kept Charles as a prisoner at Carisbrooke for almost ten months. One area of earthworks became a bowling green, which you can still see, to provide entertainment for the captive King. Charles' first bedchamber was part of what is now the great chamber in the Constable's Lodging; in March 1648 he tried to escape through the window, but got stuck between the bars. After his execution two of Charles' children were kept at Carisbrooke, with his daughter Elizabeth dying from a chill she contracted while playing bowls. There's a bust of Charles, attributed to Bernini, above the single word 'REMEMBER', in the

↑ Donkey wheel, Carisbrooke Castle. (HM)

ornate Chapel of St Nicholas. The chapel also serves as the island's war memorial, displaying inscriptions, on stone panels between the windows, of the names of 2,000 men who died in the two World Wars. Among various fascinating artefacts in Carisbrooke's museum are the so-called 'Ashburnham relics', named after one of Charles I's senior courtiers, which include a linen nightshift, silk drawers and other items of personal clothing belonging to the king.

ESSENTIALS

GETTING THERE Regular ferries run from Portsmouth, Southampton and Lymington on England's south coast via Red Funnel (⊘ redfunnel.co.uk) and Wightlink (⊘ wightlink. co.uk). The crossing takes between 22 minutes and an hour, depending on whether you bring a car or travel on foot. For an unusual alternative, take the world's last remaining commercial hovercraft service (⊘ hovertravel.co.uk) to get to the island in ten minutes. The closest airports are Bournemouth and Southampton.

STAYING You're likely to enjoy staying at Carisbrooke Castle more than Charles I did; the **Bowling Green Apartment** gives you the chance. If you're in a more Victorian than Stuart mood, Osborne House's **Sovereign's Gate** and **Pavilion Cottage** are also available (for all three options, see ⊘ english-heritage.org.uk/visit/holiday-cottages).

EATING On the island's eastern tip, with splendid sea views from its garden, the **Crab & Lobster Inn** (⊘ characterinns.co.uk/crabandlobsterinn) is an excellent place to relax. Treat yourself with the hot seafood platter for two.

TIME TO SPARE? In the northeast, **Quarr Abbey** (⊘ quarrabbey.org), which has stood since 1132, still houses Benedictine monks. **Bembridge Windmill** (NT), on the island's eastern tip, is its last surviving windmill and has stood since 1700. Four miles inland, **Brading Villa** (⊘ bradingromanvilla.org.uk) has a fine collection of Roman artefacts and beautiful mosaic floors. Also in Brading, the **Lilliput Doll & Toy Museum** (⊘ lilliputmuseum.net) started in unlikely fashion in the 1960s, with the gift of a Russian wooden nesting doll from the Russian leader Nikita Khruschev to a young collector and her mother. It now holds more than 2,000 items, some going back almost 4,000 years. Three miles south of Brading, just outside Sandown, **Dinosaur Isle** (⊘ dinosaurisle. com), a building in the shape of a giant white pterodactyl, houses the island's geology and fossil collections.

At the island's western tip, the **Needles**, a row of three stacks of chalk, rise 100ft out of the sea. High above them are the **Old and New Batteries** (NT): the former is an 1862 fort built for a war with France that never happened; the latter hosts an exhibition on the secret testing of British-made rockets a century later.

8 PORTSMOUTH

NAVAL TALES

ortsmouth, a port and island city in the county of Hampshire, has seen many naval expeditions, triumphs and defeats. The Romans built a fort at nearby Porchester; King John assembled a fleet here in 1213 to attack the French; Portsmouth was Henry VIII's first line of defence against France; Captain James Cook arrived here after circumnavigating the globe; Nelson left from Portsmouth for the Battle of Trafalgar; and aircraft carriers sailed from here to the South Atlantic in the 1982 Falklands War. Even Gilbert and Sullivan's HMS *Pinafore* is set in Portsmouth.

STAR ATTRACTIONS

Start at **Portsmouth Historic Dockyard** (AF ⏦historicdockyard.co.uk), a section of HM Naval Base Portsmouth, housing a dozen historic ships, museums and attractions. Among them are the **National Museum of the Royal Navy**, which covers more than 350 years of naval endeavours and, across the harbour, the **Royal Navy Submarine Museum**. The stars, however, are three venerable vessels spanning three centuries. The youngest, **HMS *Warrior***, was built in 1860 as one of a new class of armour-plated, iron-hulled warships, a response to France's construction of similar craft. Technological advances rendered it effectively obsolete within a decade, and decommission followed in 1883. The recreated interiors, down several steep flights of steps, include the galley and officers' cabins, though most of the crew lived on the gun deck. Presenters in character as 1860s

↑ Portsmouth Historic Dockyard. (Laurin/S)

British officers give rousing talks and demonstrations on subjects such as the uses of small arms. *Warrior*'s predecessor, the wooden-hulled **HMS *Victory***, launched in 1765 as a 104-gun first ship of the line. She served in three battles and a siege (of Gibraltar) before her most famous engagement at Trafalgar in 1805. The low ceilings and lighting demonstrate how claustrophobic conditions must have been. Opposite, the **Victory Museum**, which explores how later generations conserved and venerated the ship, displays the royal barge on which Horatio Nelson's body was brought up the Thames, and has a wonderful collection of ship figureheads. The third vessel is the ***Mary Rose***, Henry VIII's favourite warship, which sank in the Battle of the Solent in 1545 before being discovered in 1971. The **Mary Rose Museum** (⊘maryrose.org) houses artefacts found in the wreck, from weapons and surgical instruments to pocket sundials. Computer reconstructions of crew members' faces combine with displays on the carpenters, pursers, archers and many others who manned the ship. There's a skeleton of a dog, something between a modern terrier and a whippet. But the main reason to visit is the mighty hull, whose remains you can view from glass-sided walkways along its length. Projections of fictional scenes from life on board play across it, but the hull alone is an unforgettable spectacle.

ESSENTIALS

GETTING THERE Trains from London (two hours to Portsmouth Harbour, close to the dockyard) and elsewhere are frequent (GWR, SR, SW). By road take the M27, A27 or A3 from the west, east or north respectively.

STAYING & EATING **Ye Spotted Dogge** (⊘yespotteddogge.co.uk) offers individually designed period rooms showcasing 500 years of history. For refreshment, sample bacon bread and butter pudding at the **Hotwalls Studios Canteen** (⊘hotwallsstudios.co.uk/the-canteen), cakes at the **Parade Tearooms** (⊘paradetearooms. co.uk) or pies at **Pie and Vinyl** (⊘pandvrecords.co.uk).

TIME TO SPARE? At Portsmouth Harbour's northern end stand **Portchester Castle** (EH) – which has been a Roman fort, a Norman castle, Richard II's royal palace and a Napoleonic Wars PoW camp – and the mid-Victorian **Fort Nelson** (⊘royalarmouries. org/venue/fort-nelson). At the southern end, adjacent to each other, are Henry VIII's **Southsea Castle** (⊘southseacastle.co.uk) and **The D-Day Story** (AF ⊘theddaystory.com), which analyses the Allied invasion of Normandy in 1944. In central Portsmouth, **Charles Dickens' Birthplace Museum** (⊘charlesdickensbirthplace.co.uk) explores the writer's life, while **Portsmouth Museum and Art Gallery** (⊘portsmouthmuseum.co.uk) houses an exhibition on Arthur Conan Doyle, a local doctor before he created Sherlock Holmes.

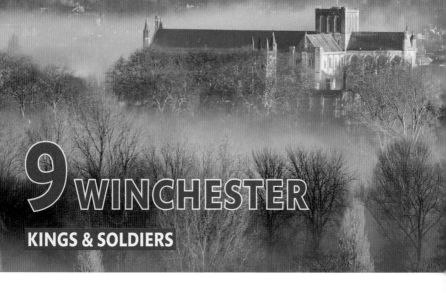

9 WINCHESTER
KINGS & SOLDIERS

Sitting on the edge of the South Downs in Hampshire, Winchester has long been associated with some of our most famous kings. In Saxon times, King Alfred based his court and capital here as he led resistance against the Vikings. Later Winchester's Great Hall became associated with the legends of Arthur and Camelot, while other royalty from Cnut to Charles I can be found in the city's medieval cathedral. William the Conqueror built a castle in Winchester and Charles II planned a palace which was never completed. Instead it became a military barracks where today you can discover the stories of soldiers and regiments who have served the British cause over the past 300 years.

THE ITINERARY

DAY 1 Start near the foot of the High Street as it becomes The Broadway, where a bronze **statue of King Alfred** stands, brandishing a sword above his head. The statue, which is 17ft tall, has been here since 1899, the 1000th anniversary of Alfred's death. Its beard may owe more to imagination than reality, however, as coins from Alfred's reign depict him as clean-shaven. A few minutes' walk along the High Street, turn left past the old Market Cross to find the **City Museum** (⌁ hampshireculture.org.uk). Across three floors, this provides snapshots of life from Venta Belgarum (the settlement the Romans established here), the Anglo-Saxon and medieval periods, and Victorian and Edwardian times. We love the 12th-century bronze horn, with four lions and two bishops as decoration, whose sound embellished city meetings and functions, and the enormous scale model representing the city in 1870. Turn left out of the museum for the impressive spectacle of **Winchester Cathedral** (⌁ winchester-cathedral.org.uk). Enter by the

↑ A view of Winchester Cathedral. (SuxxesPhoto/S)

northwest door and pause at the West End, where statues of James I and Charles I stand under a vast stained-glass window that once depicted the life of Christ with apostles and prophets on either side. Parliamentary soldiers smashed the glass during the Civil War, but the pieces were later reassembled at random, which gives a pleasing abstract effect. From here, walk down the nave which, at 246ft, is the longest surviving nave of any medieval cathedral in the country. Its early construction in the 1080s and 1090s featured Romanesque rounded arches; a remodelling three centuries later used pointed arches and large openings in the Perpendicular style, allowing more light inside. A brass memorial plaque on the left, with an accompanying black slab in the floor nearby, commemorates the life of Jane Austen (1775–1817), who died in Winchester and was buried in the cathedral. Sitting on the screens in the presbytery are six wooden chests with crowns on top. These mortuary chests contained the remains of monarchs and bishops from before the Norman Conquest, and may have included Queen Emma, wife to kings Cnut and Ethelred the Unready and mother to Harthacnut and Edward the Confessor. The results of continuing scientific analysis on the bones are displayed in a special 'Kings & Scribes' exhibition, along with the four bound volumes of the 12th-century illuminated Winchester Bible, one of the finest surviving medieval manuscripts. The cathedral's most unexpected monument is a small bronze figure of a deep-sea diver by the Langton Chapel. This is William Walker who, for six years up to 1911, dived into the flooded foundations to carry and lay sacks of concrete. His efforts enabled a team of 150 workmen to rebuild the foundations and save the building from collapse.

A few minutes away via St Swithun Street (named after one of the city's saints, who was its bishop from AD852–63) is the **Great Hall** (⊘ hants.gov.uk). Henry III, who was known as Henry of Winchester before becoming king in 1216, commissioned the building of this imposing aisled hall close to the castle (of which little remains), and it has served as a court for much of its history. The hall's highlight is high on the wall at one end: the Round Table, 18ft in diameter, weighing over a ton and made from 121 pieces of English oak. Tree-ring and radio carbon dating suggests that the table was made in the late 13th century, possibly by order of Henry's son Edward I, a strong believer in the legends of Arthur and the knights of the Round Table. The design you see today, depicting Arthur with sword and orb, 24 knights' names around the rim and a Tudor rose in the centre, came later, on the orders of Henry VIII. X-rays have shown that the original artwork of Arthur's face was, in fact, a likeness of a young Henry VIII – a none-too-subtle reminder of Henry's claim to the throne as Arthur's direct descendant.

DAY 2 A short walk from the Great Hall is the site of the King's House, the palace which Charles II commissioned Sir Christopher Wren to build, but which Charles's successor James II abandoned. It housed French, Dutch and Spanish prisoners of war, and served as a barracks for 200 years, with some of the buildings now residential developments. On the same site, the **Military Quarter** (⊘ winchestersmilitaryquarter.org) houses six museums which examine and celebrate the lives of soldiers. The **Adjutant General's Corps Museum** (⊘ rhqagc.com) traces the history of the various corps that eventually merged into the AGC and gives a useful overview of army developments since 1700, including training and pay. One sound recording recounts how an officer explained the underpayment of a soldier by £300, just after World War II, by claiming that a fly had landed on the paperwork, obscuring the crucial figure. Next door, the **Royal Green Jackets (Rifles) Museum** (⊘ rgjmuseum.co.uk) explains how four different regiments, precursors of the Green Jackets, served Britain in various wars. An excellent diorama of the Battle of Waterloo, which features models of 9,000 horses and 21,500 soldiers, is helpful if you have little prior knowledge of that crucial conflict. The **Gurkha Museum** (⊘ thegurkhamuseum.co.uk) pays tribute to the cultural heritage of the Gurkhas' home nation of Nepal. The Gurkhas and the British were adversaries in the 1814–16 Anglo–Nepalese War. Later the British recruited Gurkhas to fight for them in Afghanistan, the Falklands and elsewhere. **HorsePower** (⊘ horsepowermuseum.co.uk), which is the museum of the King's Royal Hussars, the **Rifles Museum** (⊘ riflesmuseum.co.uk) and the **Royal Hampshire Regiment Museum** (⊘ royalhampshireregiment.org) offer further insights into military life.

↑ Winchester Great Hall. (David Whidborne/S) ← Military Quarter. (irisphoto1/S)

ESSENTIALS

GETTING THERE Winchester is an hour from London Waterloo by train (SW), with good links to Birmingham and points further north. The main road is via the M3 or, from Newbury or Oxford, the A34.

STAYING **Winchester Royal Hotel** (⬧winchesterroyalhotel.com) can trace its history back over 400 years; the welcoming ambience, well-appointed bedrooms and walled garden make for a relaxing stay. Other options include bed and breakfast at **The Black Hole** (⬧theblackholebb.co.uk), suites at **Two Bare Feet** (⬧twobarefeetwinchester.co.uk) or – just west of Winchester – the luxury of **Lainston House** (⬧exclusive.co.uk/lainston-house).

EATING There are plenty of bustling cafés, including **The Square** (⏀ coffeelabuk. com) and **Café Monde**, both around the corner from the cathedral. On Jewry Street ten minutes away, **Dim T** (⏀ dimt.co.uk), one outlet of a small Hampshire/London chain, serves good-value Asian fusion food.

TIME TO SPARE? **Wolvesey Castle** (EH), near the cathedral, was the main residence of the Bishops of Winchester; most of its remains date from the 12th-century palace of Henry of Blois, King Stephen's brother. Inside a fortified medieval gateway, and once a debtors' prison, **Westgate Museum** (⏀ hampshireculture.org.uk) tells stories of the city from Tudor and Stuart times.

↑ Wolvesey Castle (Jon Mès/S)

10 AVEBURY

PRE-HISTORY MYSTERY

For anyone fascinated by pre-Roman history, the southwestern county of Wiltshire offers a wonderful prospect. Its wonders include the Iron Age hillforts at Bratton Camp, Chisbury Camp, Cley Hill, Membury and Oldbury Castle. There are the 'Seven Barrows' Bronze Age burial mounds (in fact, there are more than 30). And, of course, there's Stonehenge, Britain's most famous ancient site. Even among this concentration of attractions, Avebury in central Wiltshire stands out. The largest stone circle, the largest prehistoric mound and one of the longest burial mounds in the British Isles, one of the largest settlements of the early Neolithic period and one of the longest avenues of standing stones: they're all here, within a few miles of each other. Avebury is a Scheduled Ancient Monument and a UNESCO World Heritage Site and, while Stonehenge is not far away, we reckon Avebury's scale and greater accessibility make it more interesting. There's also the chance to travel through half a millennium in one building: Avebury Manor, a time capsule of its owners' lives from Tudor times to the 1930s.

↑ Avebury Stone Circle. (Matt Gibson/S)

THE ITINERARY

DAY 1 The best place to start with **Avebury** (EH, NT) is in the village itself, with the main **stone circle**. In fact this was not one circle, but three. The outer circle's diameter of 1,082ft makes it the largest of its type in Europe, and it comprised around 100 standing stones. Two inner circles of about 30 stones each stood within. The southern inner circle contained oblongs or trapezoids, of which one line remains. The northern inner circle's inner stones are mostly buried now, but there were three tall stones in its centre, of which two, known as the Cove, still stand. This is the most theatrical space within the overall circle; its purpose may have been to observe moonrise, the sun or the night sky. Archaeologists have recently discovered a buried arrangement of small stones in a square alignment within the southern inner circle. It's possible that the square marks the location of an early Neolithic house, perhaps part of a founding settlement – which in turn might explain the construction of the circle(s) here. Only 15 of the stones survived upright until the 20th century, but we can see a further 27 today. This is thanks to millionaire marmalade magnate Alexander Keiller who, while excavating the site in the 1930s, found those 27 buried or fallen stones and restored them to their previous positions. You can get up close – along with grazing sheep and cawing crows – or walk around the outside for a wider view. This peaceful place has a special atmosphere unlike anywhere else we know.

Keiller was one of the many inhabitants of nearby **Avebury Manor** (NT) between its construction in the 1550s (on the site of a 12th-century priory) and the end of a private tenancy in 2009. At this point, the National Trust and the BBC joined forces, due to the Trust's need to maintain the building and the BBC's hunt for an unfurnished historic house for a documentary series. With the addition of traditionally made replica items and a few original artefacts, the manor found TV fame as *The Manor Reborn* (2011). Each room represents a different point in the house's history. Part of the fun is to spot the original items, such as the fireplace in the Tudor Parlour or the Edwardian photo, in the Billiards Room, of army officer and polo player Leopold Jenner on horseback. The Keiller Parlour celebrates the life and interests of the eponymous millionaire; look down at the Art Deco carpet for some splendid artwork of cars, one of Keiller's many enthusiasms. Another owner entertained Queen Anne at Avebury; the closet features a replica 'close stool' or portable toilet, an essential Royal accessory at the time. The manor gardens are a joy in spring and early summer, with apple and cherry trees flowering alongside *Choisya ternata* 'Aztec Pearl' (Mexican orange blossom). Take the footpaths from Avebury village two miles northwest to **Windmill Hill**, a Neolithic settlement dating back more than 5,500 years. Twentieth-century excavations uncovered remains of clay pots and flint tools within its three concentric rings of ditches, as well as thousands of animal bones and around 40 finds of human remains, with three complete burials. It's a serene location now, belying the bustling place it must have been. There are great views back, on a clear day, to Avebury and **Silbury Hill** (page 58).

DAY 2 For a good overview of the site, visit the **Alexander Keiller Museum** in the Barn Gallery and the Stables Gallery. The museum displays many of Keiller's finds and provides fascinating insights into local life in prehistoric times. Before exploring to the south, take a moment to consider the remains of two trails of standing stones, the **Beckhampton Avenue** and the **West Kennet Avenue**, which head southwest and southeast from the entrance to the henge. The West Kennet is better preserved; when new, there may have been 100 pairs of stones, with a diamond-shaped example possibly representing the female form and a straight

↑ Windmill Hill. (Steve Speller/A) → Avebury Manor. (jax10289/S)

WHAT IS A HENGE?

The satirists Flanders and Swann speculated that Stonehenge's purpose was to measure when summer had come. 'Is it summer? You can't tell? Well, I'd better come and help you shovel the snow off it, then...' We still don't know everything about henges, of which Avebury is a large example. We *can* say that a henge is a prehistoric circular or oval earthen enclosure, created between 3000 and 2000BC, with a ring-shaped bank and ditch marking out the boundary. 'Henge' may be an Old English term for 'hanging'; hence Stonehenge would be 'hanging stones'. According to anthropologist Mary-Ann Ochota, speaking on an English Heritage video: 'It seems most likely that henges were

↑ Stonehenge. (Chuta Kooanantkul/S)

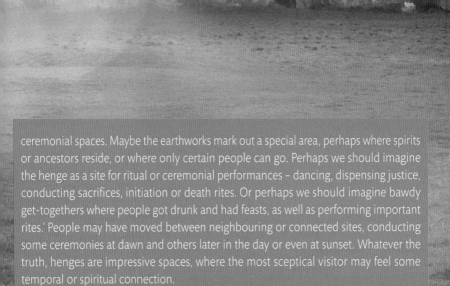

ceremonial spaces. Maybe the earthworks mark out a special area, perhaps where spirits or ancestors reside, or where only certain people can go. Perhaps we should imagine the henge as a site for ritual or ceremonial performances – dancing, dispensing justice, conducting sacrifices, initiation or death rites. Or perhaps we should imagine bawdy get-togethers where people got drunk and had feasts, as well as performing important rites.' People may have moved between neighbouring or connected sites, conducting some ceremonies at dawn and others later in the day or even at sunset. Whatever the truth, henges are impressive spaces, where the most sceptical visitor may feel some temporal or spiritual connection.

stone the male. The complete West Kennet Avenue was the longest of its type in the British Isles. A National Trust suggested walking route (6½ miles in all; ⊘nationaltrust.org.uk/avebury/trails/west-kennet-round) takes the southeastern route. You follow part of the West Kennet Avenue till you reach the **Sanctuary**, originally a setting of timber posts in concentric circles and later a double stone circle. Shortly afterwards, turning right (west) and following the NT directions, you climb a hill to arrive at **West Kennet Long Barrow**. Of the 14 long burial mounds within three miles of Avebury, West Kennet is the longest – one of the longest in Britain, for that matter. It contains five burial chambers, linked by a corridor, in the eastern part of the mound. Excavations uncovered human remains in each chamber, and radiocarbon dating has estimated the burial dates between 3700 and 3600BC. After the burials, over several centuries, people filled the chambers with pottery, animal bones, beads, flint tools and chalk rubble. If poor weather makes you think twice about the walk, consider viewing the site from a small layby off the A4.

Turning back in the direction of Avebury, a walk of just over half a mile takes you forward in time to around 2400BC and the beginning of the creation of **Silbury Hill**. There's no direct public access, but a small car park is within a minute's walk of an excellent view. At around 120ft high, 100ft across the top and 1,640ft around the base, this was the largest prehistoric mound in Europe. It began, as two tunnelling excavations revealed, with a small mound of gravel

↑ West Kennet Long Barrow. (stocker1970/S)

and clay, followed by more than 6ft of turf and soil and a capping of chalk and soil to just over 16ft, before the construction of the main mound – which seems to have occurred in many incremental stages over anything up to 400 years. Radiocarbon dating has uncovered further evidence, but not a definitive answer to the question of when the work finished. The big question of why the hill was built remains unanswered. It's still a landmark to evoke wonder; given the resources available to people at the time, Silbury Hill and the rest of Neolithic Avebury were remarkable achievements.

ESSENTIALS

GETTING THERE The nearest railway stations are Swindon or Pewsey, an hour from London and 45–90 minutes from Bristol (GWR). If you arrive at Avebury by bus, there's a £1 discount on entry. Regular buses include the X76 from Marlborough; for options see ⊘ connectingwiltshire.co.uk. The nearest main road is the A4, with links to Avebury by the A4361 from the north and the B4003 from the south.

STAYING The bedrooms at **Dorwyn Manor** B&B (⊘ dorwynmanor.com), half a mile north of Avebury village, take their names from Avebury features and people. **The Old Forge** at East Kennett (⊘ theoldforge-avebury.co.uk) is an upmarket B&B two miles south of the village. Marlborough, seven miles east, has plenty of accommodation options, including pubs with rooms such as the **Green Dragon** (⊘ wadworth.co.uk) and the **Castle and Ball** (⊘ greeneking-pubs.co.uk).

EATING There are cafés in the Old Farmyard (near the NT visitor reception) and the manor. Along Marlborough's high street, try **The Polly Tea Rooms** (⊘ thepollytearooms. com) or, for a full meal, the fresh, sustainable seafood at **Rick Stein** (⊘ rickstein.com).

TIME TO SPARE? Stonehenge (EH), just over 20 miles south of Avebury, offers the chance to walk round its world-renowned stone circle, and to see some recreations of Neolithic houses just outside the impressive visitor centre. Because of its chalk downlands, Wiltshire used to be home to 13 of the 24 white horses which various people carved into Britain's hills, and a few remain. Four miles west of Avebury is the **Cherhill White Horse** (NT), created in 1780. To the east, close to the A345 between Marlborough and Pewsey, the **Marlborough White Horse** was an 1804 school project undertaken by pupils of Mr Greasley's Academy in Marlborough's high street. Ten miles west of Avebury, **Bowood House and Gardens** (HH, RHS ⊘ bowood.org) is the historic home of the Shelburnes and Lansdownes, where Joseph Priestley discovered oxygen in 1774. Lancelot 'Capability' Brown (1716–83) designed the parkland, and the Woodland Gardens make a spectacular sight in spring and early summer, particularly the rhododendrons.

11 BATH

FROM ROMANS TO THE REGENCY

Welcome to the largest city in Somerset. The Romans built baths and a temple on this site in around AD60; by the 17th century, locals were promoting the hot springs as having curative properties. This fed into Bath's growth as a spa town in the Georgian era, by which time the creation of some remarkable and elegant architecture had added to the city's allure. Bath's reputation as somewhere to be, and to be seen, found its reflection in contemporary literature. Charles Dickens, a frequent visitor, satirised the taking of its waters in *The Pickwick Papers*. Jane Austen, who lived in four houses in Bath within six years, set two novels here; as one of her characters puts it, 'Who can ever be tired of Bath?'

THE ITINERARY

DAY 1 You enter the **Roman Baths** (AF ⊘ romanbaths.co.uk) via a terrace that dates back to the site's 1897 opening to the public. On the way in, you pass Victorian-era statues of Roman emperors and governors, including a miserable-looking Julius Caesar. Scale models, projections of filmed imaginings of Roman life and a display of finds from the site help to set the context before you go into the complex. By the 1st century BC a local tribe, the Dobunni, ruled this part of Britain. They believed the hot spring on this site was sacred to the goddess Sulis, who possessed curative powers. When the Romans arrived, perceiving similarities between Sulis and their own goddess Minerva, they combined the two, building the baths as a curative establishment and a temple to Sulis Minerva. At the front of the temple stood a great ornamental pediment. The remains survive, complete with images of helmets and an owl, symbols of Minerva's military prowess and wisdom, and the central image of a male face, which may be Oceanus or Neptune. Some of our favourite items on the site are the fragments of curse tablets, dating from the 2nd to 4th centuries AD, which appealed for the goddess's help in returning stolen goods and punishing the thieves. One example, signed 'Docimedes', states that the thief of a pair of gloves should lose his mind and his eyes; another victim claims that 'The person who has stolen my bronze pot is utterly accursed.' The gilded bronze head of Sulis Minerva, from a statue inside the temple that only priests could enter, was discovered in 1727 by workmen digging a sewer. The heart of the site is the Sacred Spring, where water at a temperature of 46°C rises naturally each day. This is where supplicants threw their curse tablets and various other objects as offerings. You can walk around the Great Bath, whose original height within a barrel-vaulted hall was about 65ft. The bath itself is just over 5ft deep, with steps on all sides and niches for benches where bathers could sit between dips, and where you may meet actors in Roman robes. Adjacent to the Great Bath, the East Baths and West Baths contain further suites of baths and heated rooms, as well as projections, soundscapes and CGI which recreate the sights and sounds of the bathhouse.

← The Roman Baths, with Bath Abbey in the background. (Bath & North East Somerset Council)

The baths' principal neighbour is another historic place of worship, **Bath Abbey** (⊘ bathabbey.org). The existing 16th-century abbey stands where a Norman cathedral and a Saxon Benedictine monastery used to be, and a Roman temple's foundations are buried deep below. The West Front's façade features ladders with angels on either side, with the ladders descending as far as the tops of the abbey doors: a clear message for pilgrims that visiting the abbey was part of the way to get to heaven. The interior is in the Perpendicular style: strong vertical lines, large windows, flying buttresses. The fan-vaulted ceiling, created by royal master masons and restored in the nave by George Gilbert Scott, is inspiring. The King Edgar Window celebrates the crowning in Bath of the first king of all England, while the walls house over 600 memorials, some to the great and the good, others to Bath residents who worshipped here. Some inscriptions are lengthy but well worth reading in full, such as the encomium to Sir William Hargood, who served in the American War of Independence and the Napoleonic Wars.

DAY 2 Bath's **Royal Crescent** was the most prestigious construction (1767–75) by John Wood the Younger. This mellow yellow arc of 30 terraced townhouses with Ionic columns was home among others to Isaac Pitman, who invented shorthand, social reformer Elizabeth Montagu and novelist and politician Edward Bulwer-Lytton. Legend has it that a Duke of York stayed here soon after its completion, hence the 'Royal' appellation. A ha-ha in front of the Crescent divides its lawn, for exclusive use by residents, from public parkland. The townhouses remain residential except for Nos. 15–17, now the Royal Crescent Hotel, and **No. 1 Royal Crescent** (AF ⊘ no1royalcrescent.org.uk), once a lodging house for clerics and then a seminary for young ladies but now a museum about Georgian life in

↑ The Royal Crescent. (Alexey Fedorenko/S)

JANE AUSTEN & BATH

Gay Street is a good place to start when looking for traces of Jane Austen. Following the death of her father, which no doubt contributed to her ambivalent feelings about Bath, the author lived at No. 25 for a year with her mother and sisters. At No. 40, **The Jane Austen Centre** (⊘ janeausten.co.uk) uses actors in Regency costume, along with period decorations and exhibits, to recreate a snapshot of the city in Austen's time and how it influenced her writing. From here, a looped walking route covers many locations that Austen would have known or which had personal significance. From the Royal Crescent, where one of her sisters lived at No. 12, follow the Gravel Walk, a means for conveying the gentry in their sedan chairs down to the baths. Along the Walk, the **Georgian Garden** is a lovely small recreation of a 1760s town garden. Continue to No 13 Queen Square, where Austen stayed with her mother and elder brother Edward in 1799. Around the block is Trim Street, where the family had their final lodgings in Bath, much further down the social scale. Continue via Union Street and Cheap Street past the Roman Baths and Bath Abbey, then walk towards the Parade Gardens and look left for a view of Pulteney Bridge, one of four bridges in the world with shops spanning both sides. Cross the bridge to Great Pulteney Street, Bath's widest street, which features in *Persuasion* and *Northanger Abbey*. At the end, turn left for No. 4 Sydney Place, where a plaque marks the house in which Jane, her sister Cassandra and their parents lived during their first three years in Bath.

↑ The Jane Austen Centre. (Jane Austen Centre/ janeausten.co.uk)

Bath. Visiting is an immersive experience, in which you 'meet' a family who lived here, with video and audio recreating a daughter's opinions on finding a husband and the parents' concerns about their son's gambling habits. From No. 1, a short walk along Brock Street brings you to **The Circus**, designed and built just before the Royal Crescent by John Wood and his namesake father. Artist Thomas Gainsborough (1727–88) used No. 17 as his studio. The Circus comprises three segments of townhouses arranged in a circle with three entrances; stone circles were the inspiration, and the Circus has almost exactly the same diameter as Stonehenge. It combines Greek Doric, Roman/Composite and Corinthian Classical styles to majestic, harmonious effect, with hundreds of pictorial emblems including nautical and masonic symbols. From the air, the Circus in combination with Queen Square and Gay Street forms the shape of a key.

From Gay Street, follow the trail of **Jane Austen** (page 63) or turn right into George Street and then left into Bartlett Street which continues into Bennett Street, home of the **Assembly Rooms** (NT). John Wood the Younger worked on the design here, too, though it has since been restored, damaged during World War II and restored again. Behind the exterior of warm Bath stone you can see the Tea Room, with its Whitefriars crystal chandeliers, the Card Room and the Ball Room – all splendid recreations of the spaces in which Georgian patrons socialised. The original card room is now known as the Great Octagon, a cheerful yellow space with four original marble fireplaces. From here a short walk, via Russell Street to Julian Road, brings you to the **Museum of Bath at Work** (⊘ bath-at-work.org. uk) on a site which was once a real tennis court. Displays include an explanation of how workmen extracted Bath stone in the days before mechanisation, and reconstructions of 18th-century furniture-making workshops. The museum's

↑ The Assembly Rooms. (ExFlow/S)

remarkable heart is the collection of artefacts from the factory and workshops of Victorian businessman JB Bowler, who described himself as a brass founder, gas fitter, locksmith and bell-hanger. He also manufactured fizzy drinks, and contemporaneous advertisements for double soda water machines and rapid syruping machines adorn the walls. Finally, a mile away on Hampton Row, **Cleveland Pools** (⚭ clevelandpools.org.uk) is Britain's oldest lido, dating back over 200 years and due to reopen in summer 2022.

ESSENTIALS

GETTING THERE Regular services run between London Paddington and Bath Spa station, taking about 90 minutes (GWR). The Cardiff–Portsmouth service also passes through Bath (SW). The main road links are the M4 and A4.

STAYING A short walk from the Roman Baths, **Harington's Hotel** (⚭ haringtonshotel. co.uk) incorporates 13 bedrooms of boutique comfort. For a self-catering alternative, try **Milliners Cottage** (⚭ milliners-cottage.bathhotels-england.co.uk), a converted Grade II-listed building with original wood beams and fireplace, about ten minutes uphill from the baths, the Circus and the Royal Crescent.

EATING The Nepalese cuisine at **Yak Yeti Yak** (⚭ yakyetiyak.co.uk) includes delicious *momos* (dumplings) as a prelude to mains as mild or spicy as you like. **Sally Lunn's** (⚭ sallylunns.co.uk) serves sweet and savoury versions of the eponymous Sally Lunn bun, or as they put it, 'the original Bath Bunn', in a house near the baths and the abbey which has stood since c1482. For a touch of elegant luxury, take afternoon tea under the chandeliers in the **Pump Room** (⚭ thepumproombath.co.uk).

TIME TO SPARE? Fascinating museums abound: on skygazing, at the **Herschel Museum of Astronomy** (⚭ herschelmuseum.org.uk), in the house where William Herschel discovered Uranus; on another famous writer who lived in Bath, at the new immersive **Mary Shelley's House of Frankenstein** (⚭ houseoffrankenstein.com); and on building Bath, at the **Museum of Bath Architecture** (AF ⚭ museumofbatharchitecture.org.uk), which is closed for repairs in 2022. For art, there's the excellent **Museum of East Asian Art** (AF ⚭ meaa.org.uk) and the **Holburne Museum** (AF ⚭ holburne.org). But one of our favourites sits in an 1820 manor house on Bath's eastern edge. The **American Museum** (⚭ americanmuseum.org) houses the principal collection of American folk and decorative arts outside the USA, within reconstructed period spaces such as Conkey's Tavern from 18th-century Massachusetts, which use original panelling and floors shipped across the Atlantic. Don't miss the wonderful quilts in the Textiles Room. The grounds feature a recreation of George Washington's garden at Mount Vernon.

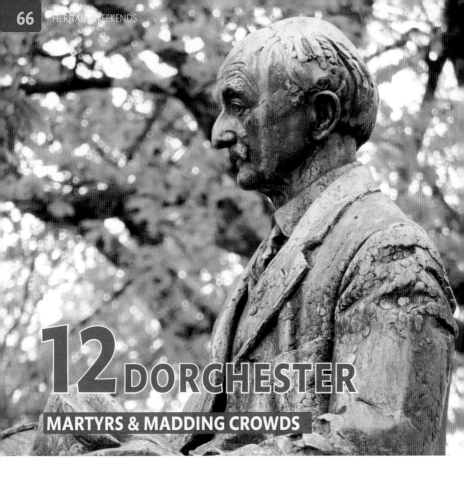

12 DORCHESTER

MARTYRS & MADDING CROWDS

The peaceful appearance of Dorchester, the county town of Dorset, belies a violent history. Maumbury Rings, in the south of town, was a Roman amphitheatre and later a public execution venue. Judge Jeffreys lodged in Dorchester during the Bloody Assizes of 1685; 74 men were hung, drawn and quartered here for treason. In and around town, a museum outlining a historic dispute between the Tolpuddle Martyrs and their employers, and the trail of a great writer, epitomise the conflict and human struggles of Dorchester's more recent past.

STAR ATTRACTIONS

Seven miles east of Dorchester, by the river Piddle, the village of Tolpuddle is world famous for a 19th-century labour dispute. Against a background of increased mechanisation of agriculture and falling wages, a group of farm labourers from Tolpuddle lobbied local landowners and employers for better recompense. But as their wages were reduced again, from nine to six shillings a week, six men formed a friendly society, an early form of trade union. For breaching an obscure law relating to oaths, the men were arrested in early 1834, tried and sentenced to

↑ Statue of Thomas Hardy in Dorchester. (Jo Jones/S)

deportation to Australia for seven years. Public outcry ensured that they returned within five years, with the union movement supporting the men's families in the meantime. The **Tolpuddle Martyrs Museum** (∂ tolpuddlemartyrs.org.uk) tells the story through interactive displays, artefacts and documents such as a letter from the local vicar, who was far from impartial despite his nominal role as an intermediary in the dispute, stating that 'these Unions must be put a stop to'. The **Martyrs' Tree**, a sycamore where the men met to discuss their grievances, stands in the centre of the village. A plaque commemorates the Martyrs outside Dorchester's **Shire Hall Historic Courthouse Museum** (∂ shirehalldorset.org), where the trials took place. One man, at least, sympathised with the working man's life more than the Martyrs' employers: the novelist and poet Thomas Hardy (1840–1928), who used local scenes and people as material for novels such as *The Mayor of Casterbridge* and *Far from the Madding Crowd*. A statue of Hardy sits at the top of Dorchester's high street; nearby, **Dorset Museum** (AF ∂ dorsetmuseum.org) examines the importance of rural poverty in Hardy's work and his creation of a semi-fictional version of the ancient region of Wessex. Hardy trained as an architect, and later designed his own home, **Max Gate** (NT), in Dorchester. Between the town and Tolpuddle in Higher Bockhampton is **Thomas Hardy's Cottage** (NT), his birthplace and home until the age of 30, where he wrote several novels and poems. In later life Hardy was a friend of the owners of the splendid **Athelhampton House & Gardens** (HH ∂ athelhampton.com), a mile west of Tolpuddle, which has stood since 1485. The current owners have recreated the room where Hardy was a frequent dinner guest and named it in his honour.

ESSENTIALS

GETTING THERE Dorchester South station is about three hours from London Waterloo and Dorchester West is two hours from Bristol Temple Meads (GWR). There are also National Express buses from London (∂ nationalexpress.com). The nearest roads are the A352, A303 and A35.

STAYING & EATING Two miles north of Dorchester, **Wolverton Gatehouse** (LT) is part of a Grade I-listed medieval and Elizabethan house. Pause in town for refreshment at the **TASTE Café** at Dorset Museum (∂ dorsetmuseum.org).

TIME TO SPARE? Dorchester's **Keep Military Museum** (∂ keepmilitarymuseum. org) covers 300 years of military endeavour. The main historic sites nearby are the Neolithic **Maumbury Rings**; **Maiden Castle**, Britain's largest Iron Age hillfort; the 4th-century **Roman Town House** (∂ dorsetmuseum.org); and the mysterious chalk carving of the naked, club-brandishing **Cerne Abbas Giant** (NT).

13 PLYMOUTH

DOCKS & DRAKES

On Devon's south coast, sitting between the rivers Plym to the east and Tamar to the west, and with the natural harbour of Plymouth Sound into which both rivers flow, Plymouth's strongest associations have always been with the sea. Sir Francis Drake played bowls here before defeating the Armada, and it was the departure point for the 102 passengers and 30 crew of the *Mayflower*, on their way to Massachusetts to found Plymouth Colony in what later became the USA. The English fleet anchored here during the Hundred Years' War and the Royal Naval Dockyard at neighbouring Devonport, completed in 1698, is Western Europe's largest naval base. Heavy Luftwaffe bombing in World War II destroyed much of Plymouth's centre, but it's still possible to find reminders of the city from Elizabethan times. The historic Barbican area claims the highest concentration of cobbled streets anywhere in England. As you find out about the many people who departed from Plymouth on journeys of exploration and discovery, and while you follow the traces of the *Mayflower* Pilgrims and Drake, pause for a sip of the drink which bears the city's name.

THE ITINERARY

DAY 1 To get a wider sense of the importance of the sea to Plymouth, start with **The Box** (AF ⌂ theboxplymouth.com), a new museum, art gallery and archive. Look up as you enter; hanging above you, like a stranded flotilla, is a selection of 14 Victorian Royal Naval figureheads. The permanent gallery '100 Journeys' brings together artefacts from various famous and not-so-famous people for whom Plymouth was a point of departure, including Sir Francis Chichester, Captain Cook, Charles Darwin, Sir Walter Raleigh… and explorer Gertrude Benham, who visited much of the British Empire. Another gallery traces the city's history as a port and a dockyard for the Royal Navy, covering innovations such as the world's first dry dock in 1692 and the introduction of nuclear submarines. From here, wander through the Barbican district, perhaps with a pause for a stiff drink (page 71), and go down to the harbour and **The Mayflower Museum** (⌂ visitplymouth. co.uk). This interactive, family-friendly museum tells the story of the religious dissidents who set sail for the New World in July 1620 (after several false starts), and what happened to them and the indigenous people they encountered after they landed near the tip of Cape Cod in November. We don't know precisely what the *Mayflower* looked like, but the star exhibit is a beautiful 1:11 scale model of a typical merchant cargo ship from that period. The museum's location is most appropriate, directly opposite the start of a ten-stage **Mayflower Trail** of just over one mile, and around an hour, taking you around parts of Plymouth surviving from 1620 and earlier; it's available via the Visit Plymouth app. The first point, the Mayflower Steps, is not definitively where the *Mayflower*'s passengers boarded – there's plenty of debate on this subject – but it's a smart 1930s memorial. The trail passes several historic buildings: the Old Customs House, where the captain of

← Naval figureheads, The Box. (HM)

every merchant ship registered their vessel and declared what they were carrying; the 16th-century Merchant's House, home of Captain William Parker, mayor of Plymouth and privateer; and Prysten House, on Finewell Street, which has stood since 1498 and contains the well that gave the street its name.

DAY 2 High above the harbour on **Plymouth Hoe**, with a large globe on his right, his left hand on his hip and a haughty expression on his face as he looks out to sea, stands a statue of Sir Francis Drake (1540–96). This, according to the stories, is where word came on 19 July 1588 that the Spanish Armada had been sighted off the Lizard in Cornwall, upon which Drake remarked that he had plenty of time to finish his game of bowls. In the subsequent battle, Drake as a Vice-Admiral helped lead the English fleet as they repelled and routed the Spanish. Drake had been a national hero since 1580 when he returned to Plymouth from a three-year journey around the world in which he raided Spanish harbours in Cuba and Peru, claimed California for England and acquired a great deal of treasure. Elizabeth I knighted him and Drake became Mayor of Plymouth, MP for Bossiney in Cornwall and the owner of various properties; not bad for a farmer's son from Tavistock. Those who romanticise Drake's life might be surprised to learn that he and his cousin John Hawkins sailed on England's first transatlantic slaving voyages. Many traces of Drake remain in the city and nearby. The small island in the harbour which has been a prison, a refuge, a religious centre and

↑ Statue of Francis Drake, Plymouth Hoe. (ian woolcock/S)

PLYMOUTH GIN

Until William of Orange's arrival in England in 1688 to claim the throne (landing at Brixham, 30 miles east of Plymouth), the English rich had drunk French wine and brandy while the poor drank beer. But William's court drank genever, a northern European version of gin; some English soldiers fighting in the Low Countries in the 17th century drank it to steady their nerves – hence 'Dutch courage'. At a time of conflict with France, the new royal court's preferences provided the perfect excuse for much of England to change its drinking habits. Government legislation restricting brandy imports, reducing regulations on distilling and encouraging gin production, along with lower food prices which left more disposable income for many, fuelled a gin craze. Just over a century later, the Black Friars Distillery in Plymouth began to distil a Plymouth version of gin, to take advantage of naval officers' growing preference for the drink over their traditional tots of rum. Plymouth Devonport was the home port for many ships, ensuring a steady demand. Plymouth Gin is still made at 'naval strength' of 57% abv or 100% 'proof', a traditional Navy measure from the time when gin and gunpowder were stored side by side. The crew would mix small amounts of both on deck and set them alight; if a clear blue flame resulted, this was 'proof' that no water had been added to the gin. The **Plymouth Gin Distillery** (⊘ plymouthgin.com) in Southside Street (point 9 on the Mayflower Trail) still operates today and runs regular tours. Cheers!

↑ The Plymouth Gin distillery. (SS)

most recently an adventure training facility is known as **Drake's Island**. Point 6 of the Mayflower Trail (page 69) lies in Looe Street, within the old Barbican area, where he owned several properties; a plaque at No. 15 marks what is believed to be his residence. Also on Looe Street, legend has it that some of the timber used to construct the **Minerva Inn**, one of Plymouth's oldest buildings, dating back to the 1590s, came from the Armada's remains. Around the time of the *Mayflower*, press gangs operated from here, tricking or intimidating men into joining the Navy.

Drake also bought **Buckland Abbey** (NT), a few miles north of the city, from Sir Richard Grenville, a fellow naval adventurer who disliked him (the purchase was through an intermediary). The house's name and unusual appearance hark back to its 13th-century origins as a Cistercian abbey; the magnificent Great Barn, now empty, once stored wool, fleeces, cattle hides, crops and fruit from the orchards. After the Dissolution of the Monasteries, Grenville converted the abbey church into his new home, with the Great Hall in the space where the church crossing used to be. The charming chapel, part of the original abbey, has one unexpected feature: a special chute to allow owls in and out to deal with mice. Beyond the beautiful Georgian staircase, the loft space incorporates displays about Drake and small reconstructions of spaces inside the ships of his era. There are mannequins of Drake and his second wife in exquisite recreations of clothes they might have worn, made by a local sewing group, and a full-scale statue of Drake, found abandoned on a Devon hillside.

↑ Buckland Abbey. (marcin jucha/S)

ESSENTIALS

GETTING THERE Plymouth is just over three hours from London by train, slightly longer from Birmingham (GWR). By road the M5, merging on to the A38, is the most direct route, about 2½ hours from Cardiff, four hours from London and 4½ hours from Manchester.

STAYING **Fox House Studio Apartments** (⊘ foxhousestudios.com) offer self-contained accommodation in a convenient location between Plymouth's modern city centre and its historic heart. Just under two miles west along the waterside, the Grade II*-listed former home of an admiral in the Royal William Yard is now **Residence One** (⊘ bistrotpierre.co.uk/rooms/residence-one), a boutique B&B retaining many period features.

EATING For a snack on the go, **Alfresco** (🛐 AlfrescoPlymouth) dispenses delicious cannoli with your cappuccino from a green South Western Trams carriage outside the Mayflower Museum. The gin distillery's **Bottling Plant** (⊘ thebottlingplant.co.uk) is a good casual dining option. A stroll along the harbour brings you to **The Boathouse** (⊘ theboathouseplymouth.co.uk), which specialises in fish caught from its own boats; we recommend the seafood linguine.

TIME TO SPARE? **Plymouth Boat Trips** (⊘ plymouthboattrips.co.uk) runs various guided cruises and trips including a one-hour harbour cruise departing daily from the Barbican Landing Stage near the Mayflower Steps. The boat gives you an excellent view of the **Royal Citadel** (EH). Looming over the eastern end of Plymouth Hoe, overlooking Plymouth Sound, this 17th-century fort encompasses an earlier fort built by Drake, and is still a military establishment; it runs three guided tours a week. Also on Plymouth Hoe, the red-and-white striped **Smeaton's Tower** (⊘ theboxplymouth.com) is a much-loved symbol of the city. It's the third of four lighthouses built to mark Eddystone Reef, a group of rocks 14 miles southwest of Plymouth. In historic New Street, the **Elizabethan House** (⊘ theboxplymouth.com), a rare surviving example from its time, runs an immersive tour on which you can 'meet' the first owner, a washerwoman and a wig maker. The recreated **Elizabethan Gardens** next door (⊘ visitplymouth.co.uk) provide a quiet retreat in which to admire the low box hedges with beds of colourful flowers and fragrant herbs appropriate to the Elizabethan era. On an artistic note, the **Cottonian Collection**, in The Box's research space, includes early portraits, letters and items from the studio of Sir Joshua Reynolds, who was born in Plymouth. Two miles west, in the Royal Dockyard, the **Devonport Naval Heritage Centre** (⊘ devonportnhc.wordpress.com; by appointment) records the dockyard's development and Plymouth's role in supporting the Navy over seven centuries; four miles east of the city stands **Saltram House** (NT), a magnificent Georgian mansion.

14 TINTAGEL

ARTHUR & OTHER LEGENDS

Stories across more than a millennium have given Tintagel Castle as the birthplace of King Arthur. This dramatic spot on north Cornwall's Atlantic coast may also have been where the lovers Tristan and Iseult, subject of another legend, met. What we do know is that Tintagel has been an Iron Age fortification and trading port, a medieval castle and a citadel.

STAR ATTRACTION

The site of **Tintagel Castle** (EH) is in two sections, with a bridge built in 2019 connecting the mainland to the headland (island). Once there was a short isthmus, until it fell into the sea: *Din tagell* is Cornish for 'the fortress of the narrow entrance'. The remains of a barbican and two courtyards are reminders of the castle which Richard of Cornwall, younger brother of Henry III, built here in the 13th century. As you cross the bridge, look down to a tunnel entrance that passes through the neck of the headland. This is Merlin's Cave, where legends tell that Merlin pulled a newborn infant Arthur from the sea; Tennyson described the scene in his poems *Idylls of the King*. Earlier aspects of the legends came from the medieval chronicler Geoffrey of Monmouth, who depicted Arthur's conception, out of wedlock, at Tintagel; Wace, a poet at Henry II's court, who

↑ The bridge at Tintagel. (Rolf E. Staerk/S)

added the Round Table; and Sir Thomas Malory, whose *Le Morte d'Arthur* inspired Victorian writers and artists. The ambiguity of the Arthurian myths finds expression in *Gallos*, a bronze sculpture of a hooded and cloaked king on the headland's northwestern tip. It might be Arthur, or one of the kings of Dumnonia, the early medieval kingdom which covered Cornwall, Devon and parts of Somerset. A small walled area nearby was probably once a garden recreating a scene from *The Romance of Tristan*. In this 12th-century poem, Tristan and Iseult meet in a garden – or possibly an orchard – pretending not to notice the latter's husband King Mark hiding up a tree. Follow the tale via engraved flagstones around the edge of the space. A medieval courtyard on the headland was the location for Richard of Cornwall's Great Hall; archaeologists have also found hundreds of pieces of pottery, animal bones and other items from the 5th to 7th centuries. Behind the Great Hall, low stone walls indicate the location of early medieval buildings from the same era, which may have formed a village within the citadel. A wall at the southeastern edge of the headland marks the likely site of an early medieval harbour. Discoveries of pieces of amphorae, glass bowls and dishes suggest that Tintagel was a major trading port with links to continental Europe and western Asia Minor. Imports of wine, food and tableware would have been powerful status symbols for the kings of Dumnonia. Whether those rulers included Arthur, who knows?

ESSENTIALS

GETTING THERE The nearest mainline train station is Bodmin Parkway, four hours from London Paddington (GWR). Direct buses include the 95 from Camelford, 181 from Boscastle and 182 from Wadebridge; the A303, A30 and A395 provide the main non-motorway driving route.

STAYING & EATING The numerous options include **King Arthur's Arms** (⌘ kingarthursarms.co.uk) opposite the Old Post Office and, for breakfast, lunch or afternoon tea, **Charlie's Café** (⌘ charlies.cafe).

TIME TO SPARE? In Tintagel village, **King Arthur's Great Halls** (⌘ kingarthursgreathalls.co.uk), built in the 1930s as a tribute to the Arthurian legends, includes 72 stained-glass windows by a pupil of William Morris. The **Old Post Office** (NT), originally a 14th-century yeoman's farmhouse, sports a distinctive wavy slate roof and Victorian-era postal equipment inside. Four miles up the coast in Boscastle is the **Museum of Witchcraft and Magic** (⌘ museumofwitchcraftandmagic.co.uk). Eight miles to the east, the **Cornwall at War Museum** (⌘ cornwallatwarmuseum.co.uk) displays 20th-century RAF, Royal Navy and Army artefacts.

15 PENWITH

IRON, TIN, LIGHT

The Penwith peninsula, in the far west of Cornwall, is not where the British Isles ends; you can get a ferry to the Isles of Scilly. But it's certainly close to where England ends, as its name, from the Cornish words penn, meaning 'headland' and wydh, meaning 'at the end', suggests. There's a strong sense of local identity; this may have been the last region of Cornwall where communities spoke Cornish. An abundance of intriguing historic sites includes a concentration of Bronze Age, Iron Age and Romano-British remains; the 'Tin Coast' and its mines, which drove the local economy through the Georgian and Victorian eras; and a 19th- and 20th-century communications hub which influences our lives to this day. Penwith has also been home to two important colonies of artists, who loved the glorious light and landscapes.

THE ITINERARY

DAY 1 In the centre of Penwith, a few miles west of Penzance, lies the enigmatic **Carn Euny** (EH). There was an Iron Age settlement of timber houses here, dating from around 500–300BC, but the remains you see today are from the late Romano-British period, CAD400. Excavations in the 1960s and 1970s revealed nine dwellings, three of which were stone courtyard houses, a type of structure specific to western Cornwall and the Scilly Isles. Each has a central courtyard around

↑ Carn Euny. (Roger Driscoll/S)

which a number of rooms are built into the thickness of a substantial outer wall. The other six dwellings were simpler, smaller roundhouses. House I is the best preserved of the courtyard houses; investigations suggest that its inhabitants slept here and used parts of the structure to shelter livestock. The layout incorporates a sloping entrance to Carn Euny's most mysterious feature: a fogou. Like the stone courtyard houses, fogous are specific to west Cornwall, where there are 15 known examples, and the Scilly Isles (similar features, known as souterrains, exist in Ireland, Scotland and Britanny). 'Fogou' comes from the Cornish for caves. Fogous are partly or wholly underground, comprising drystone walls set in a large trench with capstone roofing. Tin miners discovered this example in the 1840s and a local antiquary excavated it 20 years later. It consists of a series of passages leading to a circular corbelled chamber, although research suggests that the chamber pre-dated many of the passages; excavations of the chamber revealed drainage gullies, stone paving areas and a small recess at ground level, as well as ashes, black earth, a whetstone and red and black pottery. We don't know the purpose of fogous for certain. The cool underground setting might have been suitable for storing meat and dairy products, or they may have acted as refuges, escape routes or ceremonial settings (the discovery of pottery, beads

PENWITH'S COLONIES OF ART

Penwith has been the base for two significant colonies of artists. The first dates to the 1880s when British painters began to gravitate to the fishing village of Newlyn, south of Penzance. The area's attractions replicated what many of those artists had found in Brittany; pre-Industrial Revolution scenery, cheap accommodation and plenty of willing models. In time, more artists such as Sir Alfred Munnings and Dame Laura Knight joined the 'Newlyn school', some of them settling in Lamorna further down the south coast. **Penlee House Gallery and Museum** (⌂ penleehouse.org.uk) in Penzance showcases the work of the Newlyn school. The second colony based itself in and around St Ives in the early and mid 20th century, among them the sculptor Dame Barbara Hepworth (1903–75). The Tate now manages her two-floor studio and garden, where she lived and worked for over 25 years, as the **Barbara Hepworth Museum** (⌂ tate.org.uk). Sculptures in bronze, stone and wood are on display in the museum and garden – many in the locations that Hepworth chose for them – along with paintings, drawings and archive material. It's a beautiful, tranquil yet stimulating space. A short but steep walk away, the bright white **Tate St Ives** (⌂ tate. org.uk) above Porthmeor Beach hosts an ever-changing international programme of modern and contemporary art exhibitions.

↑ Barbara Hepworth Museum, St Ives. (Ron Ellis/S)

and burned bones in various fogous suggests the latter). As you walk with care through Carn Euny's fogou, keep an eye on the stones for a neon green glow: this phosphorescent moss, which locals call goblin's gold, adds a further eerie touch to this mysterious place. A little way northwest of Carn Euny is **St Euny's Well**, a Grade II-listed medieval monument where large granite stones enclose a well at the side of a stream. St Euny was a Celtic missionary who visited Cornwall in the 7th century and tradition associates this well with him.

From Carn Euny you can explore other ancient sites (see *Time to spare*) or go nine miles south to Porthcurno's **Museum of Global Communications** (⊘ pkporthcurno.com). A Victorian businessman, John Pender, chose Porthcurno as the place to lay an undersea cable to Bombay (now Mumbai), a key development in modern communications. The museum is based in Eastern House, once Porthcurno's telegraph station site. Colourful interactive displays tell the story of 'PK' (the station's identifier) from its earliest days, through the creation of Cable & Wireless, to the site's role in World War II and its later conversion into an international engineering college for radio, satellite and telephone technology. The equipment on display is fascinating as are the stories of those who worked at PK, on the ships that laid the cables and in other telegraph stations abroad. Necessity bred ingenuity; our favourite exhibit is a ship's biscuit converted into an electric plug.

DAY 2 Penwith's rugged landscape is famous worldwide, partly thanks to Winston Graham's *Poldark* novels and their TV adaptations. The **Tin Coast**, a seven-mile stretch of northern Penwith's coastline that forms part of the Cornish Mining World Heritage Site, offers a trail through the dangerous lives that men, women and children led as they mined for tin and other minerals in these beautiful surroundings. Some mines remained open into the 1980s, until the 'Great Tin Crash' of October 1985 caused the worldwide tin price to drop by a third within a week. Start at **Cape Cornwall** (NT) which, until the first official Ordnance Survey, was thought to be England's westernmost point. The National Trust owns much of the headland and its car park gives a spectacular coastal view. The mine here extracted tin and copper from beneath the sea and its chimney still stands at the cape's summit. At the nearby village of **Botallack** (NT), two engine houses perch on the cliff edge – on a clear day you can see the Isles of Scilly. While there's some evidence of mining from the mid-Roman era and early mining records from the 16th century, Botallack's peak arrived in the 1860s. This mine produced tens of thousands of tons of tin and copper ore and substantial amounts of refined arsenic, an ingredient of pesticides and herbicides in those days. Botallack employed more than 550 people and even became a tourist attraction (a guinea a head). There are remains of nine buildings

in all, while an adjacent holiday cottage was once the 'count house'. This was the administration centre, in which wealthy investors would meet and dine, while miners were outside, collecting their wages or applying for work. Two miles north, guided tours of **Levant Mine** (NT) enable you to inspect the restored 1840s steam-powered beam engine which was critical to raising ore from the mines, as well as the skip shaft and other remains around the site. *Poldark* fans may recognise it from the BBC TV series. Levant's neighbour, **Geevor Tin Mine** (⊘ geevor.com), remained operational until 1990; retaining much of its mining equipment, it's now an impressive museum and heritage centre. Take a hard hat tour through the tunnels of the 18th-century Wheal Mexico mine, and view the mill where workers crushed, ground and separated rock to produce the precious tin. A plaque commemorates 31 miners who died in a dreadful accident at Levant in 1919. The 'Dry', the large building where miners clocked in and out, showered and changed, is another poignant reminder of the people who risked so much for their communities.

↑ Botallack. (Lucas Nott/S)

ESSENTIALS

GETTING THERE & AROUND
Frequent train services from London Paddington include the Night Riviera sleeper to Penzance (GWR), which takes just over five hours. There are also direct trains daily from Bristol and beyond. You can travel to St Ives by rail from St Erth, the stop before Penzance (⊘ greatscenicrailways.co.uk). The main road routes into Penwith are the M4 from London or M6 from Manchester, and then the M5 to Exeter and finally either the A30 or A38. If you drive around Penwith, be prepared for narrow lanes.

STAYING
The **Egyptian House** (LT) on Penzance's Chapel Street has an unusual provenance. In the 1830s a local man bought two cottages, raised the buildings' height and added the pseudo-Egyptian frontage before selling maps, guides, stationery and minerals here; it now houses three floors of holiday apartments. With steps to Porthminster Beach, the luxurious **St Ives Harbour Hotel & Spa** (⊘ harbourhotels.co.uk) is a short walk from the harbour or the Tate and Barbara Hepworth museums.

EATING
Penzance teems with restaurants. In Chapel Street alone you can enjoy duck with pomegranate and charred cauliflower at **Blacks of Chapel Street** (⊘ blacksofchapelstreet. com), monkfish and seafood curry at **The Bakehouse** (⊘ bakehouserestaurant.co.uk) or beetroot and apple soup in the kitschly pirate-themed **Admiral Benbow** pub (⊘ thebenbow.com). For lunch, pause among the sculpture gardens at **Tremenheere** (⊘ tremenheere.co.uk), two miles northeast of Penzance, for excellent bouillabaisse or tempura vegetables.

TIME TO SPARE?
Penwith's many ancient sites include **Boscawen-ûn** Stone Circle, two miles south of Carn Euny; the nearby Iron Age hillforts of **Caer Bran** and **Bartinney Castle**; **Lanyon Quoit** (NT) and **Chysauster Ancient Village** (EH), both north of Penzance; **Tregiffian Burial Chamber** (EH) in the south of the peninsula; and **Ballowall Barrow** (EH) on the west coast. For more on ancient sites here, see the **Cornish Ancient Sites Protection Network** (⊘ cornishancientsites.com). Porthcurno hosts the open-air **Minack Theatre** (⊘ minack.com), which has perched on a spectacular cliff face for almost a century. Go east from Penzance to Marazion and walk or take a boat (depending on the tide) across the causeway to **St Michael's Mount** (NT ⊘ stmichaelsmount.co.uk). The castle here, where the St Aubyns have lived for four centuries, was a Royalist stronghold in the English Civil War; its surprises include a miniature of an unusually full-bearded Charles I and the Strawberry Hill Gothic elegance of the Blue Drawing Room. Two gardens just west of Penzance are also worth exploring: **Trengwainton** (NT), to which 1920s plant hunters brought species from around the world and **Trewidden** (⊘ trewidden.co.uk), where *Dicksonia antarctica* (soft tree ferns) flourish in the bowl of an early opencast tin mine.

16 STRATFORD-UPON-AVON

THE STAY'S THE THING

N owhere in Britain enjoys such a close association with one person as Stratford-upon-Avon with William Shakespeare (1564–1616). He was born, grew up and spent his early married life and later years in the town, and the Royal Shakespeare Company (RSC) is based here. (This isn't the place to debate whether Francis Bacon or someone else wrote Shakespeare's plays: as Laurence Olivier said, 'No self-respecting actor would belong to the Royal *Bacon* Company'.) With a handy location on the northeastern edge of the Cotswolds, Stratford was around for more than 800 years before the birth of the Bard, as a village and then a town. It gained a charter for weekly markets in 1196 and became a significant player in the wool trade in medieval times, and later a major centre for leather tanning. Nowadays tourism is Stratford's major source of prosperity, thanks to 'Bardolatry', and there are well over 300 listed buildings to admire – not bad for what is still a small market town. Our itinerary visits Shakespeare's birthplace, his school, the site of his home as a husband and father, his wife's childhood home and a local house with a legendary tale of young Will's misdemeanours.

THE ITINERARY

DAY 1 Start at the top end of Henley Street with the **bronze statue of a jester**, a gift to the town from a local businessman. The statue represents Touchstone from *As You Like It*, with quotations from that play, *Twelfth Night* and *Hamlet* on its base. On the left of the street, as you walk down it, is the half-timbered façade of **Shakespeare's Birthplace** (AF), one of several sites managed by the Shakespeare Birthplace Trust (SBT, AF ⚲ shakespeare.org.uk). William was born here, the third of eight children to Mary Arden and John Shakespeare, a glovemaker who served the town in various civic posts. Inside are two buildings. The purpose-built Shakespeare Centre houses an exhibition of memorabilia including an early Folio and a timeline of William's life; next door, furnished in period style, is the house in which he grew up. As you wander into the neat garden, actors in Tudor costumes perform famous scenes and speeches. Leaving the Birthplace, walk down to the roundabout and turn right into High Street. On the right at number 26 you'll pass **Harvard House**, whose decorated half-timbered façade dates from 1596 and which was the home of the mother of John Harvard, founder of the eponymous US university. Continuing into Chapel Street, on the left you'll find the site of **New Place** (SBT, AF), Shakespeare's family home from 1597 until his death. The house Shakespeare bought for £60 had been built a century before, from brick and timber – an innovation at the time. It had ten fireplaces and grounds large enough for two barns and an orchard. After the Bard's death, the house passed to his daughter and granddaughter, and then out of the family. A later owner demolished it, as part of a running dispute with other residents! Today, an exhibition inside the Grade I-listed Tudor house next door attempts

← Anne Hathaway's Cottage. (Shakespeare Birthplace Trust)

to recreate life as it was at New Place for Shakespeare and his family. Adjoining the house are a splendid knot garden and the recreated Great Garden, with a mulberry tree believed to have grown from a cutting of a tree Shakespeare planted. A few doors down, where Chapel Street meets Chapel Lane, the **Guild Chapel** (⌗ guildchapel.org.uk) features a splendid, rare sequence of medieval wall paintings. In 1563, as town council chamberlain, John Shakespeare arranged payment for the whitewashing over of the paintings, as part of the suppression of Catholic 'idolatry'. Ironically, the whitewashing helped to preserve the artwork in the long run. Next door to the Guild Chapel, **Shakespeare's Schoolroom & Guildhall** (⌗ shakespearesschoolroom.org) is one of the finest surviving timber-framed guildhalls in England. It has seen six centuries of continuous use, originally as a venue for the Guild of the Holy Cross, a religious fraternity. Conservation work has revealed, at the south end of the ground floor, a full-length painting of John the Baptist. After the Reformation, the ground floor became a courtroom in which authority figures such as John Shakespeare, as town bailiff (mayor) in 1568–69, heard legal cases. The upper floor turned into a schoolroom. Between c1571–78, William received his education here and watched performances by various companies of travelling players. The two principal rooms upstairs are the Master's Chamber, which contains late 15th-century wall paintings of roses and a long oak table dating from the 17th century, and the Georgian schoolroom. The latter is still in use by King Edward VI School and incorporates early 18th-century school desks. Leaving the Guildhall, turn left and continue to the end of the road and turn left again, walking towards the river to reach the Grade I-listed **Holy Trinity Church** where Shakespeare was baptised and buried. From here, take a pleasant riverside walk of less than ten minutes to the Royal Shakespeare Theatre building (page 86).

DAY 2 Today's Shakespeare sites lie outside central Stratford. A drive, a ride on a City Sightseeing bus or a pleasant walk of just over a mile west of the town centre, to the Shottery area, brings you to **Anne Hathaway's Cottage** (SBT, AF) where Shakespeare's wife was born and grew up. Young Will courted her here, and the Hathaway family remained here into the early 20th century. During Anne's time here, this was a farmhouse; later owners added a section at one end. You can still see the structure of the original 1460s house on the first floor, in the shape of two curved oak timbers supporting the roof and walls. The furniture includes 'Shakespeare's Courting Chair', on which the carvings feature a falcon holding a spear, an element from the Shakespeare coat of arms. The initials 'WAS' are a later addition, possibly by William Ireland, a notorious forger of 'Shakespeare documents'. Among nine acres of gardens, orchards and woodland, the Shakespeare Tree Garden contains over 40 trees mentioned in the Bard's

↑ New Place. (trabantos/S) ← Shakespeare's Birthplace. (Shakespeare Birthplace Trust)

THE ROYAL SHAKESPEARE THEATRE

Down by the river, the **RSC** (⌖ rsc.org.uk) performs within a 21st-century red-brick and glass ensemble that preserves elements of earlier structures. There's an observation tower, from which you half-expect an actor to call citizens, in the style of a *muezzin*, to the next performance. The complex includes two stages, the Royal Shakespeare Theatre and the smaller Swan. The main auditorium is a surprisingly intimate space: the stage reaches out into the audience, who sit on three sides of it, in a similar arrangement to theatres in Shakespeare's day. If you're not here for a performance, you can book a tour, glimpsing the vast costume store and ascending the tower for views across Stratford. For a tight budget, previews are a good option, and even seats with restricted views may enable you to see more than their equivalents in a West End theatre. If you're in the stalls, be ready for anything. You could be invited on stage for a free ice cream, as we were for *The Two Gentlemen of Verona*, in the crossfire of a food fight (*King John*) or close to some graphic goriness (hand amputations in *Titus Andronicus*). It's not all Shakespeare: recent productions in The Swan include *Don Quixote*, *Matilda* and *The Boy in the Dress*.

↑ The Royal Shakespeare Theatre. (trebantos/S)

writings, as well as sculptures of key Shakespearean characters, from a threesome of Hamlet, Laertes and Ophelia to Sir John Falstaff's belly. To find a legendary tale from Will's youth, go seven miles east of Stratford to **Charlecote Park** (AF, NT). The Lucy family has lived here since the 13th century. Sir Thomas Lucy, a local magistrate, built the current house in c1558 and entertained Elizabeth I here in 1572. Eleven years later, according to legend, Sir Thomas fined a young William Shakespeare for poaching deer from his park. It's easy to imagine the story as you watch fallow deer roaming the estate today, in parkland which 'Capability' Brown remodelled. The character of Justice Shallow in *Henry IV Part II* and *The Merry Wives of Windsor* may be a Shakespearean caricature of Sir Thomas. The interior of the house at Charlecote tells the story of its Victorian owners George Hammond Lucy and his wife Mary Elizabeth; don't miss the family's carriage collection in the stables.

↑ Charlecote Park. (wolfman57/S)

ESSENTIALS

GETTING THERE The railway station, 15 minutes from the town centre, is on a spur of the Birmingham Moor Street–Leamington Spa line; arrive from London Marylebone (CH) or Hereford (WM). The M40 is the closest motorway (exit J15), but the M1, M5 and M6 pass close by, too.

STAYING For a place to sleep, perchance to dream, there's plenty of choice. Opposite the theatre, the **Arden** (⊘ theardenhotelstratford.com) is part of the RSC's estate and the land once belonged to John Shakespeare. Nearby, the **Pen & Parchment** (⊘ greeneking-pubs.co.uk) retains some original beams and the **Swan's Nest** (⊘ swansnesthotel.co.uk) dates back to the 17th century. For half-timbered cosiness in Stratford's historic heart, try the **Mercure Shakespeare** on Chapel Street (⊘ all.accor.com). Ten miles east lies the extraordinary octagonal folly of **The Bath House** (LT).

EATING There are numerous local bistros and national chains, especially on Sheep Street where we recommend **Lamb's** (⊘ lambsrestaurant.co.uk) and **The Opposition** (⊘ theoppo.co.uk). The Royal Shakespeare Theatre's rooftop restaurant is efficient and convenient, while **Sorrento** (⊘ sorrentorestaurant.co.uk) on Ely Street offers a delicious traditional Neapolitan lasagne. For morning coffee, light lunches or afternoon tea, the dog-friendly **Other Place** café, the World War II-themed **FourTeas** (⊘ thefourteas.co.uk) on Sheep Street, or the cat café **Shakespaw** (⊘ shakespawcatcafe.com) on Union Street are all palpable hits.

TIME TO SPARE? A combined ticket for Shakespeare's Birthplace, New Place and Anne Hathaway's Cottage is available from the Shakespeare Birthplace Trust (⊘ shakespeare.org.uk). Two other Shakespeare Birthplace Trust sites closed during the pandemic, but may reopen in due course; **Hall's Croft**, where Shakespeare's daughter and her husband lived, and **Mary Arden's Farm**, just north of Stratford, where the Bard's mother grew up. There's plenty of non-Shakespearean heritage nearby. Three miles north of town, the small **Stratford Armouries** (⊘ stratfordarmouries.co.uk) has exhibits from both World Wars including parts of a Wellington Bomber. Also to the north are several other National Trust properties: the medieval moated manor house at **Baddesley Clinton** and two Tudor estates, **Coughton Court** (also RHS) and **Packwood House.** A few miles northeast lie two notable castles: **Warwick** (⊘ warwick-castle.com), still going strong after 1,100 years and set in 64 acres of 'Capability' Brown-landscaped grounds; and the remains and gardens of **Kenilworth** (EH) where the Earl of Leicester entertained Elizabeth I. Around a dozen miles east of Stratford, the **British Motor Museum** (⊘ britishmotormuseum.co.uk) houses the world's largest collection of historic British cars, while **Compton Verney** (AF) is an award-winning art gallery in a Grade I-listed Robert Adam mansion, set in 120 acres of 'Capability' Brown landscaped parkland.

17 SULGRAVE MANOR

WASHINGTON'S ANCESTRAL HOME

T he clue is in the signage. Along with directions to the house, the tea room, the shop and the toilets, an arrow points towards 'Washington DC 3,607 miles'. The significance of Sulgrave Manor, in the quiet west Northamptonshire village of Sulgrave, lies in the identity of its builder, his family and one descendant in particular: George Washington (1732–99), first President of the United States of America.

STAR ATTRACTION

Until the Dissolution of the Monasteries, the Manor belonged to the Cluniac Priory of St Andrew at Northampton. After the Dissolution, the Crown sold it to Lawrence Washington, a wool merchant who had twice been Mayor of Northampton. Lawrence had the new house built, using limestone rubble, between 1540 and 1560, living there with his wife and 11 children, and the family retained it for just over a century. In later times the house fell into disrepair, until the Anglo-American Peace Committee raised £8,000 to buy it

↑ Sulgrave Manor. (Alison Thompson/A)

in 1914 as a symbol of a century of peace between the USA and the UK. Today, a trust administers the restored **Sulgrave Manor** (HH ⊘ sulgravemanor.org.uk) and gardens, and the house has Grade I-listed status. The original Washington family arms, a combination of stars and stripes, appear above the door. As you step inside, take a moment to admire the stone floor in the great hall, as well as the salt cupboard, carved with Lawrence Washington's initials, in the original fireplace. The bed hangings in the great bedchamber, the creation of UK and US stitchers in 2005, depict mythical creatures like those on the original travelling mirror on the bedside table. The 18th-century kitchen is well equipped, its bread oven capable of baking 25 loaves of bread at a time; the oak parlour is of a similar age, and the Trust has decorated it in a style which George Washington might have found familiar, with a spinet (an early form of piano) and a Georgian tea service at the ready. From Sulgrave, Lawrence Washington's great-great-grandson John emigrated to the (then) English colony of Virginia in 1656, where John's great-grandson George was born in 1732. An exhibition at Sulgrave profiles George and debunks the more durable myths about his life. He did not cut down a cherry tree and confess the act to his father, sport wooden teeth, live in the White House or throw a silver dollar across the Potomac River. It's hard, over two centuries later, to get near the truth of the man. Nevertheless, the paintings and sculptures of George inside and outside the house, including a large bronze bust in the gardens, give an impression of serenity at one with this peaceful, charming place.

ESSENTIALS

GETTING THERE The nearest main road is the A422, accessible from junction 11 of the M40, while the M40 and A5 pass a few miles east of the village. The nearest town is Banbury, eight miles away and 80 minutes from London Marylebone by train (CH).

STAYING & EATING Sulgrave's **Star Inn** (⊘ thestarsulgrave.co.uk) offers B&B and a traditional pub menu. For a hidden refuge, stay in **Canons Ashby's** 16th-century tower (LT).

TIME TO SPARE? Five miles north of Sulgrave Manor stands another reminder of Tudor times, **Canons Ashby** (NT). The owners for four centuries were the Dryden family, whose most famous member, John Dryden, was the first Poet Laureate and an occasional visitor; his portrait is in the dining room. The decorative plaster ceiling in what is now the drawing room, and the Elizabethan wall paintings in Spenser's room (named after another poet), are breathtaking. Eighteen miles east of Sulgrave in Stoke Bruerne, the **Canal Museum** (⊘ canalrivertrust.org.uk) explores the history of Britain's canals, so crucial to the Industrial Revolution.

18 COLCHESTER

OH, WHAT A CIRCUS!

Around 50 miles northeast of London, the Essex town of Colchester has a claim to be Britain's first capital. It was the first British settlement for which there is a published reference (by Pliny the Elder in AD77) and the Romans described one of its rulers, Cunobelin, as 'King of the Britons'. Following Cunobelin's death, the Romans invaded Britain in AD43 with Colchester as a key target and stationed the Twentieth Legion here after the conquest. The rebel Boudica burned the town to the ground in AD60 and London replaced it as the British capital the following year, but Colchester rose again and prospered. Today the evidence of the Roman era is, in some ways, fragmentary, but still well worth seeking out, including Britain's only known Roman circus.

STAR ATTRACTIONS

Begin at **Colchester Castle and Museum** (⌂ colchester.cimuseums.org.uk). The building we call the castle is the keep of a much larger castle, which William the Conqueror built on the site of a Roman temple to Claudius. It's the largest intact Norman keep in Europe; only the foundations of the temple remain, which

↑ Colchester Castle and Museum. (Nicola Pulham/S)

you can see on a guided tour. Inside the castle, the museum contains several outstanding Roman artefacts. The fine tombstone of Marcus Favonius Facilis, who commanded 80 men at Colchester, shows him riding over a crouching, defeated Briton. A bronze sculpture of the god Mercury is missing its arms, which might explain his facial expression. The Colchester Vase, the most famous vase surviving from Roman Britain, depicts a gladiatorial fight, a man beating a bear with a whip and a dog pursuing a hare and stags. You can also try chariot racing, on a big screen. Fifteen minutes west across town lie the remains of a **Roman Circus** (⊘romancircus.co.uk) where the real thing took place. Local archaeologists discovered it in 2005, with a little help from TV's *Time Team*. Reconstructions of the seating and the eight starting gates give you an idea of the scale of the arena, around 1,500ft long and 250ft wide, with two long straight sections with a barrier between them. Charioteers raced down one straight, turned 180 degrees and raced down the other straight to complete a lap. The Circus was built around AD120 and in use for about 150 years. It takes imagination but, with the help of the reconstructions, the visitor centre exhibition and the castle simulations, you can picture yourself as one of the 7,000 spectators gleefully cheering the many accidents, or as a charioteer trying to control two, three or sometimes four horses. A short walk away along Balkerne Hill is a section of the **Roman wall** built after the Boudican revolt; much masonry remains visible. The Balkerne gate connected Colchester with the main road to London. Not far away in Maidenburgh Street, there's a glimpse of the remains of the **Roman theatre**; look for the darker paving in the road showing the outline of the theatre's walls.

ESSENTIALS

GETTING THERE Colchester's principal railway station (there are two others) is about an hour equidistant from London Liverpool Street and Norwich (GA). The main road links are the A12, M25 and A14. Stansted Airport (⊘stanstedairport.com) is 50 minutes away.

STAYING & EATING On East Stockwell Street, in Colchester's picturesque Dutch Quarter, stands **Peake's House** (LT), replete with cosy late Elizabethan interiors and mullioned windows. For coffee, try **Café Saison** (⊘cafesaison.co.uk) on Trinity Street.

TIME TO SPARE? Near the castle in a fine Georgian townhouse, **Hollytrees Museum** (⊘colchester.cimuseums.org.uk) displays a great collection of tall clocks made in Colchester. Above the High Street stands the **'Jumbo' Water Tower**, a Victorian construction whose weathervane is decorated with an elephant. Seven miles southwest of Colchester, **Layer Marney Tower** (AF, HH ⊘layermarneytower.co.uk) is England's tallest Tudor gatehouse.

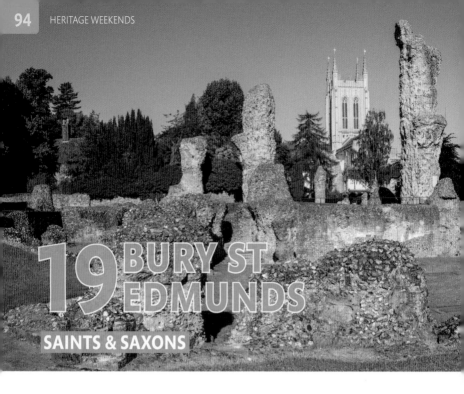

19 BURY ST EDMUNDS

SAINTS & SAXONS

The unassuming Suffolk market town of Bury St Edmunds was once a Saxon royal borough. It went by the names of Beodericsworth and Bedrichesworth before becoming St Edmund's Bury to denote the burial place of King Edmund, a 9th-century ruler of East Anglia and England's patron saint before St George. A huge abbey housed Edmund's relics and the neighbouring cathedral also bears his name; venerable civic and secular buildings enable you to find out more about the history of the town. Just outside Bury, a recreation of an Anglo-Saxon village gives a sense of local life and customs from 1,500 years ago.

THE ITINERARY

DAY 1 First stop should be the remains of **Bury St Edmunds Abbey** (EH), whose establishment in 1020 came over a century after the site received King Edmund's remains and over 150 years after the Danes shot him dead with multiple arrows and beheaded him for refusing to give up his Christian beliefs. One of the many stories of miracles to emerge after Edmund's death said that, after the disappearance of the severed head, it was found being guarded by a wolf and was re-attached to the body. The Romanesque abbey became a great pilgrimage site for visitors from all over Europe, but it was largely destroyed in the aftermath of the Dissolution of the Monasteries. Its most impressive surviving part is the Great Gate, through which you enter. This, the Norman Tower and other remains confirm how large and imposing the abbey must

↑ The remains of Bury St Edmunds Abbey, with St Edmundsbury Cathedral in the background. (chrisdorney/S)

have been; the abbey church was one of the largest in England at the time of construction. The church next door, once dedicated to St Denys and then St James, gained cathedral status in 1914 and is now **St Edmundsbury Cathedral** (⊘ stedscathedral.org). Much of the interior is relatively new, such as the Millennium Tower, or reworked by the Victorians, such as the medieval font which George Gilbert Scott redesigned. But the Susanna Window, depicting the story of Susanna and the Elders from the Apocrypha, dates to c1480. The bishop's throne references Edmund by incorporating crowns, arrows and a wolf or two into its design, and an Elizabeth Frink sculpture of Edmund graces the neighbouring Chapel of the Transfiguration.

A few minutes away via Angel Hill and Lower Baxter Street, **Moyse's Hall** (AF ⊘ moyseshall.org) has served the town for 900 years as a prison, workhouse, police station and now a museum. The ground floor is an undercroft retaining much of the original stonework; the pointed arches date from c1180. Before going upstairs, don't miss the 'Edmund Relic', a piece of metal which may have been one of the arrowheads that killed Edmund. The museum holds a collection of works by Mary Beale (1633–99), who came from West Suffolk and who was England's first female professional painter. The old Solar room houses a beautiful display of timepieces, from pocket watches to automaton inventions and grandfather clocks. A short walk from Moyse's Hall on Guildhall Street stands **Bury St Edmunds Guildhall** (⊘ burystedmundsguildhall.org.uk). Written sources confirm this was well established by 1300 as a centre for municipal functions such as elections and tax assessments. The arched doorway entrance (c1220) is an example of Early English architecture and the exterior flintwork is of a similar vintage. After 1800, Georgian design overlaid the medieval original. The long guildhall for meetings of merchants and traders gave way to a Banqueting Hall and a Court Room, with the latter serving as a court and then the town's library. Look for the portraits of a quizzical-looking James I, who granted three charters to the town, and various Bury movers, shakers and benefactors. Other features include the rebuilt Tudor kitchen, whose chimney breasts have some original brickwork, and the old council chamber where, during World War II, an Observer Corps team gathered intelligence about enemy aircraft movements.

DAY 2 We thought that the lady selling tickets for the **West Stow Anglo-Saxon Village & Country Park** (⊘ weststow.org) said: 'The re-enactors are dying today.' There was no need to worry. The volunteers were *dyeing*, to show visitors how Anglo-Saxons used plant dyes to create a range of colours. Meanwhile another

ESSENTIALS

GETTING THERE Regular trains from London take just under two hours (GA). The nearest main roads are the A11, A12 and A14.

STAYING The **Abbey Hotel** (⊘ abbeyhotel.co.uk) on Southgate Street is a sound choice, as is the **Angel Hotel** (⊘ theangel.co.uk) opposite the Abbey Gardens. The Angel, built in 1452, is a Bury landmark; guests have included Charles Dickens and Angelina Jolie. Just outside town, the **Ickworth Hotel** (⊘ ickworthhotel.co.uk) in the East Wing of Ickworth House (see below) offers a luxury touch. One mile from West Stow Anglo-Saxon Village, **West Stow Pods** (⊘ weststowpods.co.uk) offers a range of glamping accommodation in private woodland.

EATING A short walk from the abbey on Buttermarket, family-run **Cafe Kottani** (⊘ cafekottani.co.uk) does a delicious spanakopita (spinach and feta pie). On Angel Hill, facing the entrance to the abbey, the **Really Rather Good Coffee House and Tea Room** (⊘ rrgood.co.uk) lives up to its name; the coffee, tea, apple juice, beer and much of the food is made on site or by local suppliers. Nearby, **1921 Angel Hill** (⊘ nineteen-twentyone. co.uk) offers fine dining.

TIME TO SPARE? For a history of the local armed forces, visit the **Suffolk Regiment Museum** (⊘ suffolkregimentmuseum.co.uk) off Risbygate Street. Three miles southwest of town, in 1,800 acres of parkland, **Ickworth House** (NT) is an Italianate palace with

re-enactor, in period dress like the others, tuned up her lyre. West Stow, six miles north of Bury, is the site of an early Anglo-Saxon village, occupied from AD420–650. The buildings here are not the originals or adaptations of them, but experiments in archaeology, built in the past 50 years to test theories. There are eight in all, close together, including a hall, a farmer's house and a workshop. In terms of accommodation space, the Living House is the largest, with living and sleeping space for up to ten people and storage space in the roof. The display boards make it clear that investigations are continuing; for example, the Sunken House was built to test a theory that people lived in a pit (i.e. without a floor) with a roof that came down to the ground: 'We now think this idea is wrong for West Stow.' An on-site museum sets the context for the Anglo-Saxon period and displays objects found across the site and locally. The most spectacular is the Isleham Hoard of over 6,500 pieces of bronze, more than 3,000 years old, which a farmer found in 1959 buried in a pot at the end of a ditch. If you appreciate the uncertainty of historical and archaeological research, West Stow will be your cup of mead; there's so much we still don't know about how our ancestors lived 1,500 years ago.

a classical rotunda and a series of unconventional owners over 500 years. Eleven miles south of Bury, the well-preserved medieval village of Lavenham achieved its prosperity from the wool trade. Its many beautiful buildings include the Church of St Peter and St Paul and **Lavenham Guildhall** (NT).

↑ Ickworth House. (Raedwald/S)

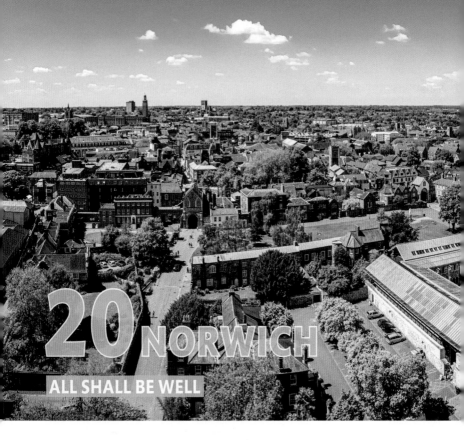

20 NORWICH
ALL SHALL BE WELL

orwich, on Norfolk's River Wensum, has adapted over the centuries to trade in wool, textiles, engineering, publishing and, for two centuries, Colman's mustard. The evidence of a millennium of human history is all around the city, most notably in the form of its castle, one of England's largest medieval cathedrals and 32 medieval churches, including one with links to a redoubtable woman who shared her visions of divine love.

THE ITINERARY

DAY 1 Start at the top, on a hill above the city, with **Norwich Castle** (AF ⊘ museums.norfolk.gov.uk), which the Normans built as a wooden fort before starting work on the stone keep with limestone from Caen in France. Royalty rarely stayed here and the castle was a prison for over 500 years. Today, while a major project undertakes to recreate the Norman-era palace by rebuilding the keep's original five floors, a sequence of galleries covers various aspects of Norfolk's past. The displays on Boudica and the Romans are notable for including coin collections not only from the Romans, but also from the Iceni and other British

↑ Norwich Cathedral. (Alexey Fedorenko/S)

tribes including the Corieltauvi and the Trinovantes. In the galleries exploring the history of the Norfolk Regiment, look out for the story of Private Abbs, who was blinded while serving during World War I. He later learned the art of string bag making, and a business card indicates that he also repaired boots and made mats. The art gallery includes works by Sir Alfred Munnings and artists from the early 19th-century Norwich School, as well as items from the collection of the Pastons of Oxnead Hall. The Pastons' meteoric 15th-century rise, from humble origins to wealth and influence within two generations, through a combination of legal training and opportunism, is documented in one of the earliest surviving collections of private correspondence in English. They remained one of Norfolk's wealthiest families for 350 years.

A few minutes' walk north of the castle, the **Museum of Norwich at the Bridewell** (AF ⊘ museums.norfolk.gov.uk) explores life here since 1700, at which point Norwich was still England's second city. Galleries recreate shop windows for outlets from butchers to taxidermists, with shop signs such as the large sheep or 'golden fleece' denoting the wealth that came to Norwich through the wool trade.

↑ Inside Norwich Castle. (SS)

Displays also remember the 'Strangers', late 16th-century settlers from the Low Countries who brought sophisticated textiles skills – and their pet canaries, from which Norwich football club got its nickname. The city's most famous firm, Colman's, made flour and starch as well as mustard. A recreation of an early 20th-century pharmacist's shop may surprise you in terms of some of the potions and pills that people were prepared to pop. The undercroft saw previous use as a house of correction and a prison.

DAY 2 The city's other great Norman building is **Norwich Cathedral** (⊘ cathedral. org.uk). Like the castle, construction combined local flint and mortar with Caen limestone. The new cathedral incorporated a Benedictine monastery, which helps to explain its great size. Fragments of wall painting are a reminder that the cathedral was much more elaborately decorated than it is today. But the bosses remain, over 1,000 of them, lower and more visible in the cloisters than elsewhere. Some are in specific sequences, such as the series in the nave's vault showing the history of the world from its creation. At the cathedral's east end lies the grave of Edith Cavell (1865–1915), a nurse from Swardeston village, just south of Norwich, who helped more than 200 Allied soldiers to escape from Belgium in the early stages of World War I before being executed by the Germans. A series of 14 small modern paintings by Brian Whelan depicts Cavell's life in the style of the Stations of the Cross. Outside, a monument by Erpingham Gate features a bust of Cavell in nurse's uniform above a laurel wreath, with a stone base incorporating a full-size relief of a soldier hanging up a second wreath. Don't miss the poem on a black wall plaque celebrating the wonderfully named Osberto Parsley, a singer and composer who served the cathedral for 50 years until his death in 1585. He sang in Latin under Henry VIII, in English under Edward VI, in Latin under Mary I and English under Elizabeth I. Less than a mile away, hidden among modern housing just off King Street, is the Grade I-listed **Church and Shrine of St Julian** (⊘ visitnorwich.co.uk). Much of it is a reconstruction of the early medieval original after bomb damage during World War II, although the Romanesque door to Julian's cell and the 15th-century font – the latter relocated from All Saints Church in 1977 – are attractive highlights. The main point of interest is the association with Lady Julian, a 14th-century anchoress (an approximate equivalent of a hermit) who inhabited a cell attached to the church. We don't know her real name, as she took Julian from the name of the church. A near-fatal illness caused Julian to see 16 visions, which she later turned into *Revelations of Divine Love*. Her theme, a controversial one for her times, was that God was not vengeful or judgemental, but loving, and that 'all shall be well, all shall be well, and all manner of things shall be well'. Even though the church is not the original, it's possible to pause here and feel an indefinable presence. Norwich now runs an annual Julian Week each May.

ESSENTIALS

GETTING THERE Norwich is 2½ hours away by train from London Liverpool Street or King's Cross, four hours from Birmingham and six hours from Edinburgh (GA). The main routes by road are the A47 and the A11.

STAYING The **Maids Head Hotel** (⌗ maidsheadhotel.co.uk), near the cathedral, has seen over 800 years as a hotel. About 15 minutes' walk from the city centre, **Number 82 The Unthank** (⌗ number82theunthank.co.uk) is a boutique hotel with serviced apartments.

EATING For a mid-visit drink and a snack, we recommend **Marmalades** (⌗royalarcadenorwich.co.uk), a friendly independent café in the picturesque late Victorian- era Royal Arcade. We can't mention Norwich and food without Delia Smith – cook, TV presenter and joint majority shareholder in Norwich City Football Club in Carrow Road, where **Delia's Restaurant and Bar** and **Yellows Bar & Grill** (⌗ deliascanarycatering. co.uk) offer fine dining and classic comfort food.

TIME TO SPARE? Ten minutes from the cathedral, **Strangers' Hall** (⌗ museums. norfolk.gov.uk) is a Grade I-listed building with parts dating back more than 700 years. Once the home of various mayors, it is now a museum of domestic history, with a Tudor Great Hall, a 17th-century bedroom and a Georgian dining room. Around the medieval **Norwich Lanes** close to the cathedral, you'll find the largest daily open **market** in Britain and the Art Deco splendour of **City Hall**; the main balcony is 200ft long, leading you to expect a politburo of the local great and the good to emerge on it at any moment, waving to the populace.

↑ The Lanes. (cktravels.com/S)

21 STAMFORD

VISIONS OF HEAVEN & HELL

This well-preserved Lincolnshire town, on the River Welland, appeared in the *Anglo-Saxon Chronicle* as early as AD922. In medieval times it grew wealthy through the wool trade, evident today in the form of numerous attractive buildings. Eccentric events and people associated with Stamford have included an annual bull run, which occurred for at least 450 years, and Daniel Lambert, who died here in 1809 weighing 52 stones and 11 pounds. You can barely turn a corner in Stamford without finding a listed building; there are over 600 in all. Elizabeth I's right-hand man built a palatial house just outside the town, an impressive testament to the family who have lived here ever since its construction, with two magnificent pieces of Baroque art inside.

THE ITINERARY

DAY 1 Start on Broad Street at **Browne's Hospital** (∂browneshospital.co.uk), which wool merchant William Browne founded in 1475. The Bishop of Lincoln dedicated the hospital in 1494, by which time Browne had died and his brother-in-law John had taken over. You can see the family crest at the top of the stairs on the left of the entrance: a shield with three mallets – a tool of the wool trade. This was a home and a house of prayer for ten poor men and two poor women under the supervision of a warden and a confrater, acting as secular priests. The Hospital still accommodates residents in 13 almshouses today. Several rooms in the main building contain original furniture, such as an iron-bound chest that stored all the key documents. The highlight is the chapel, which retains a row of original seats at its western end and stained-glass windows from the original building. The Brownes also played a key role in the history of **All Saints' Church** on the north side of Red Lion Square. This 13th-century building may conceivably be one of four Stamford churches mentioned in the Domesday Book; it has a 15th-century tower and a spire which reaches 152ft. A group of brasses commemorates William and John Browne's generosity in paying for much of the repair work after Lancastrian forces sacked and burned Stamford during the Wars of the Roses (page 17). We're fond of the timber-framed **Gothic House** on the High Street, and not just because chocolates are sold on the ground floor and there's a rather good independent bookshop upstairs... Its frontage is a Gothic Revival creation from 1849, but some original timber framing survives, and you can see the jetty of the original building inside as you head up to the first floor. At the top of the stairs stands a tall clock made by Thomas Rayment, a noted clockmaker who occupied the site for a while; he went bankrupt in 1792, as if to prove that even Stamford's story isn't one of uninterrupted success.

DAY 2 Just under two miles from the centre of Stamford stands **Burghley House** (AF, HH ∂burghley.co.uk), home of William Cecil (1520–98), later Lord Burghley, Elizabeth I's principal secretary and Lord Treasurer. The house took

32 years to complete, partly because Cecil was working on another property elsewhere. His descendants, who took the title of successive Earls of Exeter, updated aspects of the building and modernised the garden and parklands, using 'Capability' Brown's expertise. The house contains several hundred paintings, many of them purchases of the 5th and 9th Earls during their travels through Italy. House tours start in the enormous rib-vaulted Old Kitchen, one of the oldest spaces at Burghley; it showcases 260 copper utensils, including a turtle-shaped soup tureen. From here you visit a further 17 rooms on two floors, via barrel-vaulted stairs which were part of the original building at one end and a fine cantilever staircase of local stone at the other. The billiard room is worth a pause; the timber for the table came from HMS *Royal George* which sank in 1782. The most remarkable, however, is left almost until last: two masterpieces by Antonio Verrio (1636–1707), who decorated a series of rooms in the West Wing, which had been William Cecil's Long Gallery, for the 5th Earl. The first great highlight is the Heaven Room, where a vast painting across the walls and ceilings shows scenes from ancient mythology against the background of a Roman temple and blue sky. Gods and goddesses enjoying a day by the sea are 'disporting themselves as Gods and Goddesses are wont to do', as a 19th-century guidebook put it. Clothes are scarce, which might be a hazard for those figures around Vulcan's forge. See if you can spot Verrio in an Alfred Hitchcock-style

↑ The *Hell Staircase*, Burghley House. (Burghley House)

cameo appearance, looking pleased with himself. The sense of movement and action, the elaborate details, the depth of colour and *trompe l'oeil* effects lead you to expect the figures to step out of the painting at any moment. This is a classic Baroque mural, a style Verrio introduced to England. Just in case the room doesn't contain enough extravagance, a solid silver wine cooler in the centre weighs 230 pounds. From heavenly excess, you move out on to the Hell Staircase, Verrio's last commission at Burghley, which he completed over 11 months. The light pinks and blues of the Heaven Room are now blacks and reds; here across the ceiling is Hell portrayed as the enormous gaping mouth of a cat. There are no more gods and goddesses, and the men and women here are in torment, fear and despair, with Death at the centre wielding his sickle. The murals, the work of Thomas Stothard a century later, depict *Orpheus and Eurydice*, *Intemperance (Mark Antony and Cleopatra)* and *The Horrors of War*. The first two are more of a piece with artworks elsewhere in the house, but it's the claustrophobic ceiling that demands attention. From here, you descend the staircase to the spacious Great Hall – 68ft long, 30ft wide and over 60ft tall – which has served as a library and a banqueting hall. In any other house, this might be the star attraction but, in Burghley, it's a chance to catch your breath as you reflect on Verrio's visions.

ESSENTIALS

GETTING THERE Stamford is 90 minutes from London or York by train (EM) and 90 miles from London on the A1. Burghley House is a pleasant walk from Stamford, or you can take the hourly bus (⌁ delainebuses.com).

STAYING The **George of Stamford** (⌁ georgehotelofstamford.com) on St Martin's is a coaching inn which claims to have refreshed and accommodated travellers for over 1,000 years. Original gateways, passageways and the remains of a chapel, along with an oak-panelled restaurant, all add to the sense of continuity and comfort. The **Bull and Swan** and the **William Cecil** (⌁ hillbrookehotels.co.uk) are also conveniently located.

EATING The **Central Café and Tea Rooms** (⌁ centraltearoom.co.uk) on Red Lion Square serves a tempting selection of breakfasts, lunches, cakes and bakes. Its 15th-century timber-framed building was part of the Brownes' wool trade empire, and has served as a tea room for over 200 years. On St Mary's Hill, **Zada** (⌁ zadarestaurant.co.uk) offers Middle Eastern/Turkish fusion cuisine in a themed interior of colourful cushions and dark wood.

TIME TO SPARE? The remains of the Norman church of **St Leonard's Priory** just east of Stamford are worth a visit.

22 LEICESTER

FIT FOR A KING

Two thousand years ago, the Corieltauvi tribe established a settlement near the River Soar in the East Midlands. The Romans bult a fort here and the town of Ratae Corieltavorum grew around it. In Tudor and Stuart times Leicester, as it was known by then, was a centre of the wool trade, which led to the development of a local knitting industry; wealth from the hosiery trade paid for elegant buildings and the Georgian promenade known as New Walk. Leicester was also early to profit from the coming of the railway, with local businessman Thomas Cook recognising its potential for leisure travel. But it is the city's medieval legacy that has attracted attention in recent years, with the discovery in 2012 of the remains of the last Plantagenet King of England, Richard III, under a car park. The site of Richard's final, fatal battle lies ready for exploration nearby.

THE ITINERARY

DAY 1 Start at the **King Richard III Visitor Centre** (⌂kriii.com) on St Martins. The ground-floor exhibitions provide historical context. 'Dynasty' includes timelines and family trees, as well as a giant house of cards, to help unravel the complex rivalries and events of the Wars of the Roses (page 17). 'Death' covers Richard's defeat at the Battle of Bosworth in 1485 and the aftermath, including his burial in Leicester's Greyfriars church. The upper-floor exhibition 'Discovery' recounts how the dig came about, the selection of the dig site, the discovery of a skeleton and the forensic archaeological techniques that were used to identify the bones. The section on wider cultural perceptions reveals that Sex Pistols singer John Lydon apparently based his 'Johnny Rotten' stage persona on Laurence Olivier's interpretation of Richard III. Finally, you can view the trench itself, with a projected image showing exactly where the remains were found. It's a short step across the road to **Leicester Cathedral** (⌂leicestercathedral.org – closed until autumn 2023), where, after a legal tussle with York, which also claimed Richard for its own, the king's remains were reinterred in March 2015. In Richard's day the cathedral was simply the Church of St Martin. Originally a Norman church, it was rebuilt and enlarged between the 13th and 15th centuries, becoming the 'Civic Church', with strong links with the merchants and guilds, and became a cathedral when the diocese of Leicester was re-established in 1927. Opposite is the **Guildhall** (⌂leicestermuseums.org), one of the best-preserved timber-framed medieval halls in the country. Built in c1390 as a meeting place for the Guild of Corpus Christi, it was later taken over by the City Corporation and used as the Town Hall. The Mayor's Parlour hosts a magnificent 17th-century fireplace, while the medieval Great Hall has painted panels depicting the borough symbols of the cinquefoil and wyvern and the arms of the Hastings family. An upstairs room was once one of the oldest public libraries in the country. The building was a police station at one time; downstairs are cells and artefacts relating to law enforcement

← Statue of Richard III outside the visitor centre. (trabantos/S)

TRAVEL & TEMPERANCE:
THOMAS COOK IN LEICESTER

Outside Leicester's London Road railway station stands a statue of a man in formal Victorian dress, holding a briefcase and umbrella in his right hand, a large suitcase by his side. This is **Thomas Cook** (1808–92), whose company became Britain's best-known travel firm. It all began in 1841 at the old station in nearby Campbell Street, with a day trip by train to Loughborough. Cook grew his new travel firm with UK excursions, then trips to continental Europe, the USA, the Middle East and the rest of the world. He came up with the idea of the hotel coupon, a key element in package holidays for later generations. Cook's clientele was mainly middle-class, but other travel entrepreneurs followed him as foreign travel gradually opened up to working people.

Cook lived and worked in Leicester in the early years of the business. The former **East Gates Coffee House** (now a Grade II-listed building) near the city centre's Clock Tower was one in a chain of coffee and cocoa houses owned by a company of which Cook was a founder member. Cook was a lifelong believer in the benefits of temperance (abstinence from, or limited consumption of, alcohol). The 1841 train trip to Loughborough was part of his temperance campaigning, and he opened a temperance hotel (sadly no longer there) on Granby Street. The **Thomas Cook Building** at 5 Gallowtree Gate, built in 1894, housed the excursion, tourist and shipping office alongside the foreign exchange and banking departments. Friezes on the exterior celebrate the company's first 50 years. Cook is buried in **Welford Road Cemetery**, as is his son John (1834–99) who took over the business. Some of John's travel memorabilia are now in the Ancient Egypt section of **Leicester Museum & Art Gallery** (see opposite).

↑ Frieze on the Thomas Cook Building. (HM)

and punishment, the grisliest being a gibbet iron that was used for the public display of the bodies of dead criminals.

DAY 2 Fourteen miles west of Leicester, **Bosworth Battlefield Heritage Centre** (⊘ bosworthbattlefield.org.uk) provides useful context about the battle. Videos portray protagonists such as 'John the Archer', who does his weekly practice but hopes never to have to fight, and Lord Stanley, who faces the impossible choice between loyalty to his sovereign and his family. One section deals with battlefield medicine, including the story of a soldier whose jaw was smashed in battle, leaving him severely scarred but able to live and die another day. You can take a guided walk, or follow a 1.2-mile marked trail around the site, including the opportunity to hop on **The Battlefield Line** heritage railway (⊘ battlefieldline.co.uk) at Shenton station and take a 20-minute trip via Market Bosworth to Shackerstone. Between Leicester and the battlefield lie the picturesque moated ruins of **Kirby Muxloe Castle** (EH), a 15th-century fortified mansion built for the Yorkist supporter Lord Hastings. It adopted the latest fashions in domestic comfort, using local red brick with stone around the windows and doors; construction ceased in 1483 when Hastings was dramatically seized at a Council meeting and executed on Tower Green as a traitor.

ESSENTIALS

GETTING THERE Leicester station is served by CrossCountry (⊘ crosscountrytrains. co.uk) and East Midland. The city is easily reached by car using the M1 (J21) or M69.

STAYING The **Belmont Hotel** (⊘ belmonthotel.co.uk) offers boutique hotel comfort close to the station and city centre, while the **Castle Hotel** (⊘ greenekinginns.co.uk) occupies a 17th-century farmhouse building in the village of Kirby Muxloe, a short walk from the castle ruins.

EATING There are many options in the historic Lanes area east of the cathedral. **Cafe Mbriki** (⊘ cafembriki.co.uk) offers tasty lunch platters with a Greek Cypriot influence, including spinach pies with salad and pitta. **The Globe** (⊘ theglobeleicester.com) is Leicester's oldest pub.

TIME TO SPARE? **Leicester Museum & Art Gallery** (⊘ leicestermuseums.org) opened in 1849 as one of the UK's first public museums; galleries include Ancient Egypt, Victorian Art and Picasso Ceramics. Two of Leicester's most interesting historic houses, Wygston's Chantry House and Skeffington House, now form the **Newarke Houses** social history and regimental museum (⊘ leicestermuseums.org).

23 DERBY

MAKING MODERN BRITAIN

The city of Derby, on the banks of the River Derwent, has had Roman, Saxon and Viking settlements, but its main historical significance relates to more modern times. Derby is not only near the geographical centre of Britain; it's at the heart of our industrial heritage. As a remarkable new museum demonstrates, this is where much of modern Britain was made.

STAR ATTRACTION

The **Museum of Making** (⌀ derbymuseums.org), which opened in 2021, occupies the site on which John and Thomas Lombe established a silk mill exactly 300 years earlier. The mill can claim to be one of the world's first factories; its layout, with people in different buildings working on different processes, inspired other key innovations in the Industrial Revolution. Today the museum showcases 30,000 objects relating to Derby's manufacturing history. Entering through the Civic Hall,

↑ The Museum of Making. (Clive Stapleton/S)

you can see a dark outline on the brick wall where the original waterwheel once stood. There's a wall display of objects from early 20th-century working men's clogs to a bus stop sign, but you are bound to look up at two spectacular items hanging from the ceiling: a Toyota Corolla Hybrid car, and a Rolls-Royce Trent 1000 aero engine. Upstairs, a 'Flight Deck' display explores Rolls-Royce's links with Derby over the past century. One floor up, the Gateway room introduces the story of the mill within a wider context of the Derwent Valley's development. In the Throwing Room, the original location of the mill's machines, a video demonstrates a working (and very noisy) replica as you explore ten displays on the theme of making through the ages, with artefacts from a cast iron Victorian postbox to a whale's shoulder blade that saw service as a pub sign. The second floor hosts the Assemblage, where items are grouped by the materials from which they are made: wood, metal, ceramic, organic, glass, stone, textiles and synthetics. You can use workstations to find specific items or to follow themed trails, or just wander around as if inspecting the world's largest workshop. The museum also showcases the latest work by local artists and designers, and a handsome model railway with a (fictitious) scene from 1906. Derby's traditions of creativity and innovation continue to this day; one display features Core Design, the Derby-based firm that created the video game Tomb Raider and its star Lara Croft.

ESSENTIALS

GETTING THERE Derby is 90 minutes away by train from London St Pancras, slightly less from Manchester (EM). The city is 15 minutes from the M1 (J24) and accessible via the A6, A50, A38 and A52.

STAYING & EATING Just outside Derby is **Swarkestone Pavilion** (LT), a stylish 17th-century legacy of a long-gone great house. For lunch in town, try **The Dining Room** (⌂ thediningroom121.co.uk) on Friar Gate.

TIME TO SPARE? Two more Derby heritage sites form part of the **Derby Museums** group (⌂ derbymuseums.org). The **Derby Museum & Art Gallery** houses collections covering archaeology, natural history and Ancient Egypt, and works by local artist Joseph Wright, famous as a 'painter of light'; the star is a Bronze Age longboat made from a single oak trunk. A short walk away, **Pickford's House** uses the townhouse built by a Georgian architect for himself and his family to explore the everyday lives of Derby's burgeoning middle classes of the time. The Museum of Making is at the southern end of the **Derwent Valley Mills** (⌂ derwentvalleymills.org), a UNESCO World Heritage Site stretching 15 miles along the River Derwent to Matlock, in which historic mills and associated buildings explore social and industrial life in the 18th and 19th centuries.

24 LINCOLN

STEEP SALVATION

Near England's east coast, equidistant between York and Cambridge, Lincoln may trace its name from the Celtic Lindon, meaning 'by the pool'; presumably a reference to the Brayford Pool, into which the River Witham feeds. After Roman and Viking occupations, Lincoln's fortunes improved under the Normans. William the Conqueror ordered the construction of a new castle, while the building of a cathedral signified Lincoln's new status as the centre of a Bishopric stretching across much of England. Medieval Lincoln survived a few flashpoints, being besieged in 1141 as part of the civil war between Stephen and Matilda, claimants to the English throne, and being fined by King John for opposing him in the wake of the first Magna Carta. Trade in wool and cloth, meanwhile, with financing help from a prominent Jewish community, helped it to become England's third largest city. Relative decline followed and the city suffered much damage in the Civil War before recovering thanks to industrialisation. The itinerary below focuses on the city's medieval glories, and Victorian adaptations of its castle.

THE ITINERARY

DAY 1 Start at the bottom of Steep Hill – which has a 1:7 gradient – which the Romans created to help with the development of their settlement down the hill.

↑ Steep Hill. (travellight/S)

This is a good place to find some of the remaining traces of the medieval Jewish community that lived in Lincoln between 1159 and 1290 (the full Lincoln trail is available via **JTrails**; ⌕ jtrails.org.uk). Turn off Steep Hill into Danes Terrace for **The Collection** (⌕ thecollectionmuseum.com), the city's archaeological museum. Among the exhibits, a glazed decorative roof tile depicting a man with a beard, large nose and pointed hat gives a hint of the anti-Semitic attitudes of some medieval Lincoln residents. As you climb Steep Hill, look for **The Jew's House**, a 12th-century two-storey building with its façade intact. There's a large first-floor chimney breast above the entrance and two Romanesque upper windows. The house belonged to Belaset, daughter of Solomon of Wallingford and an active financier; today it is home to a restaurant. A few doors along, the **Jews' Court** is thought to be on the site of a medieval synagogue, with 'court' referring to a courtyard with communal buildings as part of a synagogue complex. The upper room is the synagogue of today's Lincoln Jewish community while the ground floor is the HQ and bookshop of the local archaeological association. Further uphill on the right at Nos. 46–47, the **Norman House** may have been built for Aaron of Lincoln, a 12th-century Jewish moneylender whose clients included Henry II. Nowadays it's a specialist tea shop.

From here it's a short walk and a left turn to **Lincoln Castle** (⌕ lincolncastle.com), where the city's Jews took refuge in 1190 to protect themselves from marauding

↑ Lincoln Castle. (Piranhi/S)

soldiers returning from the Crusades. There are three main reasons to visit the castle. The first is to see a copy of the 1215 Magna Carta, one of only four surviving copies. A short film dramatises the events leading to the sealing of Magna Carta at Runnymede, and its subsequent reissue by Henry III. The document itself, along with its sister document the Charter of the Forest, sits under glass in a simple black vault; legal and constitutional history on one large sheet of sheepskin parchment. The second main attraction, a recreation of the castle's Victorian-era prison, reflects its development away from a military installation towards a focus on justice and punishment. The prison's most unusual feature is the chapel, in which the wardens locked each prisoner into a separate wooden stall so that they could see the preacher, but not other inmates. Thirdly, a wall walk enables you to complete a circuit of the curtain wall and to enter the earlier of the two mottes, the Lucy Tower. This polygonal shell keep became, by Victorian times, a burial place for those who died in the prison; the small gravestones give the space a macabre atmosphere.

DAY 2 On the opposite side of Steep Hill from the castle, **Lincoln Cathedral** (⌀ lincolncathedral.com) is a magnificent example of the Early Gothic architectural style, using rib vaults and pointed arches to dramatic effect. The structure covers almost 54,000ft^2, with an inside length of 482ft and width of

↑ Lincoln Cathedral. (NORRIE3699/S)

78ft. The size befits its prestigious medieval status. A 14th-century spire, created after the central tower collapsed, made this the world's tallest building, according to contemporary claims, for over two centuries. Inside, on either side of the crossing, two enormous circular stained-glass windows dominate: the Dean's Eye in the north transept and the Bishop's Eye in the south transept, looking out over the city. The ten-sided Chapter House may have been the venue for three Parliaments. The cathedral's most famous inhabitant poses high on a pillar near the east window. This is the Lincoln Imp, who legend says behaved so badly that angels turned him to stone. If your eyesight isn't sharp enough to spot him, press the handy button to light him up. From the interior's many other highlights, two stand out. The tomb of Bishop Richard Fleming, near the choir, depicts him twice, once in full bishop's robes and once as an emaciated corpse – an arresting 'before and after' pair of effigies. The artwork in the Russell Chantry Chapel is even more surprising: murals by the Bloomsbury artist Duncan Grant, showing workers loading wool on to boats in Lincoln, reflecting the chapel's dedication to St Blaise, the patron saint of wool combers… and, on a side wall, two flying ducks.

ESSENTIALS

GETTING THERE Lincoln is around 90 minutes from Sheffield and just under two hours from London by train (LNER). The main route by road is the A1 linking to the A46.

STAYING A handful of cobbles away from the castle, cathedral and Steep Hill, **Bail House Hotel** (⌂ bailhouse.co.uk) is an excellent base. The building's medieval origins and antique furniture give the rooms character – remember to duck below the occasional low beam.

EATING To build energy for going up and down Steep Hill, or as a reward after the walk, visit **Browns Pie Shop** (⌂ brownspieshop.co.uk). Pie purists will sigh at the beauties they serve here, with fillings including a deliciously rich combination of pheasant, partridge, venison and hare. In nearby Bailgate, **Café Zoot** (⌂ cafezoot.co.uk) offers European cuisine and British classics; try the confit duck leg or the chicken and chorizo paella.

TIME TO SPARE? Below the cathedral, the **Bishops' Palace** (EH), medieval home to the Bishops of Lincoln, whose diocese stretched from the Humber to the Thames, is due to reopen in 2023 after conservation work. Lincolnshire housed over a third of all Bomber Command stations in World War II; find out more at the **International Bomber Command Centre** (⌂ internationalbcc.co.uk), 2½ miles south of Lincoln. Seven miles west of town, **Doddington Hall** (AF, HH, RHS ⌂ doddingtonhall.com) is a beautiful late Elizabethan mansion, with gardens that remain faithful to their original layout.

25 HULL
WHALES, TALES & TRAILS

The east coast port city of Kingston upon Hull, also known as Hull, sits on the Humber estuary in Yorkshire's East Riding. The city's reputation suffers from irritable vowel syndrome, with critics changing the vowel in its name for humorous effect. Heavy damage from German bombs in World War II and post-industrial decline hasn't helped. But Hull's character and its heritage are deep, rich and fascinating. It's been a military supply port, a trading hub and a fishing and whaling centre, and it's gained a reputation for being different. The city denied Charles I entry at the start of the Civil War; over 150 years later, Hull's MP William Wilberforce campaigned to end the slave trade. Even its cream telephone boxes hint at a certain independence of attitude. There's a creative side to the place, too, which was UK City of Culture in 2017. Hull has been home to many writers and poets, among them Andrew Marvell, Alan Plater, Stevie Smith, Andrew Motion and most famously Philip Larkin, who was the local university's librarian. The biggest tale (or tail) starts outside the city in a historic house's stables, where Hull's nautical and literary sides come together in one artefact: the skeleton that inspired *Moby-Dick*.

↑ Burton Constable Hall. (HM)

THE ITINERARY

DAY 1 Nine miles northeast of Hull lies **Burton Constable Hall** (AF, HH ⬧ burtonconstable.com). The Constable family has owned land here for over 800 years. The attractive Hall of today is Elizabethan on the outside with 18th- and 19th- century interiors. Start in the Stable Block, which houses the skeleton of a 58ft-long sperm whale stranded on the coast at nearby Tunstall in 1825. The Constables in situ at the time could claim anything that washed up on the shore, so the Burton Constable estate obtained the whale. After a local surgeon studied and dissected the creature, the estate moved its skeleton to Burton Constable Hall's parkland, where it was articulated on a wrought-iron framework. A published account of the whale attracted many visitors, including American author Herman Melville, whose novel *Moby-Dick* (1851) mentions its articulation: 'like a great chest of drawers, you can open and shut him… and swing all day upon his lower jaw…' The skeleton remained in position for over 150 years; 'Capability' Brown, who had redeveloped the parkland between 1772 and 1782, might not have approved. In recent years the Burton Constable Foundation, which now owns

LARKIN AROUND & OTHER HULL TRAILS

'That Whitsun I was late getting away…' So runs the inscription beneath the sculpture of Philip Larkin (1922–85) greeting you as you get off the train at Hull. It's the first line of *The Whitsun Weddings*, which describes a rail journey to London on which the narrator witnesses wedding parties embarking at each stop. Larkin moved to Hull in his early thirties and he infused his poems with observations of life in and around the city. The **Larkin Trail** (⬧ thelarkintrail.co.uk) follows routes through Hull centre (around 2½ hours), the wider city (three hours plus a bus to the final stop) and the surrounding area. Plaques at 25 locations detail a link to the poet, and many quote a relevant line from a Larkin poem. The website provides information on each location, including extracts from relevant poems and sound clips, such as an excerpt from Alan Plater's play about Larkin, or jazz – he was a noted jazz critic. The city centre route starts at the Royal Hotel next to the railway station; Larkin's poem *Friday Night in the Royal Station Hotel* describes 'silence laid like carpet… all the salesmen have gone back to Leeds/Leaving full ashtrays in the Conference Room'.

The circular **Fish Trail** (⬧ visithull.org) depicts Hull's fishing history through a series of artworks which Gordon Young created in 1992: 41 species from anchovy to zander, starting with anchovies at City Hall and including the Old Town, the Marina and the Fish Market – an electric eel denotes the location of an electricity substation. The **Ale Trail** (⬧ visithull.org) meanders around old(e) Hull pubs including, on a street curiously named Land of Green Ginger, the George Hotel – Hull's oldest surviving licensed pub, with England's smallest window.

the hall and parkland, has launched a campaign to find bones that past visitors may have taken from the skeleton. It promises to be a quest almost as epic as that of Captain Ahab. A modern sculpture in limestone and oak, *Constable Moby*, marks the skeleton's original position on the south avenue of the estate. The Hall itself is grand while still retaining the feel of a (large) family home. Its main cantilevered staircase stands in a hall whose original blue-grey walls are now a cheerful shade of yellow, setting off the many gilt-framed paintings and furniture. The most extravagant space is the Chinese Room, in which parrots roam all over the wallpaper and dragons curl themselves round curtains, a painted glass lantern and an elaborate chair. Much of the Hall's current splendour is down to William Constable (1721–91), a man of learning and an inveterate collector. William engaged the architect James Wyatt, the sculptor John Cheere and the furniture maker Thomas Chippendale. He also expanded his father's library and enhanced his art collection with paintings and sculptures from the Italian grand tour he took with his sister Winifred. In a reference to that adventure, the Great Hall showcases a portrait of the siblings in costume as citizens of the Roman Republic. William also assembled a Cabinet of Curiosities ('cabinet' in the sense of room rather than furniture) containing coins, medals, antiquities, fossils, gemstones, scientific instruments, shells and sporting guns, among other things. Many of these artefacts are displayed in mid-Victorian cabinets in the first-floor Museums Rooms. A Georgian generation of Constables upgraded the Gallery with a new plasterwork ceiling and frieze, new curtain hangings and elaborate carved furniture. This became a social space for games, musical evenings and amateur theatricals; look for the orange and gold costume jacket (c1840) and the playbills for productions such as *You Can't Marry Your Grandmother*.

DAY 2 Follow one of the branches of the **Larkin Trail** or the **Fish Trail** (page 119) or visit the **Museums Quarter** (⊘ hcandl.co.uk/museums-and-galleries) on the High Street in Hull's Old Town. The Quarter's museums reflect aspects of Hull's history, the most comprehensive in terms of time periods being **Hull and East Riding Museum**, which aims to depict local life from the Paleolithic era to the present. Star exhibits include Mortimer the woolly mammoth and the Wooden Warriors, small carved yew figures with quartz pebbles for eyes and wooden penises, which Victorian curators removed from display. The mosaics and other remains from local Roman settlements are also impressive. The neighbouring **Streetlife Museum** offers a powerful hit of Victorian and early 20th-century nostalgia with displays of vintage vehicles – cars from Lanchesters to Morris Minors and Isettas, buses, trams and trains – and recreations of a chemist's shop and the local Co-op: 'CO-OP COAL IS GREAT FOR THE GRATE' at ten shillings for four bags. The Quarter's most significant museum is nearby

↑ Streetlife Museum. (SS) ← **LEFT:** Wilberforce House. (HM) **RIGHT:** On the Larkin Trail. (HM)

Wilberforce House, birthplace of William Wilberforce (1759–1833), Hull's MP for 45 years and a leading anti-slavery campaigner. The museum examines how Wilberforce's activities helped to lead to the abolition of slavery in most of the British Empire, through an Act passed just before he died. It also profiles the other causes he advocated, including the SPCA, later the RSPCA, and presents a wider history of slavery up to the present day, along with details of the house and some of its other occupants. A few minutes away on South Church Side, Wilberforce's old grammar school is now the **Hands on History Museum**. Galleries explore themes of local education, home, marriage, work and Victorian children's experiences. A slightly incongruous gallery displays an Ancient Egyptian mummy and replicas from Tutankhamun's tomb that local craftsmen made for the British Empire Exhibition (1924). Outside the museum stands a statue of Andrew Marvell (1621–78), a Hull resident who, like Wilberforce, was a pupil here. John Milton's recommendation secured Marvell the role of Assistant Latin Secretary to the Council of State. During the Civil War and under Cromwell's regime, Milton was a Parliamentarian; Marvell, who had been a Royalist, changed allegiance.

↑ Spurn Lightship. (tommysmith18/S)

After the Restoration he may have helped to save Milton from an extended prison sentence. Marvell was Hull's MP for 19 years; his poetry did not gain widespread fame until long after his death.

Reflecting the city's seagoing heritage, the **Maritime Hull** project (⊘ maritimehull.co.uk) is refurbishing and restoring six sites, including two ships due to reopen as attractions over the next few years. One of the vessels, behind the Streetlife Museum, is the imposing **Arctic Corsair**, a 763-ton survivor of Hull's fishing industry. Its dramatic 60-year career included a world record for landing the greatest weight of cod and haddock from the White Sea, off Russia's northwestern coast, and ramming an Icelandic gunboat during the Cod Wars. The other is the **Spurn Lightship**, which guided vessels as they navigated the Humber estuary and served in World War II before her eventual decommission in 1975.

ESSENTIALS

GETTING THERE Hull Paragon Interchange railway station, a ten-minute walk from the city centre, has excellent connections. It's two hours from Manchester Piccadilly (TP), three hours from London (LNER or ⊘ hulltrains.co.uk) and four hours from Edinburgh (NR), and the bus station is next door. Burton Constable is 25 minutes away by taxi, or take the East Yorkshire Motor Service 277 bus (no service on Sundays) to Balk Lane, Sproatley, and walk the remaining two miles via Burton Constable Holiday Park.

STAYING The Grade II-listed **Royal Hotel** (⊘ britanniahotels.com), which Philip Larkin immortalised in verse, stands next to the railway and bus stations. In a quiet square between the station and the Museum Quarter, **Kingston Theatre Hotel** (⊘ kingstontheatrehotel. com) is a popular choice for its bright and spacious accommodation. Outside the city, **Burton Constable Holiday Park** (⊘ burtonconstableholidaypark.co.uk) offers caravanning, camping and glamping, with a scenic walking route to the Hall.

EATING Humber Street, down by the river close to the old Fruit Market, provides a range of options; try the **Humber Fish Co** (⊘ humberfishco.co.uk) for crab rarebit crumpets and generous plates of seafood. In a converted warehouse on the other side of the dock, **Al Porto** (⊘ alporto.co.uk) combines pasta with fish and meat dishes to delicious effect, with specials such as slow-cooked venison with tagliatelle.

TIME TO SPARE? In Queen Victoria Square, the **Ferens Art Gallery** (AF ⊘ hcandl. co.uk/museums-and-galleries) displays paintings and sculptures from medieval to modern, including works by Canaletto, David Hockney and Gillian Wearing. In the Victorian Grade II-listed Hepworth Arcade, off Silver Street, family-run joke shop **Dinsdales** (⊘ dinsdalesjokeshop.co.uk) has kept locals chuckling since the 1930s.

26 YORK

CITY TRADERS

There's a wealth of history to discover within the city of York, which sits at the junction of the rivers Ouse and Foss. Its original city walls were built by the Romans and strengthened with stone in the 13th century; today the streets that lead to openings in the walls are called gates, while the entrances through the walls are called bars. Each bar has points of interest, with Mickelgate Bar having seen more drama than most: ceremonial receptions for six monarchs, the heads of Hotspur and other rebels on display and a successful siege by Cromwell's forces in 1644. After the Romans left, York became variously an Anglo-Saxon settlement; the capital of Viking territories in England; a significant medieval cloth manufacturing and trade centre; and, since Georgian times, a prosperous commercial centre and a sweet spot for the confectionery industry. The itinerary below focuses on Georgian-era attractions on one day and medieval matters on the other, but you can pick and mix; every attraction below merits an extended visit if you have time.

THE ITINERARY

DAY 1 Turn right out of the railway station and, a short walk away, you'll find one of York's surprises. The **Bar Convent** (bar-convent.org.uk) is England's oldest living convent, founded in 1686 and the first to open in England after the Dissolution of the Monasteries; nuns still live here. The founding of the convent was a secret operation in the face of anti-Catholic harassment. An exhibition will tell you more, but the highlight is the Neoclassical chapel, which contains an original priest hole, eight exits and a dome built in 1769 which hides away under a pitched roof. For those who didn't have to hide, Georgian York could be a place to prosper. A few minutes' walk across the Ouse in St Helen's Square, **York Mansion House** (EH mansionhouseyork.com) was built in 1732 as England's earliest purpose-built home for a mayor. Its four floors house excellent collections of gold and silver, furniture, ceramics, glassware, paintings and photographs, and the regalia in the dining room includes a sword which may have belonged to the Holy Roman Emperor Sigismund. Recent restoration work has uncovered several unusual items, including a mummified cat which had been interred in the wall for good luck (not, in fairness, for the cat). In nearby Castlegate, **Fairfax House** (AF, HH fairfaxhouse.co.uk), the winter home of Viscount Fairfax and his daughter Anne, remains one of the finest Georgian townhouses anywhere. There's an echo of tragedy; the Viscount lost both his wives and eight of his nine children to smallpox, with only Anne surviving. However, the contents are exquisite, especially the dining room silver and several examples of early English cabinets and clocks, many from the collection of Noel Terry, chairman of the confectioners of that name.

Confectionery, and chocolate in particular, has been a York success story since 1725 when Mary Tuke, a Quaker, set up a grocer's on Walmgate selling chocolate, tea and coffee. The firms of Rowntree, Terry's and Cravens satisfied sweet-toothed customers here and all over the world for over 200 years. Find out more about them at **York's Chocolate Story** (EH ⊘ yorkschocolatestory.com), which also explores chocolate's origins in prehistoric Mexico. Displays reveal the origins of KitKat's name (after a pie maker, improbably) and the secret of its success in Japan (the name is similar to the Japanese phrase '*kitto katsu*' which means 'good luck'). You even get the chance to make a small sample of chocolate yourself. Reminders of chocolate's importance to York are all around the city; from **Rowntree Park** with its memorial to the cocoa workers who died in World War I to the gardens of the Arts and Crafts **Goddards House** (NT), Noel Terry's home, from where you can see the Terry's factory clock tower. A **chocolate trail** leaflet is available (⊘ visityork.org).

DAY 2 Just over 40 years ago, excavations in the Coppergate area of York discovered rare traces of timber buildings from the Viking era. Further digs found over 20,000 objects, including animal bones, oyster shells (oysters were once a cheap meal), building materials and pottery fragments. **Jorvik Viking Centre** (EH ⊘ jorvikvikingcentre.co.uk) divides the site into three sections. The first is a reconstruction, viewed through a glass floor, of parts of the excavations. The second is a ride in a 'time car' through an imagined Jorvik, the Viking name for York, in AD960, complete with houses, people, pets and the occasional rat. Finally, galleries show off archaeological finds, from a female skeleton to collections of combs, shoes and coins. For further insights into the Viking era and earlier, walk along Coney Street and Lendal to the **Yorkshire Museum** (AF ⊘ yorkshiremuseum. org.uk), in gardens where the remains of the church of St Mary's Abbey still stand. Within an ever-changing display, the Roman York exhibits on the ground floor and the artefacts in the basement relating to the city's medieval days are the highlights. Look for the Middleham Jewel, a late 15th-century gold pendant, set with a large blue sapphire. Engravings on each side of the lozenge-shaped pendant depict religious scenes. The museum also holds the remains of the 'Ivory Bangle Lady', a high-status resident of York in the 4th century who may have come originally from North Africa.

Three buildings in the area around the Jorvik Centre and York Minster give contrasting pictures of medieval life. In Fossgate, close to the convergence of the Foss and the Ouse, stands the **Merchant Adventurers' Hall** (AF ⊘ merchantshallyork.org), where the local great and good formed a religious fraternity and a trading association, or guild, in 1357. Various rooms were added or refurbished over the centuries; today's Guild administers charities and the Hall is a museum. Artefacts in the anterooms include a 14th-century evidence chest which contained the Company's deeds of ownership. The star of the silverware in

↑ Yorkshire Museum. (cktravels.com/S) → Merchant Adventurers' Hall. (Natalia Paklina/S)

the governor's parlour is a four-peg tankard for which the pegs indicated measures of alcohol – hence the term 'to take down a peg or two'. The Great Hall is a double nave because the builders couldn't find a single oak tree large enough to span the full width; its panelling combines Tudor and Georgian to harmonious effect. A few minutes away, **Barley Hall** (EH ⌖ barleyhall.co.uk) is on the site of property that once belonged to the monks of Nostell Priory, before the construction of a mansion which was home to William Snawsell, York's Lord Mayor, in 1468. A reconstruction project has recreated the house in an approximation of its 15th-century heyday; the great hall's central hearth, smoke hole in the roof and hand-painted wall paintings are impressive evocations. Like Barley Hall, the **Treasurer's House** (NT, timed tours) combines original fragments with a large element of reconstruction. In pre-Dissolution days it housed the eponymous Treasurers, second in seniority only to the Dean, who controlled York Minster's finances and entertained important guests. Parts of the house, such as the fireplace in the entrance hall and the ceiling in the blue drawing room, date back to the 17th century. Much of it, though, is an exercise in retrospective period redecoration by Frank Green, a local businessman who bought the house in 1897. Some of

ESSENTIALS

GETTING THERE York's excellent rail links mean it's around two hours from London, Edinburgh, Birmingham and Liverpool (LNER, TP and other services). The city is midway between London and Edinburgh and close to the M1 and M62, with six Park & Ride locations around the outskirts.

STAYING B&B accommodation is available at the **Bar Convent** (page 125). For a touch of Georgian comfort, try **Judges Court** (⌖ judgescourt.co.uk) on Coney Street, a four-storey Grade II-listed townhouse with original panelling which, as the name suggests, once provided judges' lodgings.

EATING Light options include stopping for a cinnamon bun at **Brew & Brownie** (⌖ brewandbrownie.uk) on Museum Street, enjoying a goat's cheese and apricot ciabatta roll at **Bean & Gone Coffee** (⌖ beanngonecoffee.co.uk) in Exhibition Square or going retro at the **FortyFive Vinyl Café** (⌖ fortyfiveuk.com) on Mickelgate. Or sample a fat rascal at **Bettys** in St Helen's Square (⌖ bettys.co.uk); Bettys tea rooms have been a Yorkshire institution for over a century. Close to the Minster, the **Guy Fawkes Inn** (⌖ guyfawkesinnyork.com) pays playful tribute to one of York's most infamous sons; the menu includes a fine plate of bangers and mash. On Fossgate **The Blue Barbakan** (⌖ bluebarbakan.co.uk) offers splendid Polish cuisine from pierogi (filled dumplings) to gołąbki (stuffed cabbage leaves).

Green's changes were less authentic than others, such as the creation of a Great Hall which, he was convinced, was an original feature. Spoiler: it probably wasn't.

Finally, there's the magnificent **York Minster** (⌀ yorkminster.org). There has been a church on this site since the 7th century. The existing building has survived four fires; the last, in 1984, damaged the Rose Window in the south transept, leading to a painstaking restoration programme. This window combines the red and white roses of Lancaster and York which gave the Wars of the Roses (page 17) their misleading name. Henry VII, the ultimate victor from that conflict, married Elizabeth of York here in 1486. The Minster is full of points of interest, including the 15 life-sized statues of kings in the pulpitum, the kaleidoscopic colours of the Great East Window and the Chapter House's carvings of cats, dogs, a pig and humans pulling faces. There are two more modern highlights. The first, on either side of the Great West Door, is a series of 12 contemporary headless figures in semaphore poses, a tribute to decapitated statues from the Reformation era. The other is the two-faced astronomical clock in the North Transept, a memorial to local airmen who died in World War II; its appearance suggests the sun and stars as a pilot flying over York might see them.

TIME TO SPARE? It's hard to get better views over York than from **Clifford's Tower** (EH), close to Fairfax House and almost all that remains of one of two castles that William the Conqueror built in the city. The tower has been a garrison, a prison and a royal mint. The displays and exhibitions in **York Castle Museum** (⌀ yorkcastlemuseum.org.uk) recreate past times from a York perspective. Near York's railway station, the **National Railway Museum** (⌀ railwaymuseum.org.uk) tells the story of rail transport in Britain and displays classic models from the *Mallard* to the *Flying Scotsman*. The **York Cold War Bunker** (EH), just over a mile west of the station, was ready to monitor fallout from potential nuclear attacks; a decontamination room features on the guided tour. Six miles east of York in Elvington, on the site of a World War II RAF Bomber station, the **Yorkshire Air Museum** (⌀ yorkshireairmuseum.org) covers a century of aviation up to the supersonic age.

↑ Clifford's Tower. (travellight/S)

27 RIPON
MISCREANTS & MONKS

T he pretty North Yorkshire city of Ripon is now one of Britain's smallest, but it once enjoyed great power and prestige. Ripon's medieval wool and textiles industries earned it prosperity and, in the 16th century, it became famous for manufacturing spurs. Today the city boasts the oldest structure in any English cathedral, three museums tracing the evolution of local law and order, and a public ritual that's continued for over a millennium. Meanwhile, the ruins of Fountains Abbey, one of England's greatest medieval abbeys, lie nearby.

THE ITINERARY

DAY 1 Ripon Cathedral (⊘ riponcathedral.org.uk) stands on the site of a church built by St Wilfrid, who played a key role at the Synod of Whitby (AD664) in bringing Roman religious practices to Britain. Wilfrid came to Ripon from Rome

12 years earlier and built a new church. Its last architectural remnant is the silent, atmospheric cathedral crypt – the oldest extant structure in any cathedral in England. The other reminder of Wilfrid's era is a small circular gold ornament known as the Ripon Jewel, now exhibited in the treasury display in the library. Elsewhere, the bronze-on-marble columns of the pulpit give an unexpected Art Nouveau effect, and there's a touch of fantasy in the quire stalls. The wooden carvings, dating from 1494, include a depiction of a griffin chasing a rabbit while another rabbit hides down a hole. This may have inspired Charles Dodgson – Lewis Carroll, author of *Alice in Wonderland* – whose father was a canon here.

Grimmer real-life Victorian stories await you in the **Yorkshire Law & Order Museums** (⊘ riponmuseums.co.uk), at three historic locations in the compact city centre. The **Courthouse Museum**, in an elegant Georgian courthouse near the cathedral, housed a magistrates' court until 1998; today, in the jury room, the justices' retiring room and the courtroom, you can learn about historic cases. The **Workhouse Museum** on Allhallowgate offers a piquant contrast between the areas used by residents and vagrants – including a de-infesting room – and the plush boardroom where the workhouse's guardians sat in judgement. Finally, the **Prison & Police Museum** investigates Yorkshire policing history, from medieval

FOLLOWING ORDERS: RELIGIOUS COMMUNITIES

The story of religious orders in the UK is one of continuous reform, as new groups and orders emerged to return to the original ideal. **Benedictine** monks lived in ordered communities, following a planned daily routine of prayer, work and study, according to the 6th-century rule of St Benedict. The **Cluniac Order**, founded in the 10th century, and the **Cistercian Order**, founded in 1098, both aimed to return to the strict simplicity of the early Benedictines. Cistercians sought remote sites, ideal for frugal and devotional lives, but they later acquired wealth from sheep farming and industrial activities which they spent on grand Gothic buildings. The **Carthusians**, meanwhile, followed the example of early desert hermits, wearing hair shirts, eating a simple diet and taking a vow of silence. Regular **canons** were communities of priests who lived according to a strict, almost monastic rule, preaching in parish churches. Augustinian canons, known in Britain as Austin Canons or Black Canons, followed the rule of St Augustine of Hippo. The **Premonstratensian Order** was modelled on the Cistercians. While monks withdrew from the world, **friars** were based in towns, travelling, preaching and relying on alms. The **Dominicans** or 'Black Friars' were famous as scholars and preachers. **Franciscans** or 'Grey Friars' were dedicated to a life of absolute poverty, though they were later criticised for failing to observe those standards. Other orders included the Friars Minor, the Carmelites or 'White Friars' and the Poor Clares, a sisterhood following the Franciscan way of life.

↑ Fountains Abbey. (Gareth Tandy/S)

times to the present day. Fascinating local tales feature Ripon's first policeman, who was beaten up in the line of duty and then dismissed, and two poacher brothers, one of whom was transported and returned to the city – twice. From here, head to Market Square where, at 9pm each evening underneath the historic obelisk, a man blows a horn four times before bowing to a house at one corner of the square. After the four blows, the hornblower walks to the mayor's house, or wherever he or she can find the mayor, blows the horn three more times and announces that 'the watch is set'. This ritual, dating back to 886, was originally the task of a wakeman, who maintained law and order and kept watch at night. The mayor succeeded the wakeman in 1604 and employed a hornblower, and there is now a team of four. Richard, one of the current team, told us about the ghost… The face of Hugh Ripley, Ripon's last wakeman and first mayor, is said to appear at an upper window of the house to which the hornblower bows, if he is not satisfied with the horn blowing.

DAY 2 Four miles southwest of Ripon, within the Studley Royal estate, **Fountains Abbey** (EH, NT) is a reminder of the great days of the English monasteries.

↑ One of Ripon's hornblowers. (M Barratt/S)

Thirteen monks from St Mary's Abbey in York arrived here on 27 December 1132, fleeing an establishment they felt had become extravagant in its lifestyle, no longer following the ideals of St Benedict (page 131). With the protection of York's Archbishop, who owned much of this land, and help from nearby Rievaulx Abbey, the 13 dissidents founded a new Cistercian establishment. The monks later grew prosperous thanks to revenue from wool sales, but Henry VIII forced the abbey's closure as part of the Dissolution of the Monasteries. Two centuries later the Aislabie family bought the Studley Royal estate, removing rubble from the ruins and turning them into a visitor attraction. Today's remains are of varying age; the 167ft Huby's Tower was a 15th-century addition, but you can also see the oldest part of the abbey at the crossing. In contrast to the austere principles of the monks, Studley Royal is also the site of an 18th-century pleasure garden, where the Aislabies entertained visitors. The gardens feature formal elements such as the Moon and Crescent Ponds, with their statues of Neptune and Bacchus, within a serene deer park. While on the estate, take a look at the historic watermill and St Mary's church, a Gothic Revival masterpiece from Victorian architect William Burges.

ESSENTIALS

GETTING THERE The nearest railway stations are Harrogate (NR) and Thirsk (TP), both 11 miles away, or York (LNER, NR, TP), 27 miles away, with frequent bus services to Ripon from all three. The main road routes are the M1 and A64 from the south and the A1(M) from the north.

STAYING Central Ripon options include the **Royal Oak** (⊘ royaloakripon.co.uk), a renovated 18th-century coaching inn. The **Fountains Abbey & Studley Royal** estate rents out 14 places including stone cottages and converted barns.

EATING On North Street **Realitea** (⊘ riponrealitea.co.uk), part Indian restaurant, part tea room, combines both with a British Raj themed high tea. The **Royal Oak** (see above) does an excellent pie with mash. For cafés near Market Square, try **Oliver's Pantry** (⊘ oliverspantry.com) or **Caffe Tempo** (◧ theartofgoodcoffee).

TIME TO SPARE? Of the many fascinating historic houses near Ripon, several are medieval: to the north, **Norton Conyers** (HH ⊘ nortonconyers.org.uk), whose interior inspired Thornfield Hall in *Jane Eyre* and reopens in 2023; to the south, the moated **Markenfield Hall** (HH ⊘ markenfieldhall.com) and Grade I-listed **Ripley Castle** (HH ⊘ ripleycastle.co.uk). To the southeast, elegant **Newby Hall** (HH ⊘ newbyhall.com) was built by Sir Christopher Wren and adapted by Robert Adam.

28 BARNARD CASTLE

NORTHERN FAMILY FORTUNES

Barnard Castle came to unexpected national prominence in 2020 when, during the early stages of the Coronavirus pandemic, a UK government advisor drove here in apparent breach of lockdown rules. He claimed that he was testing his eyesight, but you don't need any such excuse to visit this picturesque County Durham town. The eponymous castle goes back almost a millennium, while the Bowes Museum houses five centuries of fine art, fashion and design. Beyond town, the medieval Raby Castle was home to the powerful Neville family, while Egglestone Abbey provides a romantic location for a glimpse of austere monastic life.

THE ITINERARY

DAY 1 The original purpose of **Barnard Castle** (EH), sited above the Tees, was to control a river crossing between the lands of the Bishop of Durham and those of the lordship, or Honour, of Richmond. Building started in the late 11th century. An early owner was Bernard de Balliol, hence 'Barnard'. By the 15th century the castle was the property of the Nevilles, one of northern England's most powerful families and whose ranks included a 'Kingmaker' and two kings (page 138). Rebels hoping to replace Elizabeth I with Mary Stuart besieged and captured the castle in 1569; by 1630 Sir Henry Vane was dismantling Barnard for building material for

↑ Barnard Castle. (Dave Head/S)

Raby Castle. Now it's an impressive ruin where you can wander through towers, admiring the view of the River Tees, and find the foundations of a rectangular bakehouse. There's a trace of Richard III: a carving of a boar, his heraldic emblem, under the lintel of an oriel window in the chamber block.

Members of the Bowes family, another wealthy local dynasty, served as Barnard Castle's keepers. By Victorian times John Bowes (an ancestor of Elizabeth Bowes-Lyon, who later became George VI's queen and ultimately the Queen Mother) was conceiving the idea, and gathering the contents, for a special collection. On Newgate, Barnard Castle's **Bowes Museum** (AF ♂ thebowesmuseum.org.uk), which opened in 1892, fills three floors with fine arts, fashion, silver, furniture and more. Along with paintings by Canaletto and Goya, Sèvres porcelain and evening shoes worn by Napoleon III's wife, look out for the clockwork mouse John Bowes' wife bought him for his 60th birthday, and the 18th-century Silver Swan automaton which preens itself and catches a fish while music plays.

DAY 2 **Raby Castle** (HH ♂ raby.co.uk), a few miles northeast of Barnard Castle, has a pedigree stretching back to Cnut, who owned the estate in the early 11th century. However, the 14th-century castle standing today was built as a palace

THE NEVILLES OF RABY

The Nevilles of Raby were already a well-established, powerful northern family by the end of the 14th century, owning large blocks of land across England. Their links to both warring Houses of Lancaster and York ensured them prominence in the conflicts that followed. Ralph Neville of Raby (1364–1425), created 1st Earl of Westmorland by Richard II, did not stay loyal to his monarch for long. His second wife was Joan Beaufort, legitimated daughter of John of Gaunt, Duke of Lancaster. Ralph supported her half-brother Henry, Earl of Hereford, when he returned from exile in 1399 and claimed the throne as Henry IV. Ralph had 23 children: 11 sons and 12 daughters. One son, Richard, became Earl of Salisbury through marriage to Alice Montagu, while three other sons also married heiresses and a fourth became Bishop of Durham. Several of Ralph's daughters married dukes or lords: Cecily wed Richard, Duke of York, and was mother of two kings, Edward IV and Richard III. A generation down the line, Salisbury's son, another Richard, married the heiress of Richard Beauchamp and became Earl of Warwick, known as 'The Kingmaker' for his pivotal role in the Wars of the Roses. The Nevilles' influence died with him at the Battle of Barnet in 1471.

See also *The Wars of the Roses* (page 17) and *The Percys: Conflicts & Shifting Allegiances* (page 151).

fortress for the Nevilles. The current owners, the Vane family, have lived here for almost 400 years. Medieval towers and turrets belie the more modern, luxurious interiors. The star is the 1840s Octagon Drawing Room, in which gold silk lines the eight walls, the curtains and swags are of crimson and gold silk, and the painted, gilded ceiling is breathtaking. The high Gothic arches in the entrance hall

↑ Raby Castle. (Peter is Shaw 1991/S)

are a good example of the gradual change in emphasis from military practicality to domestic comfort: their creation, in the late 18th century, enabled easy entry for carriages.

A couple of miles southeast of Barnard Castle, in a lovely location by the Tees, lie the remains of late 12th-century **Egglestone Abbey** (EH). This was home to an order of Premonstratensian canons (page 131). After the Dissolution, and Henry VIII's death, a new owner built a mansion here. Later, the site experienced centuries of gradual decline. Some of the abbey's contents, once lost, have returned, including the effigy of a priest and the chest tomb of Sir Ralph Bowes (1449–1512), which sits at the crossing of the abbey church. The north and west walls of the nave of the original church still stand, as does a vaulted undercroft.

ESSENTIALS

GETTING THERE The nearest train station is Bishop Auckland, under four hours from London King's Cross (LNER). From the station, the X1 and X75/76 buses reach Barnard Castle in 90 minutes. By road, the A66/A67 connects with the A1(M).

STAYING Just south of Barnard Castle, the hamlet of Greta Bridge was a major stop during the 17th century for the London–Carlisle coach. Charles Dickens stayed at one of its three inns, possibly the **Morritt Hotel** (⌘ themorritt.co.uk), which is now a luxury hotel and spa, as research for his novel *Nicholas Nickleby*. Other prominent writers and artists, including JMW Turner and Sir Walter Scott, also visited, and the bar includes a mural of Dickensesque characters by John Gilroy, who created many Guinness advertising images. The **Three Horseshoes Hotel** (⌘ three-horse-shoes.co.uk) in the centre of Barnard Castle also dates from the 17th century.

EATING In the centre of Barnard Castle, **Blagraves House** (⌘ blagraves.com) is the town's oldest house, with a 15th-century pedigree (look out for the crested ceiling and oak beams in the dining room). It claims Oliver Cromwell among past diners; the menu changes monthly. **Clarendon's** (⌘ clarendonsofbarnardcastle.co.uk) in Market Place is a popular stop for breakfast, lunch or afternoon tea.

TIME TO SPARE? Another 12th-century ruin, **Bowes Castle** (EH), lies five miles southwest of town. In Bishop Auckland, 15 miles to the northeast, **Auckland Castle** (AF, HH ⌘ aucklandproject.org) was home to the Prince Bishops of Durham. Venture 15 miles east to Darlington for some modern industrial heritage: learn about the town's role in the birth of the railways at the **Head of Steam Railway Museum** (⌘ head-of-steam. co.uk) and how the Victorian-era **Tees Cottage Pumping Station** (⌘ teescottage.co.uk) revolutionised the provision of local water.

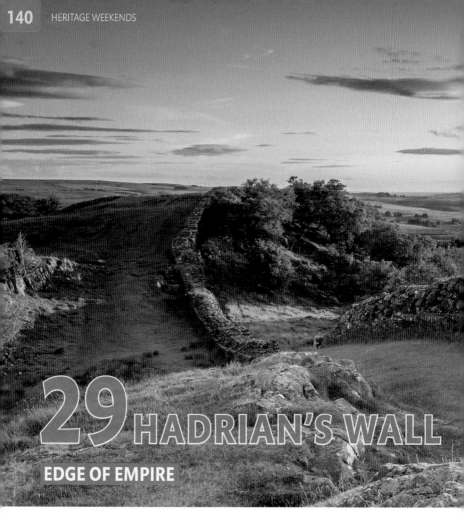

29 HADRIAN'S WALL

EDGE OF EMPIRE

Hadrian's Wall, reaching for 73 miles from North Tyneside to Cumbria, is Britain's most important Roman monument and a UNESCO World Heritage Site. For 300 years it marked the northwestern edge of an empire that covered much of Europe and reached into the Middle East and northern Africa. The emperor Hadrian (AD76–138) ordered its construction after visiting Britain in AD122, with the intention, according to his biographer, to 'separate the Romans from the barbarians'. The Wall demonstrated the Empire's power and its limits, as Hadrian opted to consolidate his territories instead of attempting to conquer Scotland. As relatively little writing survives from that time – the writing tablets from Vindolanda are an exception – much of our understanding of life on and around the Wall comes from the tireless efforts of archaeologists. This itinerary concentrates on a section of the Wall in Northumberland, which has much to tell us about the Romans, the men who joined their army from all over the Empire and the people who lived in this beautiful landscape at that time.

↑ Hadrian's Wall. (Dave Head/S)

THE ITINERARY

DAY 1 For an introduction to the Empire and its most fearsome component, start at the **Roman Army Museum** (⊘ vindolanda.com) near the village of Greenhead in western Northumberland. Slick interactive displays put the Wall in the longer context of the Empire's history, identify the known major Roman fortifications via a tactical map and lay out the Roman Army's structure, building up from basic units of eight men to legions and explaining auxiliaries (non-Roman citizens who could gain citizenship after 25 years of service). We usually think of the occupying army as Italians, but they came from all corners of Rome's Empire: northwestern, southeastern and Mediterranean Europe, the Middle East and northern Africa. There's a good display on the Hamians, inhabitants of central Syria who supplied two infantry regiments of archers, one of which came to Britain. Artefacts on display range from shields

ROMANS ROUND BRITAIN

In addition to the important sites around Hadrian's Wall, the Romans left their mark in Bath (page 61), Chester (page 163), Colchester (page 92), Dorchester (page 66), Penwith (page 76), St Albans (page 14) and Melrose (page 207). Other sites you can explore today include **Aldborough Roman Town** (EH) near Ripon in North Yorkshire, which has an outstanding collection of Roman finds, including two mosaic pavements in their original positions. Like Hadrian's Wall, which it was built to supersede, the **Antonine Wall** north of Glasgow (◈ antoninewall.org) is a UNESCO World Heritage site. The discovery of **Bignor Roman Villa** in Sussex (◈ bignorromanvilla.co.uk) was down

to farmer George Tupper, who struck it with his plough in 1811, while the Victorians uncovered **Chedworth Roman Villa** (NT) near Cheltenham. **Corinium Museum** (⌀ coriniummuseum.org) explores the archaeology of Cirencester in Gloucestershire, which the Romans called Corinium, while the nearby **Roman Amphitheatre** (EH) was one of the largest in Britain. Just west of Chichester in Sussex, **Fishbourne Roman Palace** (⌀ sussexpast.co.uk) claims to be the largest surviving Roman home in Britain. There are also extensive remains at **Wroxeter Roman City** (EH) near Shrewsbury in Shropshire, which may have been the fourth largest Roman settlement in Britain, with a population of around 15,000.

↑ Mosaic detail from Bignor Roman Villa, West Sussex. (59)

and cheekpieces to decorative brooches. Other galleries use clever films and holographic representations to help you imagine yourself into the life of a Roman soldier. You can swear allegiance to the emperor, try your archery skills, learn a little Latin with instruction from a holographic teacher and write your own Latin message. A 3D film uses an eagle's-eye view to show reconstructions of the Wall and the associated forts and towns, telling the fictional story of a new young recruit. Seven miles east of the museum is its partner site, the much larger **Vindolanda** (⏣vindolanda.com). In ancient Celtic the name means white or shining lawn or enclosure. Just over three centuries of almost continuous Roman occupation saw the creation of nine successive forts and towns here, the earliest being wooden and predating the Wall, in the days when there was an open frontier with forts along the road from Carlisle to Corbridge. There may have been up to 1,500 soldiers at one point, with a further 4,500 inhabitants comprising their families, traders, merchants, servants, slaves and local Britons. The remains through which you can walk are principally from two forts dating from the 3rd and 4th centuries. On the outskirts you encounter a butcher's shop, a tavern and workshops before reaching the heart of the site: the principia (headquarters building), the commanding officer's house, the barracks and the granary stores, with a bathhouse off to the right. Most memorable, however, are the displays within the museum. The springs at the west end of Vindolanda have kept things damp and ensured that large quantities of organic artefacts have survived, including over 7,000 leather shoes and boots of various types, charming toys such as a boy's wooden sword, and a woman's wig made from a form of moss that repels midges. A Samian dinner service which arrived damaged – and which the recipients threw away – is here in all its broken glory. The highlight is the collection of writing tablets, thin slivers of wood with ink handwriting, which excavators discovered in 1973. These comprise accounts, lists and letters, most of them predating the construction of the Wall, written by soldiers of all ranks and community members, male and female. The largest is a four-page document about business matters between Vindolanda and Catterick; it includes the phrase 'the roads are awful'. On an interactive screen you can read a selection of the tablets, including a discussion between two slaves about preparations for the feast of the Saturnalia; a request from a soldier for more beer for the men under his command; and a birthday party invitation from Claudia Severa to Sulpicia Lepidina, the wife of the garrison's commander around AD100. The handwriting on the last example is believed to be the earliest surviving female handwriting from Britain. Within the museum's tablet vault, a single display case contains nine tablets for you to examine at close quarters. We don't believe anything we have seen can get you closer than this to the lives of the Roman occupiers and the inhabitants of the villages around the forts.

↑→ Vindolanda. (both Jaime Pharr/S)

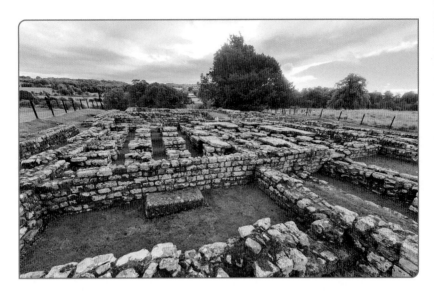

DAY 2 East of Vindolanda lie the remains of two more forts that may have been on a smaller scale, but which have many points of interest of their own. **Housesteads Roman Fort** (EH), two miles away on steep exposed hillside, was one of 15 forts built on Hadrian's Wall, about two years after work on the Wall began, and it sat around the Wall's midpoint. Roman forces, for much of the time an infantry regiment of 800 of the First Cohort of Tungrians (from territory in today's eastern Belgium), remained here for almost three centuries. Archaeological research through the Victorian era provided an early example of a complete plan of a Roman fort. Having been to Vindolanda, you'll find the 'playing card' layout familiar, with HQ, the commanding officer's house and the granaries in the centre and barracks on either side. Turn right as you enter the site and head downhill to the fort's lowest point and its most distinctive feature, the communal latrines, where a deep sewer ran beneath a wooden floor and benches with holes for multiple toilet seats. For flushing purposes, rainwater came via drains from all over the fort or, in dry spells, from the roofs of nearby buildings, with storage in stone tanks. Today this makes an atmospheric spot from which to gaze out over the hills past the local flocks of lackadaisical sheep. A small museum area displays some attractive carved slabs with depictions of deities, along with gaming counters and dice from a pub which was probably close to the fort walls. Eight miles further east, **Chesters Roman Fort** (EH) sits, in contrast to Housesteads, in a low-lying valley where the Wall bridged the River North Tyne and the fort straddled the Wall. Roman forces occupied this site for around the same period as at Housesteads, though in this case it was a 500-strong cavalry unit from Asturia in northern Spain. About one-fifth of a cavalryman's salary went towards the

cost of his horse and he had to pay the same sum if the horse was lost. This may explain why the barrack rooms were, in fact, stables and barracks combined, with three men and their horses sharing each room. Two other notable features are distinctive to Chesters. One, underneath the headquarters building, is the strongroom, or treasury, which held the soldiers' salaries. The other, down towards the river, is the bathhouse, which silt has preserved over the centuries as it washed down the slope. Its features include seven niches in the west wall, for bathers to leave their clothes in before indulging in athletic games or gambling, and then processing through a series of rooms with dry heat, steam, a heated pool and a cold plunge room. Don't miss the small but excellent Clayton Museum, with its collection of items that Victorian antiquarian John Clayton excavated here and elsewhere; the fort is on what became the parklands of his estate.

ESSENTIALS

GETTING THERE & AROUND The nearest town, Hexham, 20 miles west of Newcastle, is just over two hours from Edinburgh and four hours from London by train (LNER), with the nearest main roads being the A74(M) from the north or the A1(M) from the south, connecting to the A69. Once you're here, the AD122 bus route runs hourly for most of the day between Hexham and Haltwhistle, stopping at all the sites mentioned in this chapter and several more (⊘ hadrianswallcountry.co.uk).

STAYING Base yourself in Hexham, somewhere like the Victorian townhouse **Beaumont Hotel** (⊘ thebeaumonthexham.co.uk), or along the route of the Wall; for example, at the **Hadrian Hotel** (⊘ hadrianhotel.co.uk), which incorporates a pub and a Michelin-starred fine dining restaurant, **Hjem**.

EATING Hexham offers plenty of good food and drink options. **Bunters** (🅕 BuntersandAthenas) is one of several cafés near the Old Gaol and the abbey. For lunch, try the family-friendly **Heart of Northumberland** pub (⊘ thehearthexham.com) on Market Street, which serves up tasty Sunday lunches in a restored Grade II-listed building. **Zyka** (⊘ zykahexham.com) on Priestpopple is a boutique Indian restaurant.

TIME TO SPARE? English Heritage's other local sites include, east of Hexham, **Corbridge Roman Town**, the fortified medieval manor house at **Aydon Castle**, and **Prudhoe Castle**, a Norman construction. West of town are the longest surviving stretch of the Wall at **Birdoswald Roman Fort**, and 13th-century **Lanercost Priory**. Or you could explore Hexham itself, whose attractions include England's oldest jail, **Hexham Old Gaol** (⊘ museumsnorthumberland.org.uk), and **Hexham Abbey** ⊘ hexhamabbey.org. uk), which St Wilfrid (page 130) founded as one of England's earliest centres of Christianity.

30 ALNWICK & WARKWORTH

KINGS IN THE NORTH

The north-south divide, a staple of modern English political discourse, was even more apparent in the Middle Ages. English kings may have ruled from the south, but they needed help to maintain order in their more distant lands and to guard against incursions from across the Scottish border. Northumberland, or Northumbria as it was once known, played a key role: today, this county, the northernmost and least densely populated in England, also has the most castles, clear evidence of its place on the front line for several centuries. The Scottish royal family held the Earldom of Northumberland, by marriage ties, for two brief periods before relinquishing all claims to it via the Treaty of York in 1237; after that, the Percy family, with a succession of Henrys including 'Harry' Hotspur leading the way, took the opportunity to build power and prestige, becoming known as 'Kings in the North'. You can explore the Percy legacy in eastern Northumberland, in Alnwick and the nearby village of Warkworth, and find another Harry from a famous fictional world of wizardry and witchcraft.

THE ITINERARY

DAY 1 The small market town of Alnwick derives its name from the River Aln, on whose south bank it sits, and the Old English word for dairy farm or settlement, reflecting its past economic dependence on agriculture. Alnwick, which was a walled town in medieval times, wears its centuries of history with pride, from the medieval gate of Hotspur Tower to the old merchants' houses on Fenkle Street and the Georgian and Victorian buildings on Bondgate Within. The lion motifs in various places, representing the Percy family, give a clue to Alnwick's main attraction, on the western side of town. The exterior of **Alnwick Castle** (HH ∂ alnwickcastle.com) demonstrates its Norman origins: the position on a natural bluff above a river, a defensive bailey within the line of an outer ditch and a motte sited within the line of an inner ditch. Alnwick's location 32 miles from the Scottish border made it a focal point for possible conflicts between the English and the Scots. The castle changed hands several times during the Wars of the Roses (page 17) and Cromwell's troops occupied it during the Civil War; it was almost derelict by 1750. Today's interiors owe much to restoration work by Sir Hugh Smithson (1714/15–86), 1st Duke of Northumberland, using Robert Adam and other eminent architects, and mid-Victorian redesigns on the orders of the 4th Duke. The more recent work took inspiration from 16th-century Rome, with the Duke employing Italian and British architects and designers. Our favourite examples include the marble mosaic floor and stucco ceilings in the Upper Guard Chamber. Keep an eye out too for the lion heads on the Saloon doors, the Medusa heads in the Drawing Room, and the Percy heraldry on the ceiling in the Dining Room. The Victorian architect Anthony Salvin restored and updated the medieval chapel; its Gothic ceiling is now counterpointed by French tapestries from the 4th Duke's travels, which show scenes from the life of

← Alnwick Castle. (Visit Northumberland)

Constantine the Great and the biblical story of the blind Tobit and his son who finds a cure. After the splendour inside, it's a refreshing change to stand on the ramparts and admire the view down to the river and the surrounding parkland, designed by 'Capability' Brown. The castle and grounds have featured in various films, including two in the *Harry Potter* series; broomstick training is available for young aspiring wizards and witches.

DAY 2 Seven miles southeast of Alnwick, on a loop in the River Coquet a mile from the coast, the village of Warkworth exudes a calm that belies its violent past. There's a church at one end – its spire and windows are 14th-century, but the interior is older – and **Warkworth Castle** (EH) stands above the river. The village acted, in effect, as an outer line of defence for the castle. Warkworth's recorded history begins in 737 with the King of Northumbria granting it to the abbot and monks of Lindisfarne. A Scottish incursion in 1174 led to the deaths of some 300 villagers. By the 12th century, a timber castle was in place, with redevelopment work beginning soon afterwards. After Edward I stayed at the

↑ Inside Alnwick Castle. (Alnwick Castle)

castle, his successors granted it to the Percy family, also known as the Earls and later the Dukes of Northumberland (see below). This powerful family forfeited Warkworth for two temporary periods: firstly when the 1st Earl rebelled against Henry IV, and later after the 2nd and 3rd Earls died for the Lancastrian cause in the Wars of the Roses. Finally, the 6th Earl left Warkworth to Henry VIII in 1537 and the castle fell into disrepair. The castle is, in effect, two castles: one laid out around the outer bailey, the other in the keep. Its gatehouse has undergone many changes over the years and the bridge was originally a drawbridge, with slits in the walls at ground level in order to observe the approaches and people entering the castle. Warkworth was the Percys' preferred domestic base for many years; the remains of the principal tower show four doorways at ground level, to the

THE PERCYS: CONFLICTS & SHIFTING ALLEGIANCES

The Percy family came to England around the time of the Norman Conquest and acquired lands mainly in the north. Carving out a role as defenders of the northern border against the Scots, by the turn of the 14th century they were barons and, in 1309, they bought Alnwick Castle from the Bishop of Durham. Henry Percy (1341–1408) was created Earl of Northumberland in 1377 and acted as marshal at Richard II's coronation. The next five Earls were all Henrys. By the late 1390s disputes over royal appointments and concern about the rise of his neighbours the Nevilles of Raby, who were created Earls of Westmorland in 1397, led Northumberland to support Henry Bolingbroke when he claimed the throne as Henry IV. Over the next 80 years, concerns about their status and role on the Scottish border and intermittent disputes with the Nevilles drew the family into national conflicts. The 1st Earl's son Henry, or 'Harry', Hotspur was killed at Shrewsbury in 1403 in rebellion against Henry IV. A statue of Hotspur, wielding his sword, stands in Alnwick on Pottersgate. Northumberland himself rebelled in 1405 and fled the kingdom, forfeiting his estates and title. Henry V restored the earldom to Hotspur's son, but during Henry VI's reign the dispute with the Nevilles escalated into armed conflict. During the ensuing Wars of the Roses, the Nevilles supported York, while the 2nd and 3rd Earls of Northumberland were killed fighting on the Lancastrian side at the battles of St Albans (1455) and Towton. The 4th Earl was reconciled with the Yorkist King Edward IV when Richard Neville, Earl of Warwick (the 'Kingmaker'), in turn rebelled. When Richard, Duke of Gloucester, who had acquired the Neville lands through marriage, seized the crown as Richard III in 1483, Northumberland initially supported him. But at Bosworth in 1485, Northumberland kept his troops out of the battle. The Percys were never so powerful again, although they took part in 16th-century intrigues and the 9th Earl was implicated in the Gunpowder Plot. But the family survived and, in the 18th century, became Dukes of Northumberland.

See also *The Nevilles of Raby* (page 138) and *The Wars of the Roses* (page 17).

ESSENTIALS

GETTING THERE The nearest train station is Alnmouth, five miles southeast of Alnwick, an hour from Edinburgh and four from London (NR). The X20 bus runs from Alnmouth to Alnwick, and a regular bus service operates between Alnwick, Newcastle and other surrounding towns. The A1 passes close by Alnwick's eastern side.

STAYING The **White Swan** (⊘classiclodges.co.uk) in central Alnwick is a 300-year-old coaching inn with a nautical bonus; its dining room incorporates the original panelling, mirrors, ceiling and stained glass from RMS *Olympic*, the *Titanic*'s sister ship. Half an hour down the A1, the 14th-century gatehouse of **Morpeth Castle** (LT) provides a cosy retreat for up to seven people.

EATING Barter Books (⊘barterbooks.co.uk), in Alnwick's old Victorian railway station building, houses over 350,000 secondhand and rare books, a miniature railway running above the bookcases, a huge mural of 33 famous English-language fiction writers, a Station Buffet café and Paradise, a parlour serving ice creams, speciality teas, coffee and cake. Also in Alnwick, **Grannies** (⊘granniestea.co.uk) on Narrowgate is a popular tea room and delicatessen. Alnwick's many lunch and dinner options include **Di Sopra's** Italian fare (⊘disopra.co.uk) and **Lilburns Bar Restaurant** (⊘lilburns.co.uk).

TIME TO SPARE? Near Alnwick Castle, inside a former church, the family-friendly **Bailiffgate Museum & Gallery** (AF ⊘bailiffgatemuseum.co.uk) devotes two floors to

↑ Warkworth Castle. (Gail Johnson/S)

hall, solar (private living and sleeping quarters), cellar and chapel, while there are also traces of the buttery, pantry and kitchen. The Lion Tower served as the official entrance to the main hall for visitors; the reason for the name becomes clear if you look at the central boss of the vault under the tower's arch, where a Percy lion emblem survives.

Medieval lords were not concerned solely with matters of family, power and prestige, but also for their immortal souls. Half a mile upriver from the Castle is **Warkworth Hermitage** (EH). Like the Castle chapel (and its collegiate church, planned but never completed), this was a place of prayer for the wellbeing of the lords, their families, their followers and all Christians. The chapel and sacristy, carved into the rock, date from the 14th century and include a fine carving of the Nativity. Other rooms, now lost, included a hall, kitchen and even an entrance lobby, suggesting that the hermits who lived here did so in some comfort. By the 1530s George Lancastre received £15 6s 8d, considerably more than a skilled tradesman might typically have done, for his prayers and for acting as the 6th Earl's agent on the estate.

the history of Alnwick and the surrounding area. A few miles northeast lie the coastal ruins of **Dunstanburgh Castle** (EH), once the property of John of Gaunt, Edward III's third son and Henry IV's father. Further up the coast, 150ft above the North Sea, mighty **Bamburgh Castle** (HH ⬙ bamburghcastle.com) has seen well over a millennium of history, back to the 6th century and Ida the Flamebearer and earlier. Facing Bamburgh is the unforgettable spectacle of **Lindisfarne Castle** (NT) across a causeway on **Holy Island** (⬙ lindisfarne. org.uk), where St Aidan founded a monastery; the Priory is the burial place of St Cuthbert. Head southwest from Alnwick to **Cragside** (NT), a pioneering Victorian home and the first house in the world to use electric lighting.

↑ Dunstanburgh Castle. (David Steele/S)

31 MIREHOUSE

LAKE LEGENDS

The Lake District abounds in literary associations. William Wordsworth was born in Cockermouth, and Beatrix Potter and Arthur Ransome lived here. By the shores of Bassenthwaite Lake northwest of Keswick, Mirehouse, a historic house of understated beauty, has many literary tales to tell; the lake helped to inspire Tennyson's famous poem about Arthur, Britain's most legendary king.

STAR ATTRACTION

The 8th Earl of Derby built the current house at **Mirehouse** (HH ⊘ mirehouse. co.uk), which passed into the hands of John Spedding of Armathwaite Hall in 1802. The Speddings have lived here since, enlarging, adapting and restoring the property. It's an elegant place with a welcoming feel; as you enter the hall, there's some venerable furniture and a display of early postage stamps to admire. Before moving to Mirehouse, John Spedding and his brother Anthony attended school with Wordsworth, and their sisters befriended William and Dorothy, while Robert Southey and Samuel Coleridge were near neighbours. The study at Mirehouse displays manuscript poems and letters by Southey and Wordsworth, while other

↑ Mirehouse. (Simon Whaley Landscapes/A)

rooms demonstrate the literary endeavours and connections of Spedding's family. His younger son James wrote 14 volumes on the life and works of Francis Bacon; this, along with a collection of Bacon's papers and first editions of Bacon's own works, is on display in the smoking room. At Cambridge, James befriended Alfred Tennyson and another poet, Arthur Hallam. Tennyson brought his wife here with him in 1850, while on honeymoon. The drawing room has portraits of Tennyson and Hallam, as well as correspondence with other friends such as Edward FitzGerald, author of *The Rubaiyat of Omar Khayyam*, and the novelist William Makepeace Thackeray. John Spedding's older son Thomas was a close friend of Thomas Carlyle, a regular visitor to Mirehouse, and the library contains correspondence with him as well as letters from John Stuart Mill and Matthew Arnold commenting on Thomas's book on the Poor Laws. As you walk down from the house towards the lake, consider the enigmatic St Bega's Church, named after a 7th-century Irish princess who, according to legend, came here from Ireland to avoid marriage to a Viking prince. The church was built CAD950, while various elements date to the 13th and 14th centuries. This may be the 'chapel nigh the field' that Tennyson describes at the start of *Morte d'Arthur*. The poem, which Tennyson wrote – ostensibly about the death of King Arthur – at Mirehouse, probably had a more personal meaning for him; his friend Arthur Hallam, who was engaged to Tennyson's sister, had died in 1833. A simple open-air theatre was built by the lakeside in 1974 for a reading of the poem to members of the Tennyson Society. It's easy to envisage the poet looking out over the water, imagining the moment when Sir Bedivere throws Excalibur into the lake and 'an arm… Clothed in white samite, mystic, wonderful… caught him by the hilt, and brandish'd him/Three times, and drew him under in the mere'.

ESSENTIALS

GETTING THERE The nearest main railway station is Penrith, a three-hour journey from London (AV). From there, it's a scenic 20-mile drive on the A591 and A66, or the X4, 554 and 73 buses pass Mirehouse.

STAYING & EATING Keswick has many options, or there's self-catering for up to ten on the **Dalemain estate** (HH, ⊘ dalemain.com) – try their marvellous marmalade.

TIME TO SPARE? Drive around the top of Bassenthwaite Lake and head west for Cockermouth and **Wordsworth House and Garden** (NT), where the poet was born and lived with his parents and siblings including sister Dorothy. Four miles south of Mirehouse on the outskirts of Keswick, the **Derwent Pencil Museum** stands on the site of the UK's first pencil factory, which used graphite from nearby Borrowdale.

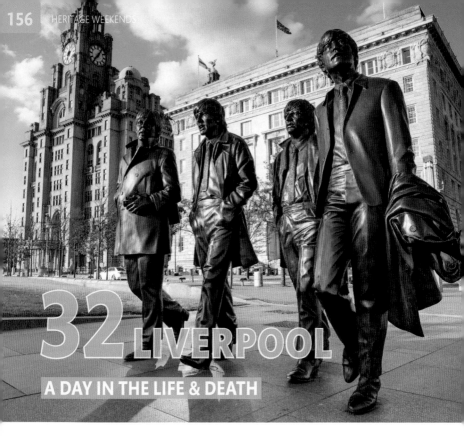

32 LIVERPOOL
A DAY IN THE LIFE & DEATH

Signs at Liverpool's John Lennon Airport used to quote the late ex-Beatle's song 'Imagine': 'Above us, only sky.' One year, after Liverpool Football Club made a poor start to the season, a piece of graffiti added: 'Below us, only QPR and Reading.' You can trace the city's obsessions with the world's most famous pop group and with football by visiting various Beatles sites and Liverpool's world-famous stadium. Liverpool manager Bill Shankly once recalled, half-joking, that 'Somebody said that football's a matter of life and death to you [and] I said "listen, it's more important than that."' A suite of museums by the docks, and a rare Tudor manor house whose later owners made their fortunes from the slave trade, demonstrate that real life and death are an inescapable part of Liverpool's legacy, too. The city's location on the estuary of the river Mersey, opening out into the Irish Sea, is key to its identity.

THE ITINERARY

DAY 1 Start by Pier Head terminal, passing a statue of the Beatles to board a **Mersey Ferry River Explorer Cruise** (⊘ merseyferries.co.uk). This 50-minute journey runs to the accompaniment of 'Ferry Cross the Mersey' by another great 1960s Liverpool group, Gerry and the Pacemakers. Commentary covers aspects of the city's history and the skyline views are great. Watch out for the two Liver Birds,

↑ The Beatles, Pier Head. (cowardlion/S)

symbols of Liverpool, on top of the Royal Liver Assurance building. 'Bella' is looking out to sea; 'Bertie' is, according to the commentary, looking the other way to see when the pubs open… You may travel on the Dazzle Ferry, whose artwork is the creation of Sir Peter Blake; the patterns are a tribute to World War I 'dazzle ships' which used combinations of colour and monochrome to make themselves more difficult to target. Back on dry land, head to three museums (⌀liverpoolmuseums.org.uk) that take you deeper into Liverpool's heritage. From the ferry terminal, turn right for the **Museum of Liverpool**, with the 'lambanana' sculptures at the entrance. The People's Republic gallery examines the impact of 200 years of social change on the city. There's an enormous architectural model of Sir Edwin Lutyens' proposed design for Liverpool Metropolitan Cathedral; a case, as Wirral-born comedian and gameshow host Jim Bowen would have said on *Bullseye*, of 'Here's what you might have had'. The Great Port gallery traces how Liverpool innovated with the use of early canals, the first timetabled passenger railway and the world's first elevated electrified railway line, while 'Global City' looks at Liverpool's significance within the British Empire and its links with cities such as Shanghai. A short walk away, by the Albert Docks, the **Maritime Museum** tells a range of dramatic stories about the city and the seas. One gallery looks at some of the nine million people who sailed from Liverpool between 1830 and 1930 in search of a new life. There are some exquisite artefacts from the age of luxury liners; look for the travelling wardrobe trunk that Gertrude Walker used on a 1911 voyage to Chile, to ensure she was dressed for every occasion. Special exhibitions examine two maritime tragedies: the sinking of the *Titanic*, with

↑ The Maritime Museum. (Graeme Lamb/S)

which Liverpool people had strong connections as officers, crew, passengers and employees of the White Star Line shipping company; and the *Lusitania*, a Cunard ship that a German submarine sank off southern Ireland in 1915 – Liverpool Irish seamen were among the 1,200 who died in that incident. The tone is equally sombre on the top floor in the **International Slavery Museum**, which opened in 2007, the bicentenary of the Abolition of the British Slave Trade Act. A 'Freedom Wall' reminds visitors of the numbers of Africans who became slaves through transatlantic trade, beginning with European exploration of West Africa in the 15th century. A model of an 18th-century slave plantation is augmented with recorded readings of contemporaneous testimonies from slaves describing their daily lives. But the most powerful area of the museum is the simplest: a dark, circular space in which an audiovisual presentation imagines the transportation of slaves across the Atlantic. Liverpool was a key player in the trade; by 1792, 131 transatlantic ships carried slaves from the city, compared with 42 from Bristol and 22 from London. Penny Lane, later immortalised in song by the Beatles, takes its name from slave trader James Penny, who opposed abolition and campaigned against a law limiting the number of slaves a ship could carry.

For a more uplifting Liverpool narrative, follow the Fab Four. The **Beatles Story** (⌀ beatlesstory.com), also on Albert Docks, recreates the Cavern Club, Abbey Road Studios and even the deck of the 'Yellow Submarine' for a cheerful romp through the band's history. It acknowledges the roles of various 'fifth Beatles': Stuart Sutcliffe, Pete Best and the band's manager Brian Epstein. Fifteen minutes' walk away, the **Beatles Museum** (⌀ liverpoolbeatlesmuseum.com) on Mathew Street, near the Cavern Club, displays memorabilia from the collection of Pete Best's brother, from posters and guitars to a humorous account of the band's origins that Lennon penned for *Mersey Beat* magazine. The final, poignant item is a copy of Paul McCartney's lawsuit against his fellow Beatles and their joint company Apple, dissolving the partnership. Years later, McCartney reflected that 'we hadn't screwed anyone… I always thought it was very clean money compared to the shipbuilders and the great sugar fortunes.'

To explore the other great Liverpudlian passion, take the 26 bus from Liverpool One Bus Station to the north of the city for a tour of **Anfield** (⌀ stadiumtours. liverpoolfc.com), home of Liverpool FC. While John Houlding founded the club in 1892, the tour focuses on its glory years from the 1970s onwards under Bill Shankly, Bob Paisley and other managers. You'll see the sign 'THIS IS ANFIELD' which players see before they go out on to the pitch. You also sit in the stands, including the famous Kop end, with a handheld video of a matchday crowd singing along to the club anthem, Gerry and the Pacemakers' 'You'll Never Walk Alone'. In the dressing rooms and the press conference room, affable tour guides reveal a few surprises: heated seats in the home team's dugout, but not the away

↑ Anfield. (cowardlion/S) → The Beatles Story. (GroovyGloryPhoto/S)

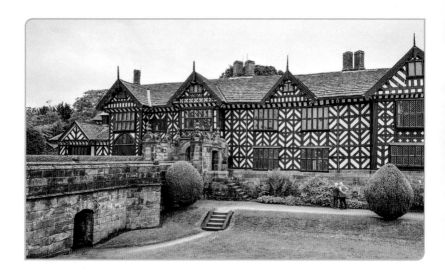

team's; soundproofing in the home, but not the away, dressing room. It's also worth wandering around the stadium and pausing at the memorial to the 96 fans who died in the 1989 Hillsborough stadium disaster, the highest death toll at any British sporting event.

DAY 2 Today we focus on Liverpool's 'blue suburban skies'. For insights into a day in the (early) lives of Lennon and McCartney, take the **Beatles' Childhood Homes Tour** (NT) in the southern district of Speke. This visits Mendips, where John lived with his aunt Mimi after his parents' marriage broke up, and 20 Forthlin Road, home of the teenage Paul and his brother Mike, later a pop star himself with The Scaffold. Mendips, a good example of 1950s semi-detached housing, has been restored to its condition at that time at the request of Lennon's widow Yoko Ono, who bought the house and donated it to the National Trust. The interiors are cosy and the Art Nouveau-style glass in the porch is attractive. But, as our guide Colin (a local contemporary of the Beatles) told us, Mimi and young John had a tense relationship. Mimi wanted John to progress to further education, and he failed all nine O levels; she refused to let him and Paul practise in the house, so they used the porch, appreciating its acoustics. Paul's time at Forthlin Road was shaped by the early death of his mother, who was ambivalent about his musical talent; after her death, Paul's father set aside a room for rehearsals. It was at Forthlin Road that Paul and John wrote early songs such as 'Please Please Me'. Money was tight, with the Chinese willow pattern wallpaper in the living room only covering one wall. In the bedrooms, there's a recording of Mike reminiscing about 'our kid'.

The Childhood Homes Tour bus departs from Liverpool South Parkway railway station and **Speke Hall** (NT), south of town near the airport. This charming Tudor

↑ Speke Hall. (Alastair Wallace/S)

timber-framed manor house has Jacobean and Victorian interiors and furnishings, including plenty of carved oak and William Morris wallpaper. Look out for the secret priest hole – the Hall's original owners, the Norrises, survived persecution as Catholics. Later owners included Richard Watt, who made his fortune from Jamaican sugar plantations, and Frederick Leyland, a wealthy ship-owner. The highlight is probably the Oak Drawing Room, with its ornate plasterwork ceiling and the carved overmantel depicting Sir William Norris, his wife and their 19 children. In the Great Hall, near some 16th-century Flemish carved panelling, hangs a portrait of John Middleton (1578–1623), born close to the Speke estate, whom contemporaries described as being 9ft 3in tall.

ESSENTIALS

GETTING THERE & AROUND Liverpool is well connected to the rest of Britain by rail, with two stations (AV and others): Liverpool Lime Street – where you can goggle at the extraordinary statue of legendary comedian Ken Dodd – and Liverpool Central. By car, from the M6, take the M62, M58 or M56. Near the waterfront, Liverpool One Bus Station (⊘ merseytravel.gov.uk) is a good starting point for explorations.

STAYING For disaster-themed bling, **30 James Street** (⊘ 30jamesstreetliverpool.co.uk) is hard to beat. Under its old name of Albion House, the building was the HQ of White Star Line. Rooms aim to combine mod cons with the trappings of a luxury liner, with some suites including double whirlpool baths. The rooftop bar gives spectacular views of the Royal Liver building and the waterfront, and it includes *Titanic* items such as an organ.

EATING The many eateries around the Albert Docks include **Lunyalita** (⊘ lunya. co.uk), with its British-Spanish fusion cuisine including a Catalan version of scouse, and **Rosa's Thai Café** (⊘ rosasthaicafe.net). Ten minutes from the Docks, **Clockworks** (⊘ clockworksliverpool.net) in Wolstenholme Square offers British classics in a 200-year-old building where exposed red brick, steel and iron combine with murals to create a steampunk vibe. In a quiet spot just off Castle Street near the Beatles Museum, **Queens' Wine Bar and Bistro** (⊘ queensliverpool.co.uk) uses seasonal produce to create little masterpieces such as haddock and brown crab fish pie and devilled quail.

TIME TO SPARE? Hope Street links two cathedrals. **Liverpool Cathedral** (⊘ liverpoolcathedral.org.uk) owes its Gothic Revival design to Giles Gilbert Scott, grandson of George. **Liverpool Metropolitan Cathedral** (⊘ liverpoolmetrocathedral.org.uk), its Catholic counterpart, was the subject of several potential designs (page 157). Its Portland stone exterior and conical shape have given it the local nickname 'Paddy's Wigwam', while the white marble and stained glass in red, yellow and blue make for a theatrical interior.

33 CHESTER

WALL TO WALL HISTORY

18 97

THIS CLOCK TOWER WAS ERECTED
IN COMMEMORATION OF THE 60TH YEAR
OF THE REIGN OF HER MAJESTY
VICTORIA QVEEN and EMPRESS.

The Romans established a fort named Deva here on the River Dee in northwest England, in a perfect position to rebuff potential attacks from nearby north Wales. Even after the Romans left Britain, some of their number stayed here and the settlement became an Anglo-Saxon stronghold. Chester Castle was Henry III's and Edward I's military HQ for campaigns in Wales; and in the Civil War, Royalists held the castle and Chester against Parliamentary attacks. You can glimpse various aspects of the city's history, including its marvellous cathedral, by walking around its Grade I-listed Roman walls. These have stood for two millennia, thanks in large part to their reinforcement with sandstone within a century of their original construction. They are the most complete Roman and medieval defensive town walls in Britain; large paving stones were laid on the walkways in the 18th century, when they became a fashionable place to stroll.

THE ITINERARY

DAY 1 From the Visitor Information Centre in Northgate Street, go to North Gate to start your two-mile wall walk. At the wall's northeast corner, the **King Charles Tower** is believed to be where Charles I stood to watch the defeat of his army at nearby Rowton Moor in 1645. Look above the doorway to the lower tower chamber for a carved phoenix, emblem of the City Guild of Painters, Glaziers, Embroiderers and Stationers who used to meet here. Continue past the Dean's Field on your right, once the site of Roman barracks, and Chester Cathedral (page 164). Climb a flight of stairs to reach the **Eastgate Clock** overlooking Eastgate Street. The East Gate was once the entrance to the Roman fortress while the elaborate clock is more recent, erected in 1899 as a (slightly late) celebration of Victoria's diamond jubilee. Continue to Newgate at the walls' southeast corner, from where you can look over the **Roman Amphitheatre** (EH) and the **Roman Gardens**. The 1st-century amphitheatre doubled as a military training site and an entertainment arena with gladiators and bear baiting. Less than half of the original is visible, including two entrances for performers, but there's enough for you to imagine the rest. The gardens display Roman fragments from across the city, including columns from the bathhouse. There was a major breach in the wall here during the Civil War. On the right stand six 17th-century timber-framed almshouses, the survivors of the original row of nine. Walk down the 'Wishing Steps', whose original purpose was to join two wall levels, and continue west along The Groves to the Old Dee Bridge, a 14th-century red sandstone creation where a Roman bridge once stood. Diverting from the wall, cross the bridge into **Edgar's Field** to find the **Shrine to Minerva**, the Roman goddess of wisdom, art, craftsmen and war. Around here, workmen excavated sandstone for the city walls, and made offerings and prayers for the success of their labours. This is the only surviving shrine of its type in the UK. Look closely to discern Minerva's spear and helmet, and an owl over her shoulder. The park gets its name from

← Eastgate Clock. (chrisdorney/S)

Edgar the Peaceable, an English king who held a council here or near here in AD973. Recrossing the Dee and rejoining the wall, a few minutes' walk to the southwestern corner brings you to **Chester Castle** (EH), whose construction in 1070 by William the Conqueror makes it a contemporary of its grander southern cousin at Windsor (page 24).

DAY 2 Around the corner from the Castle on Grosvenor Street, there are further reminders of Roman Chester and its walls in the **Grosvenor Museum** (⊘ westcheshiremuseums.co.uk). One gallery on the ground floor uses a diorama to recreate the city as a whole and a model to reimagine what the complete amphitheatre might have looked like. The highlight, however, is a display of tombstones. Most of these, having previously stood outside the city, as was the Roman custom, served a second purpose later as part of repairs to the city walls. Rediscovered in Victorian times, they commemorated various worthies including Marcus Aurelius Nepos, a centurion, and his wife (whose name is not part of the inscription) and a lady called Curatia Dionysia. The lady's tombstone, like several others here, depicts the subject reclining on a couch, drinking cup in hand; two tritons, half-man and half-fish, are blowing on sea-trumpets behind her. It seems that the afterlife could be enjoyable. Among the museum's other treasures, don't miss its silver collection or the gallery showcasing five centuries of art by and about people and places in and around Chester and north Wales.

Another way to experience more than a millennium of Chester's past is to visit **Chester Cathedral** (⊘ chestercathedral.com). This charming edifice stands where

↑ Chester Cathedral. (Steve Wilson/S)

King Wulfhere built a Saxon church in AD660. The remains of St Werburgh, later Chester's patron saint, came here in AD895, almost two centuries after her death. Near her shrine in the Lady Chapel, a modern statuette depicts the saint with a goose sheltering beneath her cloak. This refers to the famous story of how, after a servant cooked and ate one of her geese, Werburgh retrieved its bones and brought it back to life. Hugh 'Lupus', 1st Earl of Chester, founded a Benedictine monastery here in 1092, from which the cloister and 13th-century refectory and chapter house survive. The choir stalls are worth examining for their extraordinary carvings of everything from Bible scenes to a dwarf musician and an elephant with horses' feet carrying a castle. After the Dissolution of the Monasteries, Henry VIII gave the buildings new life as a cathedral, but it fell into gradual decline before major restoration work on the nave ceiling, in the cloisters and elsewhere.

ESSENTIALS

GETTING THERE Chester's train connections are good: around 2½ hours from London and three hours and 45 minutes from Edinburgh (AV). Shuttle buses run the half-mile between the station and the city centre; for local bus timetables, see ⊘ cheshirewestandchester.gov.uk. The nearest major roads are the M1, M6 and M54.

STAYING Offering self-catering for up to 16 people, **Edgar House** (⊘ edgarhouse.co.uk) sits atop the city walls overlooking the Dee. For a base with a difference, try **Gladstone's Library** (⊘ gladstoneslibrary.org), the UK's only residential library, eight miles over the border in Wales. Its collection comprises over 150,000 items and there are 23 bedrooms for bibliophiles to choose from.

EATING The many cafés in the centre include **Bridge Street Coffee** (⊘ bridgestcoffee. co.uk) and **Bridge Café & Bistro** (⊘ bridgecafebistro.business.site), both on Bridge Street. The latter's basement has the remains of a Roman hypocaust. A short walk from the amphitheatre, **The Forge** (⊘ theforgechester.co.uk) specialises in wild, sustainable British cuisine.

TIME TO SPARE? St John the Baptist Church (⊘ stjohnschester.uk), adjacent to the Roman amphitheatre, was a Saxon church and the city's original cathedral. **Cheshire Military Museum** (⊘ cheshiremilitarymuseum.co.uk), within the remains of Chester Castle, tells the stories of Cheshire soldiers over four centuries. For a different way to experience the city, walk the 700-year-old **Chester Rows**, continuous half-timbered galleries reached by steps, which form a second row of shops above those at street level along Watergate, Northgate, Eastgate and Bridge streets. The interactive **Deva Roman Discovery Centre** (⊘ devaromancentre.co.uk) has now reopened after a major refurbishment.

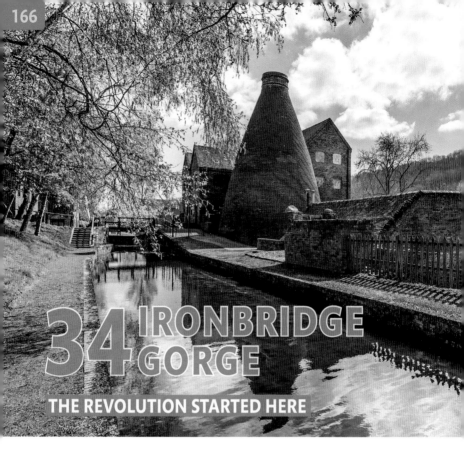

34 IRONBRIDGE GORGE

THE REVOLUTION STARTED HERE

S hropshire's geology covers 11 of the 12 geological time periods. Layers of coal, clay, iron ore and limestone eventually powered what can claim to be the Industrial Revolution's birthplace. A three-mile stretch along the Severn river, from Coalbrookdale to Coalport, comprises the **Ironbridge Gorge World Heritage Site** (⊘ ironbridge.org.uk). What happened here changed Britain and fuelled its leading world role for generations. The key was iron: the first iron barge, the first iron bridge, the first rail locomotive all had their origins here. The resurgent meadows and countryside which have flourished since the end of Ironbridge's heyday belie what a busy, noisy, smelly, smoky place this was. Ten museums tell different aspects of the area's story; we've picked out a few highlights.

STAR ATTRACTIONS

In 1709 Abraham Darby came here looking for easier and cheaper ways of producing 'iron bellied potts'. His breakthrough in producing pig iron in a coke-fuelled blast furnace is part of the narrative at the **Coalbrookdale Museum of Iron**, set in the 'Great Warehouse' of the Coalbrookdale Company. The museum explains the history of iron and improvements in smelting technology

↑ Coalport China Museum. (Nigel Jarvis/S)

from the Iron Age onwards. Key players included the 14th-century monks of Wenlock Priory who established watermills, mines and a bloomery to produce wrought iron. Coalbrookdale Company products on display include ornate garden furniture, sculpture, fireplaces and chairs. The **Coalport China Museum** explores the history of the china factories established here in the late 18th and early 19th centuries. There are many splendid examples of the factories' work, along with displays about working life; this is where you find out what a blunger and a saggar makers' bottom knocker did. Almost two miles away stands the eponymous **iron bridge** that Darby's grandson (also Abraham) built in 1779 to link Coalbrookdale with the towns of Broseley and Madeley. The other major Ironbridge attraction, **Blists Hill Victorian Town**, is an imaginary small town where you can talk with costumed volunteers as they recreate everyday Victorian life. Some of the buildings came here, brick by brick, from other places, as did the only surviving example of a Severn trow, a flat-bottomed boat that carried stone and coal. But we found the most interesting elements to be those which didn't have to be transported here, such as the remains of the blast furnaces and the Hay Inclined Plane, a rail-based way to move boats uphill in just four minutes from the river to the Shropshire Canal.

ESSENTIALS

GETTING THERE & AROUND Telford Central train station, 2½ hours from London, is six miles north of Ironbridge Gorge (WM), with the bus station a ten-minute walk away. Bus services link the various museums on many weekends during the summer holidays (⊘ telford.gov.uk/ironbridgeparkandride). By car, exit the M54 at Junctions 4 or 6 and follow the signs for Blists Hill Museums, Ironbridge Museums or Coalbrookdale Museums.

STAYING & EATING Once a grocer's house, **Iron Bridge House** (LT) enjoys a great view of the bridge. **Eley's of Ironbridge** (⊘ eleysporkpies.co.uk) serves excellent takeaway pies, made using the traditional, hand-raised method.

TIME TO SPARE? Other museums across the site include **Enginuity**, a family-friendly science and technology museum with hands-on exhibits; **Jackfield Tile Museum**, which houses reconstructions of a tiled Victorian pub and a tube station from the Edwardian era; the **Museum of the Gorge**, in what was once a warehouse for the Coalbrookdale Company, which puts the area in context; and the **Darby Houses**, elegant Georgian residences for the eponymous family. Close to the gorge is **Buildwas Abbey** (EH), a 12th-century Cistercian abbey whose church, crypt chapel and vaulted chapter house with tiled floor are largely intact.

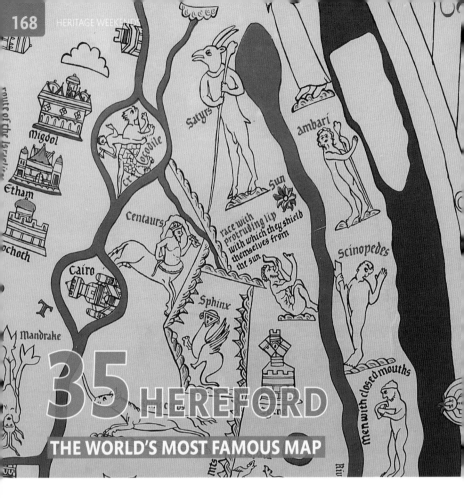

route of the Israelites

Migdol

Etham

ochoth

Cairo

Mandrake

Crocodile

Centaurs

Sphinx

Satyrs

sun

race with protruding lip with which they shield themselves from the sun

ambari

Scinopedes

Men with closed mouths

35 HEREFORD

THE WORLD'S MOST FAMOUS MAP

O nce the Saxon capital of West Mercia, later given a royal charter as 'Hereford of Wales' and now the county town of Herefordshire, Hereford has learned to adapt. In trade, it is most famous for the eponymous Hereford cattle and for cider. Actors Nell Gwyn and David Garrick came from Hereford and composer Sir Edward Elgar lived here; a statue of Elgar, leaning on his bike, stands in the Cathedral Close. Within the cathedral are two extraordinary artefacts: a map and a library, but not as we know them.

STAR ATTRACTIONS

There has been a place of worship on the site of **Hereford Cathedral** (⌗ herefordcathedral.org) for at least 1,300 years, but the earliest surviving architecture is Norman or Romanesque, from a 12th-century rebuilding. The astonishing **Mappa Mundi** (map of the world) was probably made around the year 1300; it is the largest surviving map of its kind. A single sheet of vellum, 5ft 2in tall and 4ft 4in wide, tapering towards the top with a rounded apex, rather

↑ A modern replica of the Mappa Mundi, Hereford Cathedral. (NM)

like a gabled house, it bears the name of its creator, 'Richard of Haldingham or Lafford' (Holdingham and Sleaford in Lincolnshire). This is not a map as we understand it – for example, there are no borders – but a compendium of that era's scholarly knowledge, beliefs and priorities. The geographical content, covering Europe, Asia and Africa, is within a circle, drawn mainly in black ink with red and gold highlights. The captions for Europe and Asia are the wrong way round! The seas and rivers, originally green or blue, have faded to brown. Jerusalem sits at the centre, the Crucifixion above it and Bethlehem below it to the right. East is at the top. There are over 500 drawings: around 420 cities and towns, 15 biblical events, 33 plants, animals, birds and strange creatures, eight pictures from classical mythology and 32 images of people. Some drawings are realistic while others are fantastical, such as the Blemyae in southern Africa, headless humans with eyes and mouths in their chests, or the Sciapods from India whose single enormous foot sheltered them from the sun. The cathedral's other remarkable feature is the 17th-century **Chained Library**. Here, books face you by their page edges, not their spines, and a system of chains, rods and locks enabled visitors to read books at the adjacent desks, but not to take them away. The library houses over 200 medieval manuscripts including the 8th-century Hereford Gospels. Book chaining operated in libraries until the 18th century; this is the largest example to survive complete.

ESSENTIALS

GETTING THERE Hereford is 90 minutes from Birmingham or just over three hours from London by train (WM). The nearest major roads are the M5, A438, A465 and A49.

STAYING & EATING A short walk from the cathedral, the **Castle House Hotel** (castlehse.co.uk) is a Grade II-listed Georgian villa. Try **The Bookshop** (thebookshophereford.com) on Aubrey Street for brunch or dinner.

TIME TO SPARE? Other highlights in the cathedral include, in the Lady Chapel, John Swinfield's tomb, adorned with piglets, and the south aisle stained-glass window depicting Charles I's visit to Hereford in 1645. The cathedral's copy of the 1217 Magna Carta is sometimes on display. Opposite, on Broad Street, the **Hereford Museum and Art Gallery** (AF herefordshire.gov.uk) displays artefacts and archaeological finds from around the county. A few minutes away, the half-timbered **Black and White House Museum** (herefordshire.gov.uk) was built in 1621; its top two floors recreate the Jacobean era with some splendid period furniture. Across two floors (including the cellars) of the original offices of local firm HP Bulmer on Pomona Place, the **Museum of Cider** (cidermuseum. co.uk) houses artefacts from the worldwide history of cider making.

WALES

36 TINTERN & THE WYE VALLEY

ROMANTIC SUBLIME

The ruins of medieval Tintern Abbey and the surrounding Wye Valley, straddling the border between southwest England and south Wales, were a magnet for intellectuals and tourists at the end of the 18th century. Two factors encouraged this interest: a growing fascination for 'discovering' the wilder parts of Britain, and the difficulty in travelling around Europe during the Napoleonic Wars. William Wordsworth's *Lines Composed a Few Miles above Tintern Abbey* (1798) added to the abbey's allure. His poem epitomised key ideas of the Romantic movement, exploring the individual's relationship to the natural world, and the idea of the sublime: nature's infinite majesty. JMW Turner captured similar themes with his paintings of the ruined abbey and nearby Chepstow Castle.

STAR ATTRACTIONS

When the Cistercians (page 131) built the original **Tintern Abbey** (CW) in 1131, it fulfilled the Order's preference for a secluded location, which also helped it to avoid most of the English-Welsh fighting of subsequent years. Rebuilding took place through most of the 13th century, resulting in a grander edifice, but Tintern fell victim to the Dissolution of the Monasteries in 1536, and the church lost its

↑ Tintern Abbey. (Billy Stock/S)

roof within a few years. The principal parts of what remains are from the rebuilt church of the late 13th and early 14th centuries. The West Front is an excellent example of the then-fashionable Decorated Gothic style, with much of its tracery work still intact. The chapel and nave are dotted with tall, decorated columns and corbels that have fallen from the tops of pillars. You'll see elaborate tracery in the North Transept and in the Great East Windows, which once contained stained glass; fragments of the pulpitum (a screen dividing the choir from the nave) suggest just how colourful the interior decorations were. Beyond the church lie the less extensive remains of the monks' rooms and spaces, including the dayroom, infirmary, refectory and kitchens. The abbot's residence included, after some 14th-century modifications, a grand upper hall for entertaining and accommodating distinguished guests. You can follow Wordsworth's footsteps further by wandering close to the banks of the Wye and admiring the surrounding woods. A mile around a bend in the river lies the nostalgic **Tintern Old Station** (⊘tinternvillage.co.uk), with three vintage railway carriages and an old signal box.

Three miles south, close to the English border, is **Chepstow Castle** (CW). Like Tintern Abbey, its location was crucial, but for strategic reasons; it overlooked an important crossing point between England and Wales, on steep limestone cliffs above the Wye. The original builder was William FitzOsbern, close friend of William the Conqueror. The castle was completed by c1090 and it served as a garrison against the forces of Welsh leader Owain Glyndŵr and against Parliamentary forces in the English Civil War before falling into decline. The great stone tower may be the first post-Roman stone building in Wales, and the original doors from the main gatehouse – Europe's oldest castle doors, now on display inside – are even more remarkable. Iron plates sheathed the outer wooden face, with an elaborate lattice framework of iron straps on the reverse.

ESSENTIALS

GETTING THERE Chepstow is just over an hour from Bristol Temple Meads or three hours from London by train (GWR). Via the A466, the 69 bus between Monmouth and Chepstow stops at Tintern.

STAYING & EATING The **Wild Hare** (⊘thewildharetintern.co.uk), a comfortable pub with rooms, is close to the abbey. Enjoy tea at **Tintern Old Station Café** (⊘tinternvillage. co.uk) or a meal at the nearby **Anchor Inn** (⊘theanchortintern.co.uk).

TIME TO SPARE? Eleven miles north of Tintern on the A466, tucked away in a lane off a shopping street, are the fragmentary remains of **Monmouth Castle** (CW), birthplace of the future Henry V.

37 CARDIFF

KING COAL, CASTLES, COMMUNITIES

T he armadillo-like Millennium Centre, close to Cardiff Bay, proclaims in Welsh and English that 'in these stones horizons sing'. Cardiff's story is one of expanding horizons. The Victorian patronage of the Marquesses of Bute encouraged growth, as industrialisation came to south Wales with iron, steel and coal production and a new dock exported the output. Cardiff gained city status in 1905 and recognition as the Welsh capital in 1955. The late 20th-century redevelopment of the Bay has turned Cardiff into a creative and media hub; TV viewers are familiar with its heritage sites such as Castell Coch, Cardiff Castle and the Coal Exchange Hotel, thanks to filming for *Doctor Who* and *Torchwood*. The two castles display the eccentricities of the aristocratic employers who presided over Cardiff's growth, while industrial heritage sites to the north of Cardiff give insights into working life.

THE ITINERARY

DAY 1 'Croeso i uffern', says the banner as your eyes adjust to the darkness. Welcome to hell. This is the Cast House of **Blaenavon Ironworks** (CW), 30 miles north of Cardiff, where an immersive audiovisual presentation thrusts you into the heat of the Industrial Revolution. In the Cast House, molten iron flowed into channels known as pig beds. From here, pig iron went to forges for conversion into wrought iron and then into engines, machines, rails, tools, plates and countless other objects. Blaenavon Ironworks began here in 1787, with wealthy entrepreneurs and investors opening mines and quarries, building (horse-drawn) railways and investing in canals. By 1830 south Wales, including Blaenavon, made 40% of all the iron in Britain; the Blaenavon Industrial Landscape around here is now a UNESCO World Heritage Site. A willing workforce grew the community to 13,000 at its peak before its eventual decline and closure. From the Cast House, you walk round other parts of the site including the foundry, the balance tower which lifted wagons 80ft from the lower to the upper yard, and the cottages that housed some of the workforce – including children as young as five years old. The ironworks created the first large-scale demand for coal in the area, and just under a mile to the west lies the **Big Pit National Coal Museum** (AF ⚲ museum.wales). It's an amalgamation of several mines, and while hundreds of Welsh collieries have closed without trace, Big Pit survives as a museum to tell their stories as well as its own. A former miner leads underground tours to a depth of 300ft, to give a visceral sense of the realities of mining life. The 'King Coal' multimedia experience uses galleries in the hillside above the colliery to explain how the industry evolved with the advent of ever greater mechanisation. The site takes a while to walk round in its entirety, encompassing the old electrical workshops (now waiting rooms for the underground tours), the lamp room and much else. The miners' baths are behind glass partitions, adjacent to an exhibition telling the wider story of the industry's rise and decline. It's striking to see how dangerous

← A view of Castell Coch. (Billy Stock/S)

and unhealthy this working life was – and also how the dangers and discomforts drew local communities together.

DAY 2 Two Cardiff castles reinvented in Victorian times provide a vivid contrast with the lives of working men and women. The first, **Cardiff Castle** (AF ✆ cardiffcastle.com), is in the city centre. The site was used for a series of four Roman forts after the defeat of the local Silures tribe, the first three being wooden and the fourth having stone walls. Victorian workmen rediscovered some of the latter, which were reconstructed along with a gallery within them; during World War II the gallery was a de facto air-raid shelter for almost 2,000 local people. When the Normans conquered southeast Wales, they reused the site; a 12-sided blue lias limestone keep, intended as accommodation for the lord and his household, still stands. The main castle building metamorphosed from a fortress into a comfortable mansion before, in the 1870s, the 3rd Marquess of Bute and architect William Burges (1827–81) transformed it into a riot of Gothic Revivalism. The Marquess's travels through Europe and the Near East helped to inspire more exotic developments such as the wood and gold leaf ceiling in the Arab Room, a reminder of the Marquess's travels in Sicily. In the

CARDIFF'S TEMPLE OF PEACE

The Art Deco **Temple of Peace and Health** (✆ templeofpeace.wales) in the north of the city centre, or Temple of Peace for short, is the only public building in Wales, or probably anywhere, devoted to both peace and health. It was part of the vision of Lord David Davies of Llandinam, who was so horrified by his experience of World War I that he committed the rest of his life to building peace and combating disease. The Temple housed two organisations Lord Davies helped to found: one working to eliminate tuberculosis in Wales, the other supporting the League of Nations' endeavours for worldwide peace. The building's two wings, one for Peace and one for Health, are linked by a central Art Deco portico with three large windows. These are capped by symbolic reliefs: a snake, representing Health; scales, representing Justice; and a wheatsheaf representing Peace. By a sad irony, the Temple opened on 23 November 1938, less than two months after Neville Chamberlain had returned from Munich with his ill-fated promise of 'peace for our time'. Mrs Minnie James, representing Wales's war-bereaved mothers, performed the opening ceremony; legend has it that she was buried with the ceremonial key. Today, the Welsh Centre for International Affairs, which leases part of the building, holds regular 'open doors days' with tours of the interior. To the rear of the Temple is the National Garden of Peace and Peacemakers, which is open at all times. The Temple has appeared in many TV shows including, in another ironic twist, the *Doctor Who* episode 'Let's Kill Hitler'.

↑ Blaenavon Ironworks. (INTREEGUE Photography/S) ← Big Pit National Coal Museum. (Cliff Day/S)

Banqueting Hall, murals recount the castle's history in the style of medieval manuscripts. The bronze beavers on the Roof Garden's fountain are a reference to Lord Bute bringing real beavers into the grounds in 1873, in an attempt to reintroduce a species that had been common in medieval times. The Library also takes inspiration from its medieval equivalents. This reinvented Castle is extravagant, theatrical, quasi-parodic fun, but we wonder what local miners or iron workers would have thought of it all.

Castell Coch (CW), five miles north of Cardiff on a thickly wooded hillside, was a ruined medieval fortress on the 3rd Marquess's estate, until Burges persuaded him to have it restored for use as a summer home. The circular towers with conical roofs are an early clue that, as with Cardiff Castle, understatement is not the keynote here. Not everything built for the Marquess survives today. One of his and Burges' more eccentric ideas was for a wooden chapel projecting out from the top of one

ESSENTIALS

GETTING THERE & AROUND Cardiff has strong rail links with the rest of Britain (GWR). There's easy access by road from the M4 but, as parking can be a challenge, you might consider using one of the three Park and Ride sites on the city outskirts. Or you can even sail into the harbour (⊘ cardiffharbour.com). An Aquabus service links Cardiff's centre to the Bay, departing from Bute Park (⊘ aquabus.co.uk/city-bay-link-2).

STAYING The **Coal Exchange Hotel** (⊘ coalexchangecardiff.co.uk) in Mount Stuart Square offers spacious rooms, good service and a convenient location between Cardiff Bay and the centre. For contemporary accommodation and a great view of the Bay, try **Voco St David's** (⊘ stdavids.vocohotels.com).

EATING **Giovanni's** (⊘ giovanniscardiff.co.uk) has been in Cardiff since the 1980s and there are three outlets across the city, serving good old-school Italian cuisine; try the linguine with prawns and courgettes. Close to the Bay, **Yakitori1** (⊘ yakitori1.co.uk) is a good choice for Japanese cuisine. For breakfast or elevenses, **Coffi Co** (⊘ coffico.uk) runs several Cardiff outlets. **Bill's** (⊘ bills-website.co.uk) at Cardiff Bay is worth a visit, and not just because of the excellent eggs Benedict. This Bill's is inside Cardiff's old Pilotage Building, where river pilots picked up their pay and their roster for the day, before using their local knowledge to guide large ships into the dock.

TIME TO SPARE? North of the city centre, the **National Museum Cardiff** (⊘ museum.wales) hosts Wales's national art, geology and natural history collections as well as major touring and temporary shows. Inside the Grade II-listed Old Library building on The Hayes, ten minutes' walk south, the **Museum of Cardiff** (⊘ cardiffmuseum.com)

tower into the courtyard; only the vestibule, containing ten stained-glass windows of various saints, remains. As at Cardiff Castle, the Banqueting Hall makes liberal use of medieval motifs. Through its double doors lies the steeply vaulted Drawing Room, with a minstrels' gallery on an upper level, in which a carving of the Three Fates of Greek mythology sits on the chimneypiece. The fireplace recess contains tiles illustrating zodiac signs; the vault, a brilliant sky blue, displays paintings of parrots and other exotic animals; on the lower walls, murals illustrate some of Aesop's Fables such as the tale of the hare and the tortoise, and a monkey is shown with Victorian side-whiskers. Lord Bute did not approve of the monkeys cavorting on the ceiling above the bed in Lady Bute's bedroom. Here, a luminous two-stage mirrored dome and painted panels of abstract design create a distinctly Orientalist mood, aided by rich reds and golds throughout the room and by the bed itself, a copy of a supposed 14th-century original.

tells the city's story via artefacts, photos and ephemera. Five minutes from the Bay, you can glimpse Cardiff's Victorian commercial heyday in the wood-panelled halls of the **Coal Exchange Hotel**. Coal owners, ship owners and their agents did business on the Exchange's trading hall floor; legend claims that the world's first £1 million cheque was signed here. In the Bay itself, you can't miss the **Pierhead Building** (⊘ senedd.wales/visit/our-estate), once the administrative office for South Wales Ports; its imposing red-brick Gothic Revivalist design and multi-directional clock face are unforgettable. The equally distinctive black and white **Norwegian Church** (⊘ norwegianchurchcardiff.com) nearby, now an arts centre, was once a home from home for Norwegian seafarers; Cardiff-born author Roald Dahl was baptised here. Five miles west of Cardiff, **St Fagans National Museum of History** (AF ⊘ museum.wales) presents over 50 original and reconstructed historic buildings from across Wales, from Iron Age roundhouses to an early 20th-century working men's institute.

↑ View across Cardiff Bay. (muratart/S)

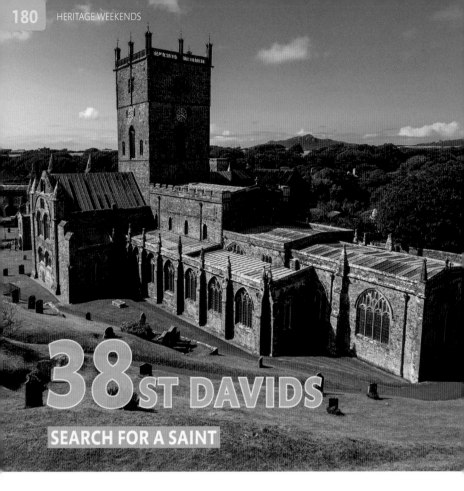

38 ST DAVIDS

SEARCH FOR A SAINT

On a peninsula in the far southwest of Wales sits the small city of St Davids, birthplace of the nation's patron saint. The 6th-century monastery he founded here became the centre point of Wales' largest and most important medieval diocese. By the Middle Ages, its bishops enjoyed quasi-royal privileges and pilgrims believed that two pilgrimages here equalled one to Rome. We can still glimpse that power and wealth in the Bishop's Palace and the Cathedral, and there's a homage to St David's mother nearby.

STAR ATTRACTIONS

Most of what remains of the **Bishop's Palace** (CW) is the legacy of Henry de Gower, the bishop here between 1328 and 1347. De Gower's palace followed the Decorated Gothic style, which used fine carving and flowing tracery. The use of purple local sandstone contributed rich colour. A doorway in the east range with a semi-octagonal head leads to an area which housed the bishop's hall, a kitchen, a solar and a chapel. There are over 100 carved figures on corbels throughout

↑ St Davids Cathedral. (Fulcanelli/S)

the palace: humans, animals, mermaids and human-animal-bird hybrids. The south range, with its great hall, great chamber and a second chapel, was the most highly decorated section. In the niches above the doorway to the great hall are the remains of two statues, possibly Edward III and Queen Philippa; the hall itself retains a beautiful wheel window carved in limestone. Some sections of arcaded parapet have been partially restored to suggest the original yellow and purple chequerboard pattern.

De Gower's influence extended to the neighbouring **St Davids Cathedral** (stdavidscathedral.org.uk), a Norman building which he repaired and remodelled after the collapse of the central tower. His tomb is in the south aisle of the nave. The building suffered damage after the Reformation, and then at the hands of Civil War troops, before another restoration, this time by George Gilbert Scott. Some of the greatest sights are above or below you. The renovated rose window incorporates William Morris Company stained glass; the nave's Welsh oak ceiling is Britain's only cathedral ceiling of this type; and the underside of the seats in the quire reveals a series of 16th-century carvings of mythical beasts and morality stories. Between the quire and the presbytery, a restored shrine to St David depicts him standing between St Patrick and St Andrew. Nearby lies the tomb of Edmund Tudor, father of Henry VII who was born 30 miles away at Pembroke Castle.

Just over half a mile south of the palace and cathedral, in a dramatic setting above St Non's Bay, a few crumbling walls mark **St Non's Chapel** (CW). Non, or Nonnita, so the story goes, gave birth to David here after being violated by Sanctus, king of Ceredigion. A nearby well enjoyed a dual reputation as a wishing well and for the curative powers of its waters.

ESSENTIALS

GETTING THERE The nearest train stations, Fishguard and Haverfordwest, are on the West Wales Line (TW), with Haverfordwest just over 4 hours, and Fishguard just over 5 hours, from London Paddington (GWR). Shuttle bus services connect St Davids with other coastal points (pembrokeshire.gov.uk). The city is 2½ hours west of Cardiff by car (M4, A40, A487).

STAYING & EATING Tower Hill (LT) offers a grandstand cathedral view. The **Mill Café** (TheMillStDavids) on New Street is popular for breakfast and coffee; try **Blas** (blasrestaurant.com) at Twr y Felin Hotel for dinner.

TIME TO SPARE? Six miles north at Abereiddi, the **Blue Lagoon** (NT) holds the remains of one of 100 slate quarries that drove Pembrokeshire's late 18th-century economy. The ruins of workmen's cottages and the foreman's house are still visible.

39 ABERYSTWYTH

BIARRITZ OF BOOKS

The small, adaptable town of Aberystwyth stands by the sand and shingle beaches of Cardigan Bay on Wales's central west coast, with the Cambrian Mountains at its back. The National Library houses several significant Welsh artefacts and acts as an inspiring research centre for students at the town's university. Aberystwyth's horseshoe bay and promenade reveal how, in Victorian times, the town reinvented itself as a seaside resort and then as a place of learning. You can find clues to earlier phases of Aberystwyth's past in the remains of a medieval castle and an engmatic Iron Age hillfort.

THE ITINERARY

DAY 1 A mile inland up Penglais Hill, with great views over the town and the bay, sits the **National Library of Wales** (⊘ library.wales). It's here because, during the planning of its creation, Sir John Williams, a local man and former surgeon to Queen Victoria, offered to donate his collection of medieval manuscripts… as long as the library was based in Aberystwyth. Among the permanent displays, there are two exhibits of particular note. The portrait *Salem* (1908) by Sydney Vosper shows Welsh women in traditional garb, including stovepipe hats, worshipping in a Baptist chapel; look closely at the fabrics and you may see the Devil. The Nanteos Cup is believed to have been made from part of the True Cross and to possess healing powers for anyone who drinks from it. Some even think it is a candidate for the Holy Grail. The library's neighbours include

↑ The view from the Pen Dinas hillfort over Aberystwyth. (steved_np3/S)

Aberystwyth University; down the hill on New Promenade, the **Old College** (⬧ aber.ac.uk) is a reminder of the university's origins. This grand golden Gothic building, with curves, bows, arches and turrets galore and even the odd gargoyle, looks particularly splendid in the early evening sun. Look up at one end of the building (which overlooks a crazy golf course) for a triptych mosaic showing technology and trade in the form of a train and a ship. The new University College Wales, Aberystwyth, as it was called then, opened in 1872 with 26 students; the university now welcomes over 6,000. The Old College sits in the middle of Aberystwyth's mile-long horseshoe **Promenade**, which features Wales' oldest pier, built in 1864 – the same year that the Cambrian Railways line arrived from Machynlleth, 20 miles north along the coast. Rail links enabled the town to market itself as a seaside holiday destination, 'The Biarritz of Wales'. New hotels and townhouses helped to meet visitor demand, and their pastel colours along the Promenade are a cheerful part of today's scene. At the Promenade's north end, it's a bracing but straightforward climb up Constitution Hill (430ft). You can also reach the top at 4mph on the **Cliff Railway** (⬧ aberystwythcliffrailway.co.uk), Britain's longest funicular electric cliff railway, in operation since 1896. From the summit, the town, the bay and up to 26 mountain peaks are visible on a clear day, with help from one of the world's largest camera obscuras, a recreation of a Victorian original with a 14-inch lens that can cover up to 1,000 square miles.

STONE CASTLES IN WALES

Medieval stone castle building in Wales happened in three broad phases. The earliest was the work of **Norman** followers of William the Conqueror, expanding territories that he had given them by moving into southern and eastern Wales. They built castles at Chepstow, Monmouth (page 173), Cardiff (page 177) and elsewhere to protect their gains. **Native Welsh princes** followed; in the late 12th and early 13th centuries Llywelyn the Great built castles such as Dolbadarn and Dolwyddelan commanding passes in Snowdonia, Castel y Bere on a rocky outcrop near his southern frontier and Criccieth (page 187) near the Llŷn Peninsula. The third phase was a result of **Edward I's** conflicts with the Welsh. After the 1277 battle against Llywelyn ap Gruffydd and subsequent settlement, Edward built or rebuilt castles at Aberystwyth (see below), Flint and Rhuddlan. Wales was under Edward's control by 1283 despite further resistance from Llywelyn's brother Dafydd. Edward redeveloped the existing castles at Criccieth and Dolwyddelan, while building new castles to the latest designs at Caernarfon, Harlech (page 186) and Conwy. After a rebellion in 1294, he commissioned Beaumaris Castle (page 195). Beaumaris, Harlech and the castles and town walls of Caernarfon and Conwy now hold UNESCO World Heritage Site status as 'The Castles and Town Walls of King Edward in Gwynedd'.

DAY 2 From the Pier, turn left to find the romantic ruins of **Aberystwyth Castle**. A Norman lord built the first castle in Aberystwyth in the early 12th century. Falling into the hands of warring Welsh princes, this was rebuilt several times before Edward I ordered the construction of a new castle in the current location in 1277 during his campaign against Llywelyn ap Gruffydd. It housed a royal mint in the 17th century until Oliver Cromwell slighted (seriously damaged) it in 1649, but traces of Edward's diamond-shaped concentric fortress remain. The absence of interpretation boards leaves much to the imagination, and the pair of tiny cannons either side of the north tower gateway makes a poignant sight. Beneath the castle, at street level, a series of alcoves contains mosaics illustrating its history. Continue left towards the end of the Promenade to find the remains of a much older fortification, the **Pen Dinas hillfort**. At just over 750ft, it's a steeper (and narrower) climb than Constitution Hill. Evidence from 1930s excavations suggests that there have been two forts here, one on the northern knoll and a later fort on the southern knoll, with later constructions of defences around both. Discoveries included shards of a jar made in the Malvern Hills between 300–50BC. Whether Pen Dinas was a major trading centre or a tribal leader's base remains a mystery. It now has a modern adornment, a stone column erected on the summit of the south fort in 1858 in tribute to the Duke of Wellington.

ESSENTIALS

GETTING THERE Aberystwyth is five hours from London, three hours from Birmingham and two hours from Shrewsbury by train (TW and others). The main road routes are via the A44, A485 and A487.

STAYING Down by the beach, try the **Glengower** (⌖ glengower.co.uk), a pub with rooms, or the **Pier Hotel** (⌖ the-pier-hotel-aberystwyth.hotelmix.co.uk) off the Promenade. **Student accommodation** is also available out of termtime (⌖ aber.ac.uk/en/visitors/bunkhouse), while just outside Aberystwyth is a touch of luxury at **Nanteos Country House Hotel** (⌖ nanteos.com).

EATING Down by the harbour at the Promenade's southern end, **Ridiculously Rich by Alana** (⌖ ridiculouslyrichbyalana.co.uk) makes raspberry blondies and other sweet treats. The takeaway **Ultracomida Delicatessen** (⌖ ultracomida.co.uk) on Pier Street is a winning Welsh-Spanish fusion concept; the spinach empanada and *barra gallega* (artisanal Spanish half-baguettes) are excellent. **Sweet Vice with Poly** (⌖ sweetvicewithpoly.co.uk) on Eastgate is a family-run Bulgarian restaurant.

TIME TO SPARE? **Ceredigion Museum** (⌖ ceredigionmuseum.wales), in a preserved Edwardian museum on Terrace Street, covers the region's heritage, culture and art. The popular **Vale of Rheidol Railway** (⌖ rheidolrailway.co.uk) runs restored Edwardian steam trains from Aberystwyth to the nearby Devil's Bridge and waterfalls. To explore Welsh mining history, head 11 miles east of town to the family-friendly **Silver Mountain Experience** (⌖ silvermountainexperience.co.uk), in what was once a silver-rich lead ore mine.

↑ Vale of Rheidol Railway. (David Hughes/S)

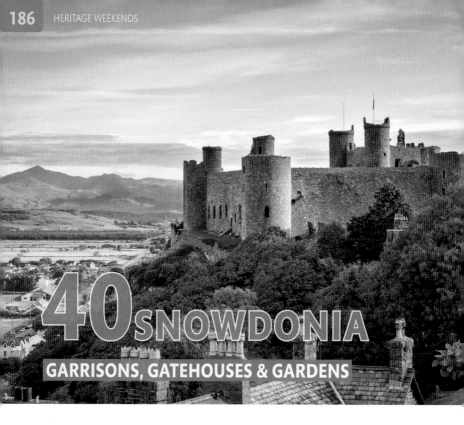

40 SNOWDONIA
GARRISONS, GATEHOUSES & GARDENS

While Snowdonia, in northwest Wales, is known best for its great beauty, the evidence of centuries of toil and conflict – and also of great creativity – lies all around. Medieval castles in dramatic locations remain from the wars between the Welsh and the English. Quarries of local slate offer tangible reminders of how, in the wake of the Industrial Revolution, this region built an industry with worldwide demand for its product. Meanwhile, celebrated architect Clough Williams-Ellis's work at Portmeirion and Plas Brondanw marries wit and imagination with respect for the environment, in scenic, peaceful spaces which are perfect for reflection.

THE ITINERARY

DAY 1 After his second war against the Welsh in 1283 (page 184), Edward I decided to build **Harlech Castle** (CW) on a rocky crag above Tremadog Bay, an inlet of Cardigan Bay. Its concentric plan of two circuits of stone walls, the inner walls with towers at the four corners, made for a formidable fortress. Even under siege, as in 1294, a 'Way from the Sea' – a path of 108 steep steps in the rockface – enabled the castle to receive supplies. But Harlech was also intended as a sumptuous residence, and you can see traces of the two upper floors of accommodation as well as the chapel, great hall, buttery, pantry and kitchen. Unlike other castles, the construction of Harlech finished on time, in 1290. A great

↑ Harlech Castle. (Valery Egorov/S)

deal survives, including those massive towers, which is remarkable considering Harlech surrendered three times: to Owain Glyndŵr's forces in 1404 (before the English recaptured it in 1409), to the Yorkists in the Wars of the Roses (page 17) and to the Parliamentarians in the English Civil War. The song 'Men of Harlech' may commemorate the heroic effort of resistance against the Yorkist siege of 1461–68. The views, with the mountains of Snowdonia as a backdrop and Cardigan Bay and, beyond it, the Irish Sea to the front, are as majestic as you're likely to find. Fifteen miles around the bay, on the southeastern part of the Llŷn peninsula, is the small town and seaside resort of Criccieth, with **Criccieth Castle** (CW) above it. In this case the Welsh, in the person of Llywelyn the Great, built the first castle here in the 1230s, combining a massive gatehouse with two elongated D-shaped towers. His grandson Llywelyn ap Gruffydd, or Llywelyn the Last, added the outer ward, curtain walls and two new towers. After the English captured Criccieth in 1283, they rebuilt and enhanced the castle, adding an extra storey to the towers. Since 1404, when Owain Glyndŵr's forces captured it, tore down the walls and set it alight (try to spot the scorch marks), it has been a ruin. The inner gatehouse remains impressive and the north tower gives a hint of the military past, as it may have had a stone-throwing trebuchet on the roof.

To learn about the industry that powered this region in the 19th century, head inland to the east. South Wales had coal; the north quarried and exported slate. Between the 1760s and the end of the 19th century, mines at Dinorwig, Penrhyn, Llanberis, Bethesda and Blaenau Ffestiniog supplied Britain, continental Europe and North America with slate. At its height, the industry employed around 17,000 people. The **Llechwedd** site (⊘llechwedd.co.uk), a few miles from Snowdon and a mile north of Blaenau Ffestiniog, runs deep mine tours – with a train descending 500ft into ten chambers that tell the stories of the slate miners – and off-road

THE PRISONER: BE SEEING YOU!

A British intelligence agent resigns and is abducted to a mysterious coastal destination known as 'The Village'. His unidentified captors want to know why he resigned; he wants to escape. This is the premise of *The Prisoner* (1967), a 17-episode British TV drama series filmed at Portmeirion (page 191) which blends spy fiction, psychological drama, allegory, science fiction and fantasy. Patrick McGoohan's agent, known as Number Six, locks horns with Number Two, whose identity changes in every episode, and tries to evade large white balloon-type security devices known as 'Rover'. The Village residents, most of whom exude cheerful false bonhomie, have numbers, not names; some help Number Six while others betray him. The phrase 'Be seeing you!' is a conversation stopper and a reminder that everyone and everything is under surveillance.

↓ Criccieth Castle. (travellight/S)

tours of the quarries. For the daring, there's a network of zip-line and adventure courses, above and below ground.

DAY 2 The creator of **Portmeirion** (⏣portmeirion.wales), Clough Williams-Ellis (1883–1978), was an architect, an advocate for National Parks and an opponent of rural urbanisation. He bought the coastal village of Aber Ia, two miles southeast of Porthmadog, in 1925, changing its name to Portmeirion and developing it over the next 50 years as a playful evocation of Italian resorts such as Portofino. An old house on the shore served as a hotel which, along with self-catering cottages in the village, brought in money to fund the work. Portmeirion has been a popular visitor attraction and holiday village since its early days, and found international fame as the setting for *The Prisoner* (page 187). The government awarded protected status in 1973 and today a charitable trust manages the site. Williams-Ellis wanted 'to show people, with a sort of light-opera effect, that architecture could be fun, could be entertaining, interesting, intriguing.' The Gate House is a good example: a pale terracotta cottage above a deep arch (with its own ceiling mural), whose window shutters are not real, but lines cut into the render and painted green. From here, you walk through to the centre of the village, with the Bell Tower and the Pantheon – a dome in the style of Brunelleschi's work in Florence – overlooking a central piazza. Starting at the Piazza, moving past two statues of Burmese dancers, you climb a low stone stairway to the Gloriette, named after a monument at Vienna's Schönbrunn Palace. The Gloriette is, in reality, a façade with five *trompe l'oeil* windows along with four 18th-century columns from Hooton Hall in Cheshire, while the pink-walled Gothic Pavilion facing it across the piazza was a gift from Nerquis Hall in nearby Flintshire. The Jacobean vaulted plasterwork inside the Town Hall came from Emral Hall in Wrexham, after Williams-Ellis heard of the Hall's imminent demolition and rushed to the auction. Deception and playful humour are everywhere. Unicorn House, which looks from a distance like a small stately home, is a one-storey 1960s bungalow, while the 1920s petrol pump outside Neptune House has a 19th-century pine figurehead (looking understandably bemused). From the Observatory Tower, below the village on the beach, Portmeirion is visible through a camera obscura said to have come from a German U-Boat. Temples and gazebos lurk in 74 acres of sub-tropical forest around the village, along with an Edwardian wild garden containing Himalayan flowering trees and exotic plants. **Morfa Harlech National Nature Reserve**, one of Britain's most important actively growing sand dune systems, lies beyond the Observation Tower.

Four miles north of Portmeirion, **Plas Brondanw** (HH, RHS ⏣plasbrondanw. com) was Williams-Ellis's family home; he received it as a 21st birthday present in 1904. He had to restore the estate twice, once from the state of disrepair in

↑ Portmeirion. (EddieCloud/S) ← Llechwedd. (David Pimborough/S)

which he inherited it and then after a fire gutted the house in 1951. The Grade I-listed gardens are set within two long lines of Irish and English yew hedges and cypresses, with a 200-year-old oak tree at the centre of a large lawn with apple trees along the border. The layout is formal, with touches of wit. Within a series of garden 'rooms', the statuary includes three classical busts under blue painted arches ('Cupid's Folly') and a cherub dressed as a fireman, complete with hosepipe. Light blue handrails are decorated with gilt fish and mermaids

ESSENTIALS

GETTING THERE & AROUND Harlech and Criccieth are 3 to 3½ hours from Shrewsbury by rail (TFW). The A487/A497 is the nearest main road route (or the A496 for Harlech). Trains run from London Euston to Llandudno Junction or Bangor (AV), both of which are around an hour away from Portmeirion by car (Llandudno Junction also connects to Blaenau Ffestiniog along the Conwy Valley line). Alternatively, the Cambrian Coast Line runs from Pwllheli to Machynlleth with a station at Minffordd, from where a footpath of 0.7 miles takes you to Portmeirion. A daily bus service from Porthmadog runs to Portmeirion between March and October. Snowdonia is a great place for vintage rail journeys. **Ffestiniog and Welsh Highland Railways** (⊘ festrail.co.uk) runs two steam lines to Portmeirion, one from Blaenau Ffestiniog and one from Caernarfon, while the volunteer-run **Welsh Highland Heritage Railway** (⊘ whr.co.uk) operates short steam trips and 'diesel days' between Porthmadog station and Pen-y-Mount Halt.

STAYING **Portmeirion Village** (⊘ portmeirion.wales) has two hotels (Hotel Portmeirion and Castell Deudraeth, an early Victorian castellated mansion); various rooms and suites dotted around the village; and 13 historic self-catering cottages with full access to hotel facilities. **Llechwedd's** glamping facilities (⊘ llechwedd.co.uk) comprise six lodges, each sleeping four or five people, overlooking moorland, valleys and local slate quarries. Ten miles northwest of Snowdon, castle lovers will enjoy a stay in **Bath Tower**, one of the eight towers of Caernarfon's medieval town wall (LT).

EATING Opposite Harlech Castle, **Caffi Castell Harlech** (⊘ cafficastell.co.uk) promises three Welsh cheeses in its Welsh rarebit. In the small village of Maentwrog, there's delicious home-cooked food on offer at the **Grapes Hotel** (⊘ grapeshotelsnowdonia.co.uk). Portmeirion's hotel restaurants and cafés cater for most needs; the on-site gelateria **Caffi'r Angel** combines Welsh and Italian themes with bara brith ice cream, along with more traditional flavours.

TIME TO SPARE? Add to your castle collection by heading north to **Caernarfon**, the ruins at **Dolbadarn**, near Llanberis, and **Dolwyddelan** (all CW). Near Dolbadarn,

in mustard yellow. From every angle, and especially at the Belvedere roundel or 'full stop', the views of Snowdonia are awe-inspiring. Above the gardens is the small, whimsical Folly Tower, which Williams-Ellis built with wedding present funds from army officers with whom he had served in World War I. These are peaceful gardens, whose use of local stone celebrates the wonderful surrounding landscape. They live up to Williams-Ellis's wish to 'cherish the past, adorn the present, construct for the future'.

the **National Slate Museum** in Dinorwig quarry (⊘ museum.wales) recounts the history of this key north Welsh industry. For a more personal story, take the A497 nine miles west from Portmeirion to Llanystumdwy and David Lloyd George's childhood home, now the **Lloyd George Museum** (⊘ lloydgeorge.net). The **Snowdonia National Park** (⊘ snowdonia.gov.wales) is a great destination for walkers, climbers, bikers and stargazers; it received International Dark Sky Reserve status in 2015. Clough Williams-Ellis was personally responsible for the demarcation of the park's boundaries.

↑ National Slate Museum. (Andrew Chisholm/S)

41 ANGLESEY

MOTHER OF WALES

Wales's largest island lies off the country's northwestern coast, resembling a teapot with the handle on the western side and the spout to the east. The English name, Anglesey, may come from the Old Norse for 'Hook Island'; its Welsh name is Ynys Môn. The Romans knew it as Mona. More poetic alternatives have included Môn Mam Cymru, which translates as 'Môn, Mother of Wales'. The medieval chronicler Gerald of Wales suggested that this last name derived from the island's fertility and its role in supplying mainland Wales with agricultural produce. The low-lying terrain, mild climate, relative inaccessibility for aspiring invaders from the mainland and access to the Irish Sea enabled farming and fishing to flourish. Anglesey now welcomes almost two million visitors a year. Some arrive via Thomas Telford's Menai Suspension Bridge and Robert Stephenson's Britannia Bridge, which connect the mainland to the island's south coast; others come on ferries from Ireland to Holyhead in Anglesey's northwest. The itinerary below, travelling clockwise from the southeast, is a delight for lovers of history and archaeology. It encompasses Edward I's last great Welsh castle, an elegant country house with a remarkable mural, romantic hidden gardens, ancient monuments full of mystery and the startling site of what was once the world's largest copper mine.

↑ South Stack Lighthouse. (Lukassek/S)

THE ITINERARY

DAY 1 By 1295, after two wars against the Welsh and one rebellion, Edward I had had enough. He ordered the building of **Beaumaris Castle** (CW) on Anglesey's southeast coast as an addition to English strongholds in the region, and the creation of the new town of Beaumaris – along with the forcible evacuation of the residents of Llanfaes a mile away. The castle was to be a masterpiece: two lines of curtain walls and towers; luxurious accommodation within two gatehouses and in the inner ward. However, despite the efforts of a workforce of 1,500 and spending of £6,000 within six months (equivalent to millions today), progress slowed and funds ran out as Edward focused on Scotland. The incomplete castle functioned as a governing hub, as a fortress against Owain Glyndŵr's rebellion a century later and sometimes as a prison, falling out of use after the Civil War. Nowadays the only garrisons are flocks of seagulls, their mocking cries occasionally interrupted by the sardonic interjections of crows, but the castle remains impressive. Its defensive attributes include hundreds of vertical slits in the walls through which crossbowmen could shoot, and a south gateway with two portcullises and 'murder holes' in the ceiling. Traces remain of a chapel, a kitchen and a bakehouse.

A handful of miles west along Anglesey's south coast lie two properties with contrasting histories. **Plas Newydd** (NT) is home to the Marquesses of Anglesey, many of whom have been colourful characters. Henry Bayly, the 1st Marquess, did his bit for the family dynasty by having 18 children by two wives; he had eloped with the second, who was the future Duke of Wellington's sister-in-law. Henry lost a leg in action at Waterloo, where he was Wellington's second-in-command, and wore a replacement articulated leg thereafter. The house is an eclectic mix of Gothic and Neoclassical. Its highlight lies in the long dining room, where a 58ft mural by Rex Whistler merges Snowdonia's mountains with classical scenes from Italy and Austria to evoke memories of the family's holidays, along with in-jokes such as the inclusion of the family's favourite pug dog. Nearby **Plas Cadnant** (HH ⊘plascadnant.co.uk) was the early 19th-century creation of a father and son, each named John Price. The Prices both worked for the Marquess of Anglesey and would have known the Plas Newydd estate, whose grounds Humphry Repton had redesigned in fashionable Picturesque style. The Prices created their own walled garden with a valley garden below, but all was overgrown and lost in later years; the current owner rediscovered and recreated the gardens. The slight acidity of the soil encourages camellias, rhododendrons and magnolias in the spring, but there is plenty of colour and interest in summer and autumn too, with more than a mile of footpaths.

The approach to the house at Plas Newydd features five large boulders which once formed a cromlech (the burial chamber of a Neolithic chieftain), and many ancient monuments remain around the island. Some five miles southwest of Plas Newydd, off the A4080, are **Caer Lêb** (CW), a rectangular enclosure of double banks and ditches, which may have its origins in the Iron Age, and **Castell Bryn Gwyn** (CW), once an enclosure with a bank and external ditch built in the late Neolithic era, which later became a Roman settlement. Two miles northwest of Plas Newydd is **Bryn Celli Ddu** (CW), whose name translates as 'The Mound in the Dark Grove'. There was once a henge here but, towards the end of the Neolithic period, inhabitants built a new stone burial chamber and covered it with a large mound that extended into the henge's original ditch. Inside is a passage tomb, a long passage that leads to a polygonal stone chamber. Excavators have found burned and unburned human bones in the passage, as well as quartz, two flint arrowheads, a stone bead and limpet and mussel shells. Outside is a replica of a decorated pattern stone (the original is in the National Museum in Cardiff). The site's unique feature among Anglesey tombs is its precise alignment with the rising sun at dawn on the day of the summer solstice; at that time, sunlight travels down the passage and lights the

↑ Plas Newydd. (JIcst/DT) → Bryn Celli Ddu. (HM)

inner chamber. There's no definite agreed reason for this arrangement, but it adds an uncanny touch to a truly fascinating site.

DAY 2 Continuing a clockwise route around Anglesey, start in the northwest corner in Holyhead which, strictly speaking, is on Holy Island, separated from Anglesey by the narrow Cymyran Strait. In the centre of town, **Caer Gybi** (CW) comprises three historic sites in one: a 3rd-century Roman coastal fort whose walls remain; a 6th-century monastic foundation granted to St Cybi (or Cuby in Cornish – he was a Cornish bishop, saint and king who worked mostly in north Wales); and a late medieval church within the fort walls. Outside Holyhead are various further ancient sites, all managed by Cadw: **Holyhead Mountain Hut Group**, up to eight distinct homesteads which may date back to the Mesolithic period; an Iron Age hillfort at **Caer y Twr**; two Bronze Age standing stones at **Penrhos Feilw** and one at **Tŷ Mawr**; and a Neolithic burial chamber at **Trefignath**. From Holyhead, a 20-mile drive to the northeast of Anglesey brings you to the **Copper Mountain** (also known as Parys Mountain; ⊘ copperkingdom.co.uk). The presence of copper here was known in Bronze Age times, but the discovery of a mass of ore close to the surface in 1768 led to a Welsh copper equivalent of the Gold Rush, with hopefuls from around the UK arriving with the dream of making their fortunes. On a larger scale much of the copper became sheaths which helped to protect the ships of the Royal Navy from

ESSENTIALS

GETTING THERE & AROUND Regular trains run to Holyhead from London, Birmingham and Manchester, changing at Chester and sometimes Crewe (AV). The main road routes via the mainland are the A55 from the north and the A487 from the south; the A55 runs through Anglesey to Holyhead. There are daily flights between Cardiff and Anglesey Airport in Holyhead (⊘ flybe.com) and ferries from Dublin to Holyhead (just over three hours; ⊘ stenaline.co.uk). For Anglesey bus timetables, see ⊘ traveline.cymru.

STAYING Joseph Hansom, who invented the hansom cab, was also an architect. His creations included the Neoclassical Grade I-listed **Bulkeley Hotel** in Beaumaris (⊘ bulkeleyhotel.co.uk), to host a visit in 1832 by Princess, later Queen, Victoria. For self-catering, **Plas Cadnant Estate and Gardens** (⊘ plascadnant.co.uk) offers five holiday cottages, including the old Coach House which sleeps up to 12 guests.

EATING Good options in Menai Bridge town include excellent antipasti at **Plus 39** (◆ Plus39MenaiBridge) or seafood at **Dylan's** (⊘ dylansrestaurant.co.uk) while you gaze over the Menai Strait. For a coffee break, the delectable homemade cakes at **Happy Valley Café**, right by Beaumaris Castle, go down a treat.

timber worm and barnacle growth. By following the well-signed routes around the site, you can view various aspects of the operation such as a sampling pool, a smelter, processing yards, the offices and a mortuary. The open cast mines, where 1,500 people a day would dig by hand, are a kaleidoscopic mixture of reds, oranges and golds, with the colours even more vibrant early or late in the day. It's as close to a lunar landscape as most of us will ever walk upon. Just over two miles away in the harbour of Amlwch, the **Copper Kingdom** exhibition centre (⊘copperkingdom. co.uk) tells the history of copper on Anglesey, while a listed building known as the Sail Loft gives information about the shipbuilding industry that grew up to serve the copper mine. Halfway down Anglesey's east coast is another cluster of three Cadw-managed ancient monuments, around Ffordd Lligwy in Moelfre: a Neolithic burial chamber; an early medieval church; and **Din Lligwy Hut Group**. To see this last site, walk through a small, wild-garlic-laden wood which resounds to the car-horn cries of pheasants; you'll arrive at the remains of an ancient village that was probably a native settlement of the 3rd and 4th centuries AD. A 50ft-thick wall encloses two round huts and several rectangular buildings; the latter may have served as barns and workshops, while the outer wall kept livestock in rather than fulfilling a defensive purpose. Excavations found the remains of smelting hearths, suggesting that metalworking occurred here. It is possible, but not certain, that the site was inhabited during the Bronze Age.

TIME TO SPARE? See ⊘ cadw.gov.wales for locations and further details of **Anglesey's 22 ancient monuments**. Beaumaris's old **Gaol and Courthouse** offer insights into the town's history of crime and punishment. Classic vehicle aficionados will head for **Tacla Taid** (⊘angleseytransportmuseum.co.uk), in the south of the island, where over 100 exhibits include military transport, tractors and a jet plane. **Oriel Môn** (⊘orielmon.org), near the county town of Llangefni in central Anglesey, houses a museum of the island's history and a gallery of works by its contemporary artists and makers. Holyhead's Newry Beach is home to Wales's oldest lifeboat station, now **Holyhead Maritime Museum** (⊘ holyheadmaritimemuseum.co.uk). Anglesey's many churches include Wales's oldest, **St Patrick's, Llanbadrig** on the northern coast, said to have been founded by St Patrick after his ship ran aground, and four disused churches in the care of **Friends of Friendless Churches** (⊘friendsoffriendlesschurches.org.uk). While in southern Anglesey, drop in for a photo – with a wide angle lens – in **Llanfairpwllgwyngyllgogerychwyrndrobwll-llantysiliogogogoch (Llanfair PG)**, whose residents combined the names of several local places in 1869 for publicity purposes. To explore 19th-century engineering history at either end of Anglesey, find out about the Menai Straits' two bridges at Menai Heritage's **Thomas Telford Centre** (⊘ menaibridges.co.uk) or visit the **South Stack Lighthouse** (⊘southstack.co.uk), on a small island just off Holyhead.

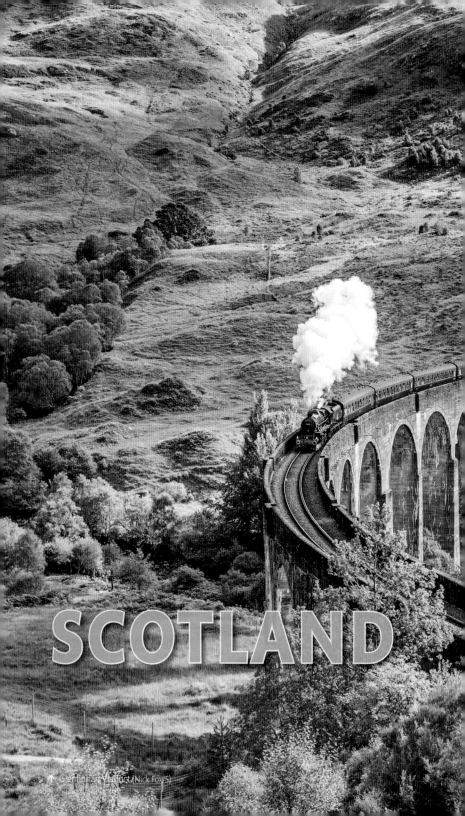

SCOTLAND

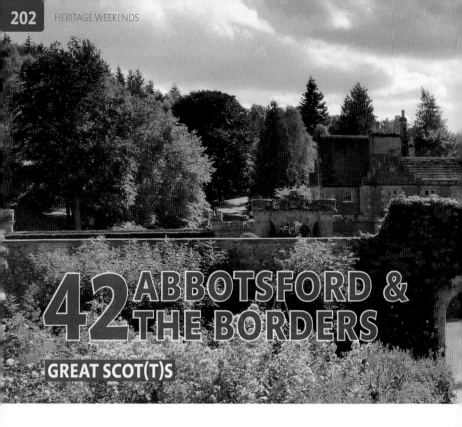

42 ABBOTSFORD & THE BORDERS

GREAT SCOT(T)S

I n the southern shadow of Edinburgh, the Scottish Borders offer a delightful, scenic, invigorating prospect. The region covers about 1,800 square miles of hills, moorland, valleys and agricultural plains, along with an eastern coast of attractive fishing villages, and has long attracted walkers, cyclists and anglers. It was also home to two authors whose works millions still read today and whose influence on other writers was immense. Sir Walter Scott (1771–1832) was perhaps Scotland's most famous writer. As the author of *Rob Roy* and *Ivanhoe*, he was arguably the greatest exponent of the historical romance novel, and in popularising the idea of clan tartans, among other things, is regarded as 'the father of modern Scotland'. The 'shilling shocker' thrillers of John Buchan (1875–1940), meanwhile, foreshadowed Ian Fleming's James Bond and the ambivalent spy novels of John le Carré and Graham Greene. The Borders also hold a remarkable botanical garden; the oldest inhabited house in Scotland, its gates still closed in memory of Bonnie Prince Charlie; and an impressive monastic ruin where Robert the Bruce left his heart.

THE ITINERARY

DAY 1 The range of objects in the entrance hall at **Abbotsford** (AF, HH 𝒸 scottsabbotsford.com), near Galashiels, suggests the breadth of interests that Sir Walter Scott cultivated during his busy life as advocate, judge, legal administrator, writer and historian. Abbotsford became Scott's home, monument and millstone:

↑ Abbotsford. (Wapted/S)

his involvement in a publishing firm which went bankrupt meant he had to place the house in trust while he wrote in order to work off his debts. Those same publishers had given Scott the Italian mosaic which sits on top of the large table near the front door. Other gifts on display include skulls on the mantelpiece and a pair of elk antlers. Look up to admire the coats of arms of Scott's ancestors. (He sometimes got his facts wrong; thanks to Scott, generations of amateur historians have mistakenly believed that a 'bar sinister' on a coat of arms denotes illegitimacy in a family.) From here you go on to see a splendid sequence of rooms. There's a heavy emotional heft to the study, which contains the desk at which Scott wrote the *Waverley* novels and whose secret drawers held letters to his wife. In the little octagonal closet at the back of the study, known as a 'speak-a-bit', Scott held private business meetings. The drawing room, where the ladies knitted, read, chatted and sang, with Scott's daughter Sophia playing the harp, is distinguished by splendid green Chinese wallpaper, a gift from a cousin who worked for the East India Company. As a manly counterpoint to the drawing room, the small armoury comprises Scott's antiquarian collection of suits of armour, helmets, daggers, guns, battleaxes, maces and swords. After passing through the dining room and the anteroom with its casts from ancient stones of old ecclesiastical buildings (Scott had a *very* bad case of collector mania), your house tour concludes. You can then look in on the Catholic chapel, added

after Scott's death, three beautiful garden 'rooms' or an exhibition on the writer's life in the visitor centre. There's also the prospect of a walk around Abbotsford's woodland estate, much of which Scott planted.

Three miles east of Abbotsford, along winding roads with glorious views of the countryside, you come to **Melrose Abbey** (HS), founded in 1136 by Cistercian monks and rebuilt more than once. The last monk to live and work there died in 1590, but enough remains to suggest how impressive the Cistercians' chief house must have been. Robert the Bruce left his heart here, or so the legend says; a lead container which is supposed to contain it was found in the Chapter House. (The rest of Robert is at Dunfermline Abbey.) As you wander round the exterior, look out for carvings of saints, dragons, gargoyles… and a pig, playing the bagpipes. You can view medieval objects from the cloisters in the abbey's museum.

DAY 2 Eight miles southwest of Peebles lie the **Dawyck Botanic Gardens** (⏀rbge.org.uk): 65 acres which burst into colour throughout the year, notably in summer with a double border of red, pink, orange and yellow azaleas. Plants from mountainous parts of North America, Asia and Europe flourish here, including mosses, liverworts, lichens and fungi in the innovative Cryptogamic Sanctuary. Many Dawyck plants are the first examples collected and brought to Scotland; some owe their presence to David Douglas (1799–1834), the botanist and explorer after whom the Douglas fir is named. In contrast, in the early 18th century the owners of Dawyck discovered an upright variation of the common European beech tree, now known as the Dawyck beech, on the estate. The tallest of the tall trees here are Giant Sierra redwoods, a species which can live for over 3,000 years.

Unlike Sir Walter Scott, John Buchan left no substantial memorial. But his grandfather and later his uncle lived in Peebles, in Bank House at the end of the High Street, and Buchan was a parliamentary candidate for the local constituency. He's one of a colourful cast of Peebles figures to feature on a splendid mural, covering over 2,000 years of Peebles' history, in Pennel's Close just off the high street. The artwork also depicts a young Robert Louis Stevenson (1850–94), who holidayed here as a boy and featured Peebles in several of his novels. Back on the high street in a 16th-century building with Scottish baronial turrets, the **Chambers Institution** stands as a monument to the philanthropy of publisher William Chambers (1800–83). He established it in 1859 as a reading room, museum and meeting hall, and his name lives on in Chambers dictionaries. The complex still incorporates art galleries and a small museum; the star exhibit is a reproduction of a section of the Parthenon's frieze. The Chambers also houses the **John Buchan Story** (⏀johnbuchanstory.co.uk), a small but potent exhibition on Buchan's life and times. He's best known now for writing *The Thirty-Nine Steps* (published in 1915 and filmed by Alfred Hitchcock and three more times since).

↑ Melrose Abbey. (Richard Melichar/S) ← Mural depicting local history, Peebles. (HM)

But he led a polymathic life as a barrister, thriller writer, novelist, historical biographer, government propaganda director in World War I, MP and finally Canada's Governor-General. In the courtyard outside, the **Peeblesshire War Memorial** (which uses distinctive Sicilian mosaic motifs) commemorates the fallen of both World Wars including Alistair Buchan, John's younger brother, who died in action in 1917.

Eight miles southeast of Peebles, near the village of Innerleithen, **Traquair House** (AF, HH ⌂ traquair.co.uk) is the oldest continuously inhabited house in

ESSENTIALS

GETTING THERE This area is about an hour from Edinburgh by car and public transport. For Abbotsford, trains from Edinburgh Waverley run to Tweedbank, a mile away (SC), or buses from Edinburgh to Galashiels link with the X62 and 72 local buses (⌂ bordersbuses.co.uk). For Traquair, the 62a/x62 bus from Edinburgh goes to Innerleithen leaving a scenic walk of 15 minutes or so, or the Edinburgh–Galashiels train links with the 62 bus to Innerleithen. The x62 also stops in Peebles and Melrose, while the 91 bus stops outside Dawyck Botanic Gardens on request.

STAYING The **Peebles Hydro** (⌂ peebleshydro.co.uk) dates back to 1878 when, as its name suggests, the idea of 'taking the waters' for your health while on holiday was popular. There's a spa, gym and swimming pool along with archery, air rifles, giant-sized games, a putting green – and the chance to try the hotel's own 1881 Gin, created using its private spring. In Innerleithen, the 200-year-old **Traquair Arms** pub (⌂ traquairarmshotel.co.uk) has 16 en suite rooms and two self-catering cottages; **Traquair House** (⌂ traquair.co.uk) offers B&B accommodation, and self-catering at Howford House on the Traquair estate.

↑ Traquair House. (SS)

Scotland. It dates back at least to 1107, possibly earlier. Originally a royal hunting lodge, it came into the Stewart family's ownership in 1491 and the Stewarts (or Stuarts, now Maxwell Stuarts) have been here ever since. The main house, tall and white, was complete by the 17th century, its turrets evoking a medieval tower house and its many rooms fulfilling the needs of the inhabitants of a comfortable country house. The 7th Laird John Stuart (1600–59) became Chief High Treasurer of Scotland, but the family later returned to Catholicism, reducing their influence, especially when they offered support to the Jacobites. The Bear Gates on the main drive closed after Bonnie Prince Charlie's visit in 1745, with a promise that they would not reopen until a Stuart returned to the throne. They remain closed, a majestic and melancholy sight; visitors and members of the household still use the 'temporary' drive which runs alongside the main drive. Up a stone spiral staircase lies an array of secrets and treasures. The High Drawing Room contains an exquisite and rare harpsichord, made in Antwerp in 1651. Mary, Queen of Scots stayed in what is now called the King's Room; the wooden cradle used for her son, later James VI and I of Scotland and England, is at the end of the bed. Other highlights include the museum on the upper floor, two rooms containing an 18th-century library, and a secret passage and Priest's Room, where the resident chaplain lived in hiding until the 1829 Catholic Emancipation Act. Portraits, old prints and maps cover the walls. Traquair is an extraordinary place, a historic house on a human scale which remains a family home.

EATING The theatrically red **Adam Room** in Peebles' Tontine Hotel (⊘ tontinehotel. com) delivers authentic Scottish dining, from Cullen skink and scallops with black pudding to local beef and lamb. For Sunday roasts and scrumptious desserts, head for the **Traquair Arms**: banoffee profiteroles, anyone? You could also satisfy a sweet tooth at **Cocoa Black** (⊘ cocoablack.com) at the end of Peebles' high street: a high-quality boutique café offering every imaginable chocolate indulgence.

TIME TO SPARE? The Borders' independent historic houses include **Mellerstain** (AF, HH ⊘ mellerstain.com), a Robert Adam creation; **Paxton House** (AF, HH ⊘ paxtonhouse. co.uk), a Palladian house with collections of Chippendale and Trotter furniture; **Floors Castle** (HH ⊘ floorscastle.com), Scotland's largest inhabited castle and **Bowhill House** (HH ⊘ bowhillhouse.co.uk), home of the Dukes of Buccleuch, with an art collection including works by Canaletto, Gainsborough and Reynolds. Historic Scotland manages the remains of **Jedburgh Abbey**, a distinctive blend of early Gothic and Romanesque styles, and **Dryburgh Abbey**, burial place of Sir Walter Scott and Field Marshal Earl Haig. Just east of Melrose, the remains of the largest Roman fort and settlement north of Hadrian's Wall lie at **Trimontium** (⊘ trimontium.co.uk).

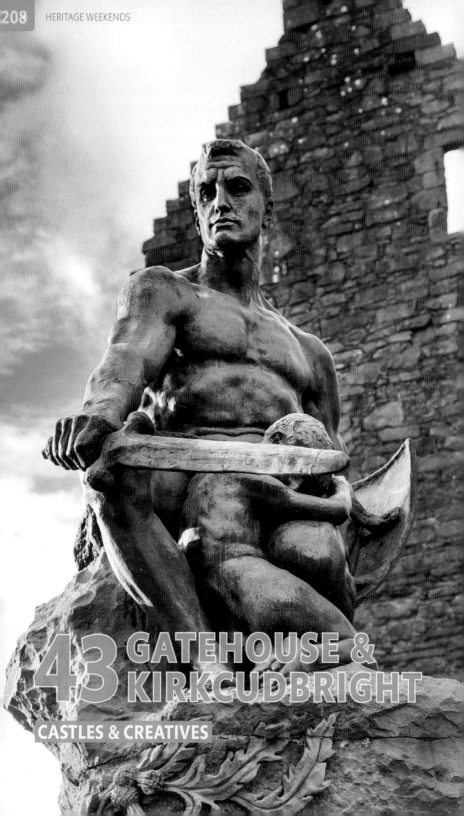

43 GATEHOUSE & KIRKCUDBRIGHT

CASTLES & CREATIVES

'I fixed on Galloway as the best place to go... the nearest wild part of Scotland... not over thick with population.' Such is Richard Hannay's reasoning as he goes on the run in John Buchan's *The Thirty-Nine Steps* (1915). Over a century later Galloway, now part of Dumfries and Galloway, with the Solway Firth separating it from England to its south and west, seems little changed: a low-key region of small towns, moorland and machars (low, undulating hills). On the southwestern coast, the triangular Wigtown Bay, a large inlet of the Irish Sea, was the testing site for the temporary portable harbours that Allied forces used while invading Normandy during World War II. Three significant rivers, including the Fleet, enter the bay, which is now a large local nature reserve. Fewer visitors venture to Dumfries and Galloway than to Scotland's Borders, Highlands or islands, but you can find splendid castles, memories of vanished industries and thriving creative arts here. Two contrasting settlements epitomise the region's charm. Gatehouse of Fleet, near Wigtown Bay's northeastern shore, was a mere staging post on the way to Ireland until industrialisation brought a tannery, breweries and a cotton mill. Nine miles southeast of Gatehouse, Celts, Romans and Picts settled in Kirkcudbright (pronounced kir-coo-bree). The town's modern renaissance owes much to its late Victorian community of artists, and it served as a commercial port for over 800 years. Robert Burns, Scotland's national poet, and renowned crime writer Dorothy L Sayers visited both Gatehouse and Kirkcudbright; the latter also featured in an infamous horror film.

THE ITINERARY

DAY 1 **Gatehouse of Fleet** (⌀ gatehouse-of-fleet.co.uk), a pretty village of around 1,000 people, provides an excellent place to take a deep breath and relax. At either end of its main street stand two buildings with literary links. At the northern end, Robert Burns is said to have visited the **Murray Arms** (⌀ themurrayarmsgatehouse.com) in 1793, where he wrote the first draft of *Scots Wha Hae*. The Arms is on the site of the original gatehouse. At the southern end of the street, in its previous incarnation as the Anwoth Hotel, the **Ship Inn** hosted Dorothy L Sayers as she researched material for her novel *Five Red Herrings* (1931), which she dedicated to the hotel's owner. The story takes place in Gatehouse and also in Kirkcudbright, where Sayers rented a studio in 1929. Halfway along the street sits the solid, square **Mill on the Fleet**. The name is slightly misleading as, after 1788, there were two mills on the site. They did not last long as cotton mills, due to competitive pressures, and by the mid 19th century they were making wooden bobbins for the textile industry and processing oak for the local leather tanning industry. They ceased trading in the 1930s. Today, one floor focuses on the history and heritage of Gatehouse, which local laird James Murray of Cally hoped would become the 'Glasgow of the south'. The rest of the mill is devoted to promoting the work of local artists and craftmakers, temporary exhibitions, the Gatehouse Tourist Information

← MacLellan's Castle, Kirkcudbright. (Jan Holm/S)

Centre, an excellent café and, on the second floor, a secondhand bookshop with 20,000 volumes.

Two miles west of Gatehouse is the village of Anwoth and **Anwoth Old Kirk** (⌂ gatehouse-of-fleet.co.uk). You can reach Anwoth from Gatehouse by a choice of circular routes: northwest on Old Military Road; or southwest, which takes rather longer and detours via Trusty's Hill, site of an ancient hillfort and Pictish rock carvings. The shell of the kirk, now devoid of its roof, dominates the space. There is a dedication to Samuel Rutherford, minister here between 1627 and 1638; he is also commemorated by a granite obelisk above Anwoth to the east. The kirk features in a key scene of cult British horror film *The Wicker Man* (1973) in which a grave digger investigates a child's coffin to find a hare inside. Even today, in sunny broad daylight, there's an air of mystery, with skulls and crossbones on some graves, as seen in the film, and eggs and apples placed as offerings. Allan Brown's description of Anwoth in *Inside The Wicker Man: how not to make a cult classic* (2000), as being 'like a pocket of the distant past, pickled in its own solitude', is apt.

Returning to Gatehouse, take a footpath from the southern end of the high street to head along the riverside where information boards describe some of the industrial history of the area. This was the site of Port Macadam, where medium-sized ships came in the early Victorian era to unload coal, lime and construction materials, with wood and agricultural products going in the other direction. The use of the port declined, partly due to the arrival of the railways in 1860, and it stopped operating around 1930. Follow the river for just under a mile until you come to the remains of **Cardoness Castle** (HS) at the top of a short but steep hill. This six-storey tower house was the creation of the McCullochs, a wealthy local family, in the late 15th century. The new building balanced defence (walls over 6ft thick, small window openings, an inner door beyond the main entrance) with home comforts, such as a dining hall on the third floor with a special wall space for showing off the best tableware.

DAY 2 For a day in Kirkcudbright, start in Castle Street with **MacLellan's Castle** (HS), built about a century after Cardoness. While this too is a tower house, the emphasis here was less on defence against invading forces and more on domestic comfort, with about 15 family rooms on the upper floors. A 'laird's lug' behind the fireplace enabled the host to eavesdrop. From here you can bear right or left to discover Kirkcudbright's artistic story. Go right towards the old Town Hall on St Mary Street, where **Kirkcudbright Galleries** (AF ⌂ kirkcudbrightgalleries. org.uk) explain how it all started in the 1880s, with painters John and Thomas Faed returning from success in Edinburgh and London to settle in Gatehouse and mentor young artists in the area. Kirkcudbright was attractive to creative

↑ The Mill on the Fleet, Gatehouse. (Terence A R Watts/S) → Cardoness Castle, Gatehouse. (Heartland Arts/S)

types for its historic character, the variety of local landscapes, the quality of the light and the relative cheapness of housing and studio space. Some of these young artists focused on domestic life and agricultural scenes; they became known as the Glasgow Boys, as many had studios close to the city. If you bear left from MacLellan's Castle on to High Street, you come to **Broughton House and Garden** (NTS), the home of one of those Glasgow Boys, Edward Atkinson (EA) Hornel (1864–1933). The young Hornel was born in Australia before his parents moved back to Kirkcudbright, studied in Antwerp and spent over a year in Japan before returning to Scotland. Broughton House was his home, gallery and showroom/salesroom all in one; many of his works, and some by contemporaries, hang in the house today. Pause to admire the fireplace and Parthenon frieze in the gallery, before enjoying the gently sloping garden with views over the town harbour and the River Dee (and trying not to trip over the black and white cat that follows you around). Further up the High Street, the old Tolbooth, built in the 1620s,

ESSENTIALS

GETTING THERE the nearest railway station is around 25 miles northeast at Dumfries, which is 1 hour 45 minutes from Glasgow (SC). From Dumfries the 501/502 bus will get you to Kirkcudbright; the 431 and 517 buses cover the eight miles between Kirkcudbright and Gatehouse. For drivers, the A75 links all three places, and many others along the coast, all the way west to Stanraer.

STAYING Gatehouse's modern **Ship Inn** (⚭ theshipinngatehouse.com) sadly makes little of the Dorothy L Sayers connection, but it's comfortable and the staff are extremely helpful. In Kirkcudbright, **Selkirk Arms** (⚭ selkirkarmshotel.co.uk) has been around since 1777, and its blue and white exterior is one of the town's highlights; Robert Burns stayed here in 1793. For an unusual self-catering option, drive 30 miles west of Gatehouse on the A75 to **Castle of Park** (LT) just outside Glenluce, a 16th-century tower house which sleeps seven.

EATING In Gatehouse, the Ship Inn's restaurant **1 Fleet Street** mixes Scottish classics and modern cuisine; our pea and ham ravioli in Cullen skink, followed by trout with almonds and broccoli, disappeared in a trice. At the other end of the main street, the curry of the day is excellent in the **Masonic Arms** (⚭ masonicarms.co.uk). For a filling lunch, try the **Galloway Lodge** café (⚭ gallowaylodge.co.uk): their preserves are yummy, too. Kirkcudbright's **Selkirk Arms** (see above) offers local and Asian dishes – the oyster mushroom bao bun and steak pie are winners. On the banks of Wigtown Bay and 12 miles west from Gatehouse, **Galloway Smokehouse** (⚭ gallowaysmokehouse.co.uk) is a good option for a lunchtime stop, with fish and game prominent on the menu.

has spent time as a council office, sheriff's court and prison, and now houses the **Tolbooth Arts Centre** (⊘ dgculture.co.uk). Displays relate to the building itself and the town, with contemporary works by exhibiting artists; the Tolbooth and some nearby passageways featured as locations in *The Wicker Man*. A short walk along from Kirkcudbright Galleries, the **Stewartry Museum** (AF ⊘ dgculture.co.uk) offers wider insight into the history of the town and surrounding area. 'Stewartry' is an old name for Kirkcudbrightshire, a corruption of 'Steward' dating from the 14th century when a steward collected revenue from the locals for the Lord of Galloway, the wonderfully named Archibald the Grim. The upper floor displays stuffed animals, birds and fish – the ones that didn't get away, it turns out, are quite large after all – and glass-fronted wooden cabinets on the ground floor show off an eclectic collection. A Bechstein piano from 1898, a stuffed cockatoo and a World War II walking stick with a battery-operated light in the tip (to find one's way during blackouts) are all here.

TIME TO SPARE? A few miles from Gatehouse to the west you can wonder at **Cairnholy Neolithic tombs** and **Glenquicken Stone Circle** (both ⊘ gatehouse-of-fleet. co.uk). Either side of Wigtown Bay lie the colourful **Gem Rock Museum** (⊘ gemrock. net) at Creetown, and the ruins of 16th-century **Carsluith Castle** (HS) and **Sorbie Tower**, ancient seat of the Clan Hannay. A wooden cross in **Wigtown Parish Church** (⊘ wigtownparishchurch.org.uk) commemorates two 'Wigtown Martyrs', women put to death in 1685 for religious dissension. Wigtown itself, **Scotland's National Book Town** (⊘ wigtown-booktown.co.uk), is replete with wonderful independent bookshops, several of which double as tea shops.

↑ Cairnholy Neolithic tombs. (Doubleclix/S)

44 GLASGOW

CITY OF ARTS & SCIENCES

O nce the second city of the British Empire, Glasgow is a port city on the River Clyde in Scotland's central belt. Its reputation for shipbuilding and heavy industry has somewhat overshadowed its other successes. The university, which dates back to 1451, has led research into crucial medical and scientific advances; Glasgow School of Art, meanwhile, has produced a succession of brilliant creatives, including five recent winners of the Turner Prize. But no GSA graduate has left such a distinctive stamp on the city as Glasgow-born architect and designer Charles Rennie Mackintosh (1868–1928), some of whose work – for public commission and for his own home – remains on view.

THE ITINERARY

DAY 1 Start just under two miles west of Glasgow's centre in the imposing red-brick Victorian Gothic **Kelvingrove Art Gallery and Museum** (AF *&* glasgowlife. org.uk), which opened in 1901, a legacy of the 1888 International Exhibition in neighbouring Kelvingrove Park. Before venturing into one of the 22 galleries, pause in the Centre Hall and look up to admire the magnificent concert pipe organ, which also dates back to 1901. The galleries contain everything from Renaissance art to Ancient Egyptian artefacts and a 1940s Spitfire. 'Glasgow Stories' summarises the city's development over the past millennium and its emergence as a 19th-century powerhouse of industry, shipbuilding and export,

↑ Kelvingrove Art Gallery and Museum. (Ulmus Media/S)

and the associated growth of socialist and trade union political movements. There's a marvellous banner promoting the Clyde District of the United Society of Boilermakers, Shipbuilders and Structural Workers (founded 1834). Kelvingrove's curators aren't afraid to take a holistic approach to their displays; the armaments gallery illustrates the influence of nature upon the design of suits of armour with the inclusion of the odd pangolin and armadillo. Other galleries look at the Glasgow Boys (page 212) and their work, and you can also see furniture and partial recreations of dining rooms from Catherine Cranston's tea rooms (page 217). A few minutes' walk away, in two buildings facing each other across University Avenue, the **Hunterian Museum and Art Gallery** (AF ⌀ gla.ac.uk/hunterian) is part of Glasgow University. It owes its name, and much of the contents, to William Hunter (1718–83), an obstetrician and teacher whose bequest of his private collection enabled the museum to open in 1807. Hunter was part of a new wave of privileged people who collected not just for curiosity, social prestige or economic gain, but also to share that knowledge: this is, like many museums but more explicitly than some, a collection of collections. Bernard Hague's wind instruments, Emily Dix's fossil plant specimens and Ina Smillie's 28 fine oil paintings are all highlights. However, the Hunterian is perhaps most significant for its coverage of Glasgow's role in medical history. Displays explain

the important innovations in obstetrics, neurosurgery and orthopaedics for which Hunter and other eminent Glasgow medical practitioners were responsible. Another section examines the career of the physicist William Thomson, 1st Baron Kelvin (1824–1907) who taught at the university and invented an international system for absolute temperatures. Exhibits of Kelvin's teaching aids include the French horn he used to liven up his lectures on acoustics.

DAY 2 By no means all of Charles Rennie Mackintosh's work survives intact (the Glasgow School of Art's devastation by fire in 2018 being a tragic case in point). But two substantive examples do, as outstanding reminders of Mackintosh's unique talent. The first, at the Hunterian Art Gallery, is the **Mackintosh House** (⊘ gla.ac.uk/hunterian). This is a reassembly from 78 Southpark Avenue, a Victorian terraced house which Charles and his artist wife Margaret Macdonald remodelled and lived in for eight years. The fixtures were preserved after the house's demolition in the early 1960s, enabling the recreation of key rooms and spaces just a few feet from where it once stood. The furnishings are either originals or based on contemporary descriptions of the house's contents. The journey begins as you step into the dark hall with its petal wall lamps and beaten lead mirror. Next door, the dining room, its dark colour scheme offset by stylised pink roses, furnished with characteristic Mackintosh high-back chairs, contrasts with the light and calm of the studio-cum-drawing room upstairs. Here Margaret's influence is apparent from the painted gesso panel 'The White Rose and the Red Rose' above the fireplace. As John McKean observes in his *Pocket Guide* to Mackintosh's work: 'There is no warm clutter; no patterned wallpaper, upholstery or rugs.' Another floor up, the white L-shaped bedroom holds a cheval mirror with tiny built-in drawers on either side, under light fittings with a teardrop in each side and an enclosing saucer above. The gallery on the top floor showcases a changing collection of Mackintosh artefacts from the Hunterian collection and a partial reconstruction of the bedroom from 78 Derngate, Northampton – Mackintosh's final major commission and the only house he designed in England. As you descend back through the rooms, the overall effect is one of subtle, streamlined sensuousness, with rose and teardrop motifs offsetting austere black and white lines.

Just over a mile from the Hunterian, the second Mackintosh must-see is **Mackintosh at the Willow** (⊘ mackintoshatthewillow.com), one of four Glasgow tea rooms owned by Catherine Cranston (1849–1934), now a café, visitor centre and exhibition. As tea rooms became more fashionable due to the temperance movement, and votes and other rights for women rose up the political agenda, Cranston promoted attractive venues where unaccompanied women could socialise. (Despite being married, she traded as Miss Cranston.) To make the venues stand out from the competition, Cranston turned to Mackintosh. The

↑ The Hunterian Museum and Art Gallery. (HM) ← **LEFT:** A statue of Charles Rennie Mackintosh in Glasgow. (HM) **RIGHT:** Mackintosh at the Willow. (HM)

CHARLES RENNIE MACKINTOSH

The son of a superintendent clerk with Glasgow's police, Charles Rennie Mackintosh began his architectural training aged 15, as an apprentice during the day and an evening student at the Glasgow School of Art. He and fellow apprentice J Herbert MacNair met their respective future wives, the sisters Margaret and Frances Macdonald, as students and formed a creative alliance known as the 'Group of Four'; Charles was also one of the Glasgow Boys (page 212). He joined the firm of Honeyman & Keppie in 1889, rising through the ranks to become a partner. Over the next two decades he achieved national and international acclaim, with exhibitions in Vienna and Turin and commissions for various Glasgow design projects. The latter included Scotland Street Public School; the second phase of a redesign of the School of Art; and The Willow Tea Rooms on Sauchiehall Street (now Mackintosh at the Willow). Mackintosh's work drew on eclectic inspirations, from Scotland's late medieval tower houses to Art Nouveau, the emergence of Art Deco and the West's increasing appreciation of Japanese art, design and architecture. However, by 1913 work had dried up. The Mackintoshes moved to Suffolk, then London, and finally the south of France, with Charles working on textile designs, still-life watercolours and landscape painting. He died in relative obscurity, but today Charles Rennie Mackintosh may be as firmly associated with Glasgow as Gaudí is with Barcelona.

Willow, which opened in 1903, got its name from its location in Sauchiehall Street, which translates from Scots dialect as 'the way of the willow'. Mackintosh reworked the front and rear as well as reorganising the interiors and staircases; even today, the façade stands out with four levels of windows, each with a different degree of recession. First point of entry is the front saloon, where the high-back chairs and white plaster reliefs, suggesting willows, add to the impression of light and space. A baldacchino, a quasi-religious centrepiece of wood, metal and glass, dominates the room. The transition to the back saloon with its pink roses and purple teardrop motifs on the walls is marked by a large, curved chair with a lattice back. A sequence of mirrors over the fireplace add to the theatrical effect; people came here to dine, but also to see and be seen. From here you proceed up two flights of stairs: to the mezzanine gallery whose coffered ceiling dispenses dappled light on diners; to the male domain of the billiards room (now sans billiards table, to enable the use of the room for corporate events); and to the Salon de Luxe. Here the designs and tricks of the other rooms come together in a glorious whole; high-back chairs in purple with a silver finish; chandeliers with glass crystals of pink and green; arrays of mirrors to magnify the space; and a gesso panel by Margaret Macdonald illustrating a line from Dante Gabriel Rossetti's poem *Willowwood*. The tea room menu included, improbably, baked herring in custard and sheep's head.

ESSENTIALS

GETTING THERE Glasgow Central railway station connects to all UK cities south of Glasgow, while Glasgow Queen Street links to central and northern Scotland (AV, SC, TP and others). It's between three and four hours from London, Birmingham, Manchester, Liverpool or York and 50 minutes from Edinburgh. Principal road links include the M74 from England and the M8 from Edinburgh, or you can fly into Glasgow Airport (⊘ glasgowairport.com) or Glasgow Prestwick (⊘ glasgowprestwick.com).

STAYING On the sixth floor of a building overlooking Glasgow Central station, **Grasshoppers** (⊘ grasshoppersglasgow.com) is a modern and stylish choice. The complimentary cake awaiting you on arrival is a nice touch. Around the corner from Sauchiehall Street, the five-star **Kimpton Blythswood Square Hotel** (⊘ kimptonblythswoodsquare.com), dating from 1823, offers an on-site spa.

EATING Follow in the footsteps of Catherine Cranston's clients and take breakfast, lunch or afternoon tea at **Mackintosh at the Willow** (⊘ mackintoshatthewillow.com). The dinner menu in the wood-panelled **Café Gandolfi** (⊘ cafegandolfi.com) on Albion Street includes the classic Cullen skink. A few minutes from the Hunterian, Byres Road offers a range of options including excellent eggs Benedict at **Café Francoise**, cheese toasties with kimchi at **Oaka** (⊘ oakasupercity.com) or noodles at Japanese restaurant **Esushi** (⊘ esushiglasgow.co.uk). Glasgow's two outlets of **Bibimbap** (⊘ bibimbap-glasgow.com) showcase the eponymous Korean comfort food.

TIME TO SPARE? For more insight into Charles Rennie Mackintosh's work, visit the Interpretation Centre at **The Lighthouse** (⊘ thelighthouse.co.uk – closed at the time of writing), Scotland's leading design and architecture centre, on Mitchell Lane. The building, which housed the offices of the *Glasgow Herald*, was Mackintosh's first public commission. On the banks of the Clyde, the **Riverside Museum** (⊘ glasgowlife.org.uk) explores Glasgow's transport and technology heritage; facing it across the river, the **Fairfield Heritage Centre** (⊘ fairfieldgovan.co.uk) focuses on shipbuilding, in which Glasgow excelled for over a century. The **People's Palace** (AF ⊘ glasgowlife.org.uk) in Glasgow Green examines Glaswegians' working and leisure lives, while **St Mungo's Museum** (⊘ glasgowlife.org.uk), which takes its name from the city's patron saint, reveals the importance of religion to its citizens. St Mungo's is in the medieval quarter, where you can also see the 550-year-old **Provand's Lordship** (⊘ glasgowlife.org.uk) and **Glasgow Cathedral** (⊘ glasgowcathedral.org), the only medieval cathedral on the Scottish mainland to have survived the Reformation virtually intact. Close by is the extraordinary 37-acre Victorian **Necropolis** (⊘ glasgownecropolis.org). This space was a fir park and then an arboretum before its conversion into a cemetery, with the first burial in 1832. Since then, over 50,000 burials have taken place here.

45 FORT WILLIAM

HEROES & BETRAYALS

To see one major reason why so many visitors come to Fort William, on the eastern shore of Loch Linnhe in Lochaber, look up and to the south: Ben Nevis, the UK's highest mountain, attracts about 125,000 climbers each year. In 1911 Henry Alexander, the son of a local car dealer, drove a Model T Ford to the summit in an attempt to prove the Ford's superiority to hand-crafted British motorcars. A bronze statue of man and car in Fort William's Cameron Square commemorates the feat. This charming Highlands town and the surrounding countryside has its share of military heritage, too: as a fort which the English hoped would keep the Highland clans under control; as the scene of a massacre infamous in Scottish history; and as the rallying point for the final phase of the Jacobite rebellions.

THE ITINERARY

DAY 1 Start with remains: the surviving fragments of the **Old Fort**, the original Fort William, five minutes north of the railway station. The fort took its name from William III, who ordered its construction in 1690 on the site of a 1654 fortification which Oliver Cromwell had hoped would keep local Royalists in check. A thousand troops had a stronghold with 20ft high stone walls, with additional protection from deep ditches, the River Nevis and Loch Linnhe. A basic

↑ Glenfinnan Monument. (MarcvanKessel.com/S)

settlement of around 100 local Highlanders, who supplied provisions to the fort, was just outside the walls; it was originally called Maryburgh after William's wife. Troops remained here until 1855, after which the Old Fort was sold, converted into other uses and eventually disappeared almost completely. You can find a reconstruction of the governor's office from the original Old Fort, and much else from the region's past, in Cameron Square at the **West Highland Museum** (⊘ westhighlandmuseum.org.uk). Its eight rooms pack in plenty of fascinating material, from the origins of tartan to St Kilda's postal solution to its remote location (islanders floated their letters to the mainland in a piece of hollow wood attached to a sheep's bladder). The main attractions, though, are military. The first room on the ground floor records the activities of the Commando unit established in World War II who trained at Achnacarry Castle near Spean Bridge, about ten miles north of Fort William. Upstairs, a long room displays an outstanding collection of objects relating to Charles Edward Stuart (1720–88), also known as Bonnie Prince Charlie, and the Jacobite cause. The most noteworthy artefact is the 'secret portrait', an anamorphic painting used by the Prince's supporters. It appears to be a tray with random smears of paint but, if a polished cylinder or claret goblet is placed in its centre, a portrait of the Prince becomes visible.

↑ The Glencoe Monument (Steve Meese/S)

DAY 2 Outside Fort William, two monuments mark key events from the Jacobite rebellions (page 230). The first is 15 miles south of town, within the remarkable cocktail of natural and human drama that is Glen Coe. In the village of Glencoe itself, down a quiet side road, the **Glencoe Monument** commemorates the Massacre of 13 February 1692. William III had demanded an oath of allegiance from Highland chiefs by 31 December 1691. Some equivocated, including Maclan, chief of the Macdonalds of Glen Coe. Maclan reached Fort William on 30 December, but the governor was not empowered to administer the oath, and Maclan had to travel down to Inverary, taking the oath there on 2 January. It was too late. Soldiers from the Argyll regiment, billeted in houses in Glen Coe's various settlements, were ordered to kill the Macdonalds. Maclan and 35 of his people were killed, while 40 more died trying to escape through the hills. Some soldiers had tried to warn the Macdonalds; two companies arrived too late, possibly to avoid being involved. The beauty of the surrounding mountains is a poignant contrast to this notorious episode. Nearby, **Glencoe Visitor Centre** (NTS) is worth a visit, for its geological explanation of the shape of the glen (massive volcanic eruptions and a glacier) and for the reconstruction, using traditional techniques, of the type of 17th-century turf and creel house in which Macdonald clan members lived.

The second monument, 15 miles west of Fort William on Loch Shiel, stands at **Glenfinnan**. It marks the spot where, on 19 August 1745, Bonnie Prince Charlie came to rally his supporters. A small band of loyalists had accompanied him but, by the end of the day, 1,200 clansmen had swelled the Prince's ranks and watched

↑ Glencoe village. (markferguson2/A)

him raise his father's standard. The monument is 60ft high; buy a ticket from **Glenfinnan Visitor Centre** (NTS) and climb the spiral staircase inside to enjoy splendid panoramic views. It was built in 1815 by local landowner Alexander Macdonald, whose ancestors had supported the Prince. You won't be alone at the top; a statue of a kilted Highlander was added up here 15 years after it was built. The visitor centre's exhibition, in English and Gaelic, includes a model of the gathering itself. There's also a good view of the Glenfinnan Viaduct, Scotland's longest concrete railway bridge.

ESSENTIALS

GETTING THERE The train from Glasgow's Central or Queen Street stations (SC), which takes around four hours, rewards you with superb views of Loch Lomond and the Trossachs National Park; the A82 from Glasgow takes a similar route. For journeys from further afield, there's a sleeper service from London Euston (SC), and the nearest airport is Inverness (𝒽 invernessairport.net).

STAYING Close to the railway station, **Alexandra Hotel** (𝒽 strathmorehotels.com) is a reassuring presence, with comfortable rooms. At the other end of the High Street, the **Garrison Hotel** (𝒽 thegarrisonhotel.co.uk) offers something different: a night in an old police cell, albeit with mod cons not available to the original inmates.

EATING Close to the museum, the queue outside **Rain** (𝒽 rainbakery.co.uk) is always a good sign: try one of their outsize pains au chocolat or a rhubarb and custard pastry. Opposite Rain, the **Highland Cinema Café Bar** (𝒽 highlandcinema.co.uk) serves tasty tapas and pizzas. **Crannog** seafood restaurant (𝒽 crannog.net) enjoys superb views of Loch Linnhe from its red-roofed base on the Town Pier. On a warm day, a blackberry yoghurt ice cream from **The Kilted Camel** coffee shop on the High Street is a great refresher. **Lochaber Café** at Fort William train station offers reasonably priced food along with tea in pots with strainers and additional hot water; there's also a good selection of leaf teas and infusions at **Glencoe Café** (𝒽 glencoecafe.co.uk) in the village of the same name.

TIME TO SPARE? The 'massacre room' in the **Glencoe Folk Museum** (𝒽 glencoemuseum.com) tells the gruesome story of the events of 1692. Two miles north of town, **Inverlochy Castle** (HS) was a 13th-century stronghold for the lords of Badenoch and Lochaber. Four miles north of Fort William, in the small village of Banavie, is Scotland's longest staircase lock, **Neptune's Staircase** on the Caledonian Canal, the work of Thomas Telford. For a stunning steam train ride, **The Jacobite** (𝒽 jacobitetrain.com) makes a 84-mile round trip between Fort William and Mallaig, passing over the Glenfinnan Viaduct, famous for its appearances in the *Harry Potter* films.

46 INVERNESS

DEFEAT & REMEMBRANCE

T here has been a settlement on the site of modern Inverness, the unofficial capital of the Highlands, for at least 1,500 years. The city today has a serene Georgian and Victorian flavour, from the Ionic columns of the Old Post Office on the High Street to the 150ft Tolbooth Steeple at the corner of Church and Bridge streets. There are clues, though, to a more turbulent past. Twin sculptures of grinning wolves outside the Town House on Castle Street represent dangers beyond the city. Around the corner stands a statue of Jacobite heroine Flora Macdonald (page 236) outside the redstone Victorian Inverness Castle. The 1745-46 Jacobite rebels destroyed the previous castle on this site. Inverness is the perfect base from which to discover some key aspects of Highlands history. Within easy reach lie a mysterious Bronze Age cemetery complex; a remarkable collection of Pictish art; Culloden Moor, on which Scotland's most famous battle took place; the fort built in Culloden's wake; and Cawdor Castle, whose location was chosen, according to legend, by a donkey.

THE ITINERARY

DAY 1 A misty morning is the perfect time to be standing at **Clava Cairns** (HS), in a quiet spot six miles east of Inverness. Four circular chamber tomb cairns, three of them surrounded by stone circles, carry teasing hints of life up to 4,000 years ago. There was certainly one cemetery here around 2000BC, and there may have been a second a thousand years later. Excavations have found traces of white quartz inside a 'kerb cairn', a smaller monument dating from around 1000BC. The most significant point of the cairns may be that they point towards the southwest, aligning with the midwinter sunset; the tallest of the standing stones also face the setting sun. The cairns are grey now, but the original builders chose red and pink stones to face the sunset; traces of those bright colours remain. It seems likely, from similar monuments elsewhere, that these cairns only housed one or two deceased people, which suggests that they were important. Cup marks on the northern cairn add an artistic touch of mystery. Wandering among the cairns and stone circles, you lower your voice instinctively. It's a strange, unsettling place. From Clava Cairns, return to Inverness and drop into **Inverness Museum and Art Gallery** (AF ⬙ highlifehighland.com) on Castle Wynd for an excellent overview of the history of the city and the region, from the Highlands' geological origins thousands of years ago to Inverness' recent economic developments. Then cross the Moray Firth and travel 15 miles north to the Black Isle, which, despite the name is a peninsula. Here, in the pretty village of Rosemarkie, further enigmatic artefacts await you at **Groam House Museum** (⬙ groamhouse.org.uk). The centrepiece is a great collection of stones and sculpted art of intricate design, the work of the Picts. These descendants of the Iron Age inhabitants of northern and eastern Scotland (and possibly Scandinavia before that) were in this part of the country between CAD300–900. Their beliefs focused on various pagan gods, at least until they began to adopt Christianity in the later part of this era. The star of the stones in this collection is a slim cross-slab, over seven feet tall, which probably stood at an entrance to a monastic enclosure. It divides at the front into three panels, with the middle panel the most complex in terms of design, while the reverse comprises a riot of Pictish symbols such as crescents with V-shaped rods and an equal-armed cross of the type you might usually see in a Gospel book such as the *Book of Kells*. A number of other stones come from inside the church which stood in those days. We don't know for sure the purpose of every stone, as captions like 'A church fitting?' emphasise. Helpful notices draw your attention to the complex geometry the craftspeople used, and sometimes point out mistakes: 'The sculptor has copied out the spiralling snake on the right-hand side. If the craftsperson was being exact the spiral would have been inverted.'

DAY 2 Five miles east of Inverness, on the fields of Culloden Moor on 16 April 1746, government troops defeated the army of Charles Edward Stuart, grandson of James II. Thus ended over half a century of Jacobite-inspired attempts to restore the Stuarts to the throne (page 230). The **Culloden Visitor Centre** (NTS), which stands beside the battlefield, explores the run-up to Culloden including the wider global context, the battle itself and its aftermath. By the simple device of red displays on one wall for the government perspective, and blue displays on the other wall for the Jacobites, the exhibition effectively sets out the strategic and tactical considerations which drove both sides. Audio clips recounting eyewitness accounts and a 360-degree 'battle immersion theatre' recreate the small- and large-scale human dramas, and there are live demonstrations of how to use weapons such as the Highland targe (shield), dirk and basket-hilted sword. The battlefield uses the same red/blue colour coding, with flags to map out the armies' positions. Plaques indicate places of special interest, with heather and white roses or carnations left on some of the stones in memory of fallen Highlanders. Ten miles north of Culloden, on a level spit of land near Ardesier commanding the sea entry to Inverness, **Fort George** (HS) was built in the years following that battle to prevent any further rebellions. This was the second Fort George; the Jacobites seized and blew up the first (the medieval Inverness Castle) in 1746. The second fort never had to defend itself against attack. It became a training base for regiments recruited in Scotland – especially, irony of ironies, from the Highlands – and remains a working fort today. The main defence, the rampart, was equipped with over 70 guns; bastions and demi-bastions were designed to absorb artillery shot. Barrack rooms recreate historical living conditions for officers and soldiers, and the Highlanders Museum explores the history of Highland soldiers and regiments since 1792. While admiring the view over the Moray Firth, you may spot a bottlenose dolphin or a minke whale.

↑ Fort George. (Rico Baumann135/S) → Culloden Visitor Centre. (Marina Hannus/S)

THE JACOBITES

The Jacobite rebellions began after the exile of the last Stuart monarch, the Catholic James II, in 1688 and the confirmation of his Protestant older daughter Mary and her Dutch husband William of Orange as joint monarchs. Jacobites wanted to restore James: 'Jacobite' derives from Jacobus, the Latin for James. Support for Jacobitism was strongest in Ireland, the Highlands and other parts of Scotland and northern England, with foreign powers sometimes providing help. William III's attempts to suppress rebellions by extracting oaths of loyalty from Highland chiefs led to the Glencoe Massacre of 1692 (page 224).

There were five distinct attempts to restore the Stuart line:

- 1689–90: James' landing in Ireland, and the defeat of his Irish-French army by William's Anglo-Dutch army at the Battle of the Boyne
- 1708: a French invasion which misfired
- 1715: the 'Fifteen Rebellion' on behalf of James II's son James Edward, which ended with James leading his supporters into exile in France
- 1719: a Highlands rising aided by Spain, quickly aborted
- 1745–46: the 'Forty-Five' began in July 1745 with Charles Edward Stuart (Bonnie Prince Charlie) landing in Scotland, hoping to raise enough support to persuade the French to invade England and aid him. Charles' newly raised Jacobite army gained control of Scotland and marched as far as Derby. However, the absence of French support weakened the prince's position and his army retreated. Eventually, at Culloden, the prince's army faced forces under the command of George II's youngest son, the Duke of Cumberland. The brutal battle lasted just one hour. It ended in conclusive defeat for the Jacobites and, eventually, Charles' escape to Skye (page 233).

Eight miles southeast of the fort, brimming with intriguing artefacts and stories, stands **Cawdor Castle** (HH, RHS ⟊ cawdorcastle.com). The wall by the front stairs displays a set of French muskets from a raid on Fishguard in western Wales in February 1797. The French invaders surrendered to forces under the command of the 1st Lord Cawdor. The castle is a 14th-century creation, originally a fortress for the Thane of Cawdor. In a vault, next to an ancient holly tree, a caption recounts the legend that the Thane loaded gold on to a donkey's back and let it wander, resolving to build a castle wherever the animal came to rest... which turned out to be under a tree. Twenty-three generations of Cawdors – first Calders, then Campbells – have lived at the castle, and there are beautiful collections of ceramics, fine art and rare tapestries to admire while you chuckle at the amusing room notes and the stories they tell. Look out for the Landseer portrait of a small dog in the first-floor Tower Room. The female Cawdor who owned the dog was a lady-in-waiting to Queen Victoria. Her Majesty loved the dog so much that she arranged for its 'kidnap' for the portrait, which she gave the lady-in-waiting as a surprise present. A later Cawdor sold the painting, which 'was bought back… by a bevy of furious aunts.' In the Drawing Room, a label identifies a medal as 'the Chinese Order of Wen Hu, 4th class', which was awarded to Colonel Ralph Campbell. At the time he had a desk job at the War Office in London and in fact was off work with 'flu.' Cawdor's supposed link with *Macbeth* is, in reality, the creative work of certain pre-Shakespearean Scottish historians. But the castle has so many great tales of its own that it doesn't matter.

ESSENTIALS

GETTING THERE Edinburgh and Glasgow are 3½ hours away by train and the Caledonian Sleeper connects Inverness with London (SC, not on Sat). Bus options include ⊘ megabus.com and ⊘ nationalexpress.com. The main road routes are the A82 from Fort William, the A9 from Glasgow, Edinburgh and southern Scotland and the A96 from Aberdeen and eastern Scotland. Inverness Airport (⊘ invernessairport.net), nine miles northeast of the city, connects to Birmingham, Bristol and Manchester and three London airports.

STAYING The **Glen Mhor Hotel** (⊘ glen-mhor.com) comprises 110 bedrooms across ten Victorian buildings, 11 self-contained apartments and a four-bedroom villa, along one side of the River Ness and ten minutes' walk from the railway station.

EATING On the site of a former dancehall where the Beatles played on their first tour, the **Rendezvous Café** (⊘ rendezvous-cafe.co.uk) in Church Street has a vintage cinema theme, serving pancakes and other treats as you enjoy Laurel and Hardy's antics on two screens. **Café Ness by the Cathedral** (⊘ invernesscathedral.org) serves sandwiches, cakes and snacks. **Mustard Seed** (⊘ mustardseedrestaurant.co.uk), in a disused church on Fraser Street, offers an excellent menu including smoked haddock and pea frittata, Highland beef, and apple sorbet from nearby **Miele's Gelateria** (◼ mielesgelato).

TIME TO SPARE? Ambitious plans are afoot to reopen **Inverness Castle** with a museum, gallery and other facilities. Near Rosemarkie, in a quiet square in the town of Fortrose, stands the red stone shell of **Fortrose Cathedral** (HS), which was part of the medieval diocese of the bishops of Ross. Half an hour southwest of Inverness by the A82, on Loch Ness's banks, is the ruin of **Urquhart Castle** (HS), which saw 500 years' service as a medieval fortress until government forces blew it up during the Jacobite Risings. A few minutes away, the **Loch Ness Centre and Exhibition** (⊘ lochness.com) explores the the loch's history and its mysterious monster.

47 SKYE

CLANS, CASTLES, LEGENDS & GHOSTS

'The Skye Boat Song' is a beautiful piece of music, but unreliable as history. After defeat at Culloden (page 228), Charles Edward Stuart hid among the Highland moors before fleeing, with the help of Flora Macdonald, to Benbecula and then to Skye, the largest and most northerly of Scotland's Inner Hebrides. His pursuers may have been, as the song says, 'baffled' by being unable to capture Charles, but their triumph was otherwise complete. By September 1746, Charles was in France and, apart from one secret visit to London, he never returned to Britain; the dream of the 'lad that's born to be King' never came true. Historical reminders of Charles, or Bonnie Prince Charlie, and Flora remain on the island, along with plenty of evidence of Skye's earlier, turbulent history. After periods of Pictish and Norse rule, various clans sought to establish their power here, the Macdonalds and the Macleods in particular. On a tour from south to north, three castles in contrasting states of repair offer insights into Skye's history, as do a cemetery with a moving tribute to Charles' saviour and a reconstruction of a traditional local settlement.

THE ITINERARY

DAY 1 Five minutes from the ferry landing point at Armadale, **Armadale Castle** (⊘ armadalecastle.com) is an excellent place to start. The castle itself had a relatively short lifespan, beginning as a mansion house built c1790, with an extension commissioned in 1815 and a new mock-Gothic wing after a serious fire in 1855. The owners moved out in 1925, leaving the castle to fall into disrepair. A trust bought the building in 1972, but had to demolish it a few years later due to its derelict condition, while saving remnants where possible. Now, although parts of the original building survive as offices and conference rooms, the castle is a picturesque shell. In its heyday, with arcaded public rooms of fan vaulting and Gothic mouldings, it must have been an impressive sight. The centrepiece was a stained-glass window of the legendary Somerled, the first known great historical figure of the medieval Hebrides. Somerled, who had Gaelic ancestry, defeated Norse armies on two occasions, before dying in 1164. His kingdom, poised between the King of the Scots and the King of Norway, evolved over the centuries into what became known as the Lordship of the Isles, covering the western islands and the Scottish mainland's west coast. The descendants of one of his grandsons Donald, the Macdonalds ('sons of Donald') came to control Somerled's kingdom in the late 14th century and for most of the 15th, until the forfeiture of the Lordship in 1493. They were Clan Donald, and the Armadale Castle estate is the last piece of the lands they once ruled. The castle's **Museum of the Isles** traces Clan Donald's timeline, from its heights as Lords of the Isles through the low point of the murder of many Macdonalds at Glencoe (page 224) to its dispersal around the globe in the 19th century. It also places the clan within the wider history of the Highlands and Islands. Perhaps unsurprisingly,

← Armadale Castle. (H0nzaM/S)

the most memorable artefacts on display are weapons such as a fine early 19th-century flintlock pistol of gilt brass and blued steel. Just over an hour away in the northwest of Skye, **Dunvegan Castle** (HH, RHS ⊘ dunvegancastle.com) has sat on an elevated rock overlooking an inlet of Loch Dunvegan for eight centuries; the Macleod family has lived here all that time. The original Leod was a younger son of a Norse King of Mann, before the Vikings relinquished control of the Hebrides. He inherited Lewis and Harris along with various pockets of land on Skye, which he bequeathed to his two sons. Despite various attempts by the Macdonalds to wrest the castle from them, the Macleods have remained, true to their motto 'Hold Fast'. Different eras from the castle's architectural development are still visible, such as the Fairy Tower (1500), a traditional Scottish castle tower with a medieval spiral staircase connecting its four floors, and Rory Mor's House (1623) – a reference to the 15th clan chief Roderick MacLeod. A Victorian mock-Gothic scheme of dummy pepper pots and defensive battlements brought a belated unity to the exterior. Like many of the best historic houses, Dunvegan is grand but on a human scale. Stories are everywhere. A bull's head at the top of the stairs in the entrance hall relates to the legend that 'Hold Fast' was the cry of clansmen who watched the 3rd Chief wrestle with, and kill, a bull. The castle holds the remains of a Fairy Flag, which was believed to have the power to turn defeat into victory if unfurled on the battlefield. The V&A attempted to provide evidence-based

↑ Dunvegan Castle. (Nataliya Hora/S)

historical explanations for the origins of the flag, only for the Macleod Chief of that time to say: 'I know it was given to my ancestor by fairies.' The North Room, once part of a block which accommodated soldiers of the Black Watch, now displays precious artefacts including Jacobite relics: a corset and pincushion which belonged to Flora Macdonald and a lock of Charles Edward Stuart's hair. Our favourite is Rory Mor's Drinking Horn, which holds 2½ pints of claret and which tradition dictates that each male heir must drain in one draught when they come of age. John Macleod, the 29th Chief, managed the feat in 1956 in one minute and 57 seconds, having 'practised considerably beforehand'.

DAY 2 While the castles of Armadale and Dunvegan enjoy enviable locations, **Duntulm Castle** may trump them both. Its remains perch on almost the most northerly point on Skye, the northwestern coast of the Trotternish peninsula. Take care as you explore, as a notice warns that 'the site is structurally unstable'. Duntulm may have been fortified in the Iron Age; the Norse rulers of Skye did fortify it. The castle whose remains you see today was a 14th-century creation of the Macleods, though three centuries later it fell into the Macdonalds' hands. Fragments of stone walls represent various elements of what once stood: the keep; a barrel-vaulted cellar; perhaps a great hall. In front of the ruins, a modern cairn is a memorial to the Macarthur clan, who were pipers for the Macdonalds during

the 18th century. It seems Duntulm is popular in the spirit world as, according to legend, three apparitions haunt the site. One is the ghost of Hugh Macdonald, who tried and failed to become clan chief by murdering his cousin Donald. Hugh went mad as he starved to death in prison, which explains the ghost's screams. The second is Donald Macdonald himself, who tries to fight other ghosts, while the third is a screaming nursemaid who, so the story goes, dropped the baby boy of a Macdonald chief out of a castle window to his death. We don't know whether the three spirits run a rota. Three miles south along the coast, a host of other stories awaits you at **Kilmuir Cemetery** (⏣skyeforall.co.uk). The road splits the graveyards and monuments into two sections, with one of the more recent and illustrious additions to the newer section being a gravestone for the designer Alexander McQueen, whose father came from Skye. In the older section, dominating all around it is the tall white cross and memorial to Flora Macdonald, 'preserver' (as the inscription has it) of Charles Edward Stuart. After aiding the Prince's escape – against the wishes of her family, who supported George II – Flora married, had seven children, emigrated to North Carolina and later returned to Skye. As many as 3,000 people may have attended her funeral in 1790. The memorial records Dr Johnson's judgement that 'Her name will be mentioned in history and if courage and fidelity be virtues, mentioned with honour.' Another grave of note is that of piper Charles Macarthur, whose son drowned after commissioning it. The sculptor concluded that payment for his work would not be forthcoming, so he didn't complete the inscription. And there's a slab with the figure of a knight denoting the death of Angus Martin, known as Angus of the Wind because of his insistence on going to sea, whatever the weather. The slab was allegedly the marker of an early Scottish king's grave, to which Angus took a fancy. Along the

↑ Kilmuir Cemetery. (Matteo Provendola/S)

road from the cemetery, the **Skye Museum of Island Life** (skyemuseum.co.uk) helps you to imagine life in a Highland or island village, as reconstructed within a small group of traditional thatched cottages. There's a comprehensive display of agricultural tools, some as much as 200 years old, a distaff of similar vintage for wool working and a smithy to see to the needs of working horses. Though working hours were long, the old ceilidh house is a reminder that neighbours would gather in the evenings to make their own entertainment through storytelling and song.

ESSENTIALS

GETTING THERE To go 'over the sea to Skye', take the ferry from Mallaig to Armadale in Skye's south (calmac.co.uk), or from Glenelg to Kylerhea on Skye's eastern corner (skyeferry.co.uk) – the latter is the last manually operated turntable ferry in Scotland. In addition, a road bridge connects Kyle of Lochalsh on the mainland with Kyleakin on Skye's southeastern coast. For island hopping, other ferry routes from Skye include Sconser to Raasay and Uig to Lochmaddy on North Uist or Tarbert on Harris.

STAYING Numerous accommodation options in the capital Portree, halfway up the eastern coast, include the historic **Portree Hotel** (theportreehotel.com) on the main street, with a bus stop and taxi ranks on its doorstep. For something different, try self-catering for two at the **Spinning Wheel Pod** just behind Dunvegan's high street. The pod is cosy and well equipped, there's private garden space and, as the owners run a local bakery, the supply of rolls, teacakes and scones is outstanding.

EATING Near Skye's southeastern tip, **Café Sia** (cafesia.co.uk) in pretty Broadford is a convenient stop for a coffee or a pizza. In Dunvegan, the **Old School Restaurant** (oldschoolrestaurant.co.uk) includes vegetarian haggis with neeps and tatties as a starter, while **The Dunvegan Hotel** (thedunvegan.com) combines local produce with Argentinian influences.

TIME TO SPARE? On Dunvegan's high street, the **Giant MacAskill Museum** (dunveganmuseums.co.uk) is a charming tribute to the life of Angus MacAskill (1825–63) whose family settled on Skye in the 12th century. Angus was notable for his height (7ft 9in) and various feats of strength; he eventually died in Canada. On the eastern side of the Trotternish peninsula, **Staffin Dinosaur Museum** (staffindinosaurmuseum.com) displays fossils and other evidence from Skye's distant past, including the footprints of a Coelophysis, the tail verterbra from a Cetiosaurus and some beautiful ammonites as well as items from everyday island life. If you travel to or from Skye by the road bridge, **Eilean Donan** (eileandonancastle.com), at Dornie on the mainland nine miles from Kyle of Lochalsh, is well worth a visit.

48 PERTH

THE STONE & THE SLAVE

etween the Borders and the Highlands, Perth has seen plenty of military and political action including Jacobite occupations. Three miles north of the city, the abbey and later palace at Scone, and its famous Stone of Destiny, played a central role in Scottish history for 1,500 years. Scone was the first recorded location for a Scottish parliament, and the crowning place of 38 Scottish kings including Macbeth and Robert Bruce, but it also has other significance. An 18th-century owner of Scone Palace made a legal judgement with enormous implications for slavery within Britain's empire.

STAR ATTRACTION

Scone Palace (AF, HH, RHS ⊘ scone-palace.co.uk) came to Sir David Murray in 1604 as a reward for helping to save James VI's life from a conspiracy; his descendants, various Viscounts Stormont and (from 1776) Earls of Mansfield, have lived here ever since. Before entering, pause in front of the chapel to admire

↑ Scone Palace. (Courtesy of Scone Palace)

the palace's most famous item: a replica of the Stone of Scone (also known as the Stone of Destiny), an oblong block of red sandstone which was kept here for nearly 500 years. Scottish kings were crowned while sitting upon the original Stone, until Edward I removed it to Westminster Abbey in 1296; it was another 700 years before the Stone returned to Scotland and it is now in Edinburgh Castle. It was through Scone's Long Gallery, which at 150ft is the longest room in Scotland, that kings walked on their way to coronations. The oak and bog oak marquetry floor has had other uses, too; Queen Victoria witnessed a demonstration of curling here in 1842. Other highlights include a series of European ivories in the dining room and the playful lions on the bed canopy in the Ambassador's Room. Two portraits hint at a family story with wider historic implications. The 1st Earl of Mansfield, whose portrait is in the Drawing Room, rose to become Lord Chief Justice of England. In a 1772 case he freed an African slave called James Somerset, preventing Somerset's owner from returning him to Jamaica for sale, on the grounds that slavery was 'odious' and unsupported in English law. The second portrait, in the Ambassador's Room, shows Dido Elizabeth, a mixed-race woman born to an African slave and a British naval officer, the nephew of the 1st Earl. When the mother died, the Earl raised Dido with his own family. It's uncertain whether Dido's presence, dramatised in the film *Belle* (2013), influenced the Earl's views; but his judgement on Somerset v Stewart helped to start the process of slavery's abolition.

ESSENTIALS

GETTING THERE Perth is just over an hour from Edinburgh or Glasgow by train (SC). Roads include the M90 from the south and the A9 from the north. Stagecoach buses 3 and 58 travel between the city and Scone Palace (⊘ stagecoachbus.com), which lies off the A93.

STAYING & EATING On Perth's Tay Street, enjoying great river views, the **Royal George Hotel** (⊘ theroyalgeorgehotel.co.uk) marks 250 years in business in 2023. **Hinterland** on St John's Place (⊘ hinterlandcoffee.co.uk) serves excellent coffee.

TIME TO SPARE? Don't miss Perth's own historical attractions. Fans of Sir Walter Scott's *The Fair Maid of Perth* can seek out the **Fair Maid's House** on North Port, and a sculpture of the maid by Graham Ibbeson sitting on a bench in the High Street. In Perth's historic Balhousie Castle, the **Black Watch Castle & Museum** (AF ⊘ theblackwatch.co.uk) tells the stories of Scotland's oldest Highland regiment. Just over two miles west of the city is **Huntingtower Castle** (HS), which Mary, Queen of Scots visited in 1565. There were once two towers here, with a 10ft gap between them; legend states that a young girl leapt from one to the other to avoid her mother finding her in a lover's bedroom.

49 ABERDEEN

GRANITE CITY

They built this city on rock and oil. Aberdeen is Britain's oil industry capital; and constructions from London's original Waterloo Bridge to the state Capitol in Austin, Texas, USA all used granite from Aberdeen's Rubislaw quarry. Hence its nickname, 'Granite City' – or, more romantically, 'Silver City', because the granite's mica content sometimes sparkles. There have been human settlements here, where the rivers Dee and Don flow into the North Sea, for over 8,000 years, and reminders of the city's fishing and building legacies are all around.

STAR ATTRACTIONS

Start in the harbour, where you may see a visiting ship such as the *Balder Viking*, standing out like a giant yellow toy against the battleship-grey buildings. For insights into Aberdeen's relationship with the sea, the **Maritime Museum** (⌘ aberdeencity.gov.uk/AAGM) is a short walk away on Shiprow. On four floors of a modern building and the neighbouring 16th-century Provost Ross's House, displays cover almost a thousand years of maritime history from the earliest days of trading, fishing and shipbuilding to the discovery of North Sea oil and gas. There are ship models from three centuries, a complete lighthouse lens assembly and a remarkable 29ft model of an offshore oil platform. Near the museum, through Exchequer Row, is the old area of Castlegate, the site of

↑ Fishing Industry Memorial at the Maritime Museum. (Adam Wrobel/S)

Aberdeen's original medieval castle. Here stands the Mercat Cross, a mark of a town or city's right to hold a regular market or fair; its hexagonal base features illustrations of Scottish monarchs and a Corinthian column with the royal symbol, a unicorn. Visit at full moon, says a legend, and you may see a ghostly unicorn circling Castlegate. A statue nearby celebrates the **Gordon Highlanders**, who have a dedicated museum in the city's western outskirts (⊘ gordonhighlanders.com). Pausing here to admire the Salvation Army Citadel, modelled on Balmoral, you can follow a maritime or a granite theme. For the maritime option, a stroll east to the far end of Aberdeen's harbour brings you to **Footdee**, known as Fittie, a charming mid-19th-century fishing village. Across the mouth of the Dee you can see **Torry Battery**, built in 1860 against a possible French invasion. For the granite alternative, walk from the Mercat Cross through Union Street and the surrounding streets to find a compelling architectural spectacle. Some buildings hail from the 19th century, such as the Music Hall, formerly the Assembly Rooms, with its splendid Ionic columns. Others, such as **Provost Skene's House** (⊘ aberdeencity.gov.uk/AAGM) on Broad Street, showcase the pre-industrial use of granite. On one corner, a sculpted effigy of a baker snarls at the neighbour whose complaints about his hygiene standards allegedly got the business closed. Also on Broad Street, **Marischal College** (⊘ abdn.ac.uk) is the world's second-largest granite building, a symphony of 1890s Perpendicular Gothic. An equestrian statue of Robert the Bruce is outside.

ESSENTIALS

GETTING THERE Trains run hourly from Glasgow and Edinburgh, taking about 2½ hours (SC); there are links from Newcastle, York and London (LNER), and the Caledonian Sleeper (⊘ sleeper.scot) runs overnight from London. Flights (⊘ aberdeenairport.com) connect to various British and Irish destinations. The nearest main roads are the M8 or M90, then the A90, from Glasgow and Edinburgh.

STAYING & EATING The historic **Station Hotel** (⊘ stationhotelaberdeen.com) is a good base. Snack at the **Union Café** on Union Street (⊘ ucbistro.com) or at **Upperkrust** (⊘ upperkrustaberdeen.co.uk) on Upperkirkgate near Provost Skene's House. For dinner, try **Thaikhun** (⊘ thaikhun.co.uk).

TIME TO SPARE? In Aberdeen's medieval quarter, the walls of **St Machar's Cathedral** (⊘ stmachar.com) contain, it is said, William Wallace's left arm. The **Brig O'Balgownie**, one of Scotland's oldest bridges, is a short walk away. West of the city, **Crathes Castle** (NTS, RHS) and **Drum Castle** (NTS) have Robert the Bruce connections; Crathes' painted ceilings are exquisite.

50 ORKNEY
THE MARKS OF MILLENNIA

E ight miles off the northern coast of Scotland, between the Atlantic Ocean and the North Sea, the archipelago of Orkney hangs above the rest of Britain like an ironic raised eyebrow. These 70 islands offer ample natural beauty and an abundance of wildlife; as many as one in six of all seabirds breeding in Britain nest here. Just over 21,000 people call the islands home. Many more, from Picts to Vikings, have settled here over the past 5,000 years, and much of the archaeological heritage of Orkney predates the Pyramids at Giza. Its greatest monuments lie on the west coast of the largest island, which Orcadians call Mainland. The capital Kirkwall is home to a magnificent medieval cathedral and the remains of two palaces, while a few miles to the south stands a moving, beautiful example of wartime art.

THE ITINERARY

DAY 1 In the west of Mainland stands the collection of Neolithic and early Bronze Age buildings and monuments which gained recognition in 1999 as the **Heart of Neolithic Orkney UNESCO World Heritage Site** (HS). It's a spectacular testament to the everyday lives and beliefs of our ancestors. Moving from west

↑ The Ring of Brodgar. (John Braid/S)

to east, start with the 5,000-year-old chambered tomb of **Maeshowe** (pronounced Mays How). This mound sits on a circular platform, with a ditch and bank surrounding it. Inside, a long passage leads to a stone-lined chamber with cells on either side. The largest stones which comprise the passage weigh around three tons. Simple geometric designs mark the walls at various points, but their meaning has been lost to time. It seems probable that Maeshowe's main purpose was to mark midwinter, with its passageway and main chamber in alignment with the setting sun for the winter solstice and three weeks either side of the shortest day, 21 December. Excavations revealing human bones at similar monuments suggest there may have been burials here. Norse travellers discovered Maeshowe during the 12th century. The runic graffiti they left on its southeast wall includes the immodest 'The man who is most skilled in runes west of the ocean carved these runes with the axe which Gauk Trandilsson owned in the south of the country [Iceland]'. Just over a mile away, on a small strip of land called the Ness of Brodgar, between the lochs of Stenness and Harray, are the foundations of up to 14 houses from a late Neolithic village, **Barnhouse**, or rather a partial reconstruction of the

houses. Barnhouse's discovery in 1984 indicated that the wider landscape was not just ceremonial, but residential, although the more complex layouts of House 2 and Structure 8 suggest they may have been more than houses. Less than half a mile away, the **Standing Stones of Stenness** is the oldest ceremonial monument in the World Heritage site, dating to 3100BC, possibly earlier. A stone hearth stands at the centre of four monoliths; there might once have been 11 or 12 set out in an ellipse for a ceremonial or ritual purpose. A further mile along the causeway stands the **Ring of Brodgar**: a henge of 36 monoliths of old red sandstone – there may have been 60 originally – with some standing and others prone or in bits, some oblong and others thin. The ring, which is about 340ft in diameter, was probably built over 4,000 years ago, as a place for ceremonies and to remember the dead. A number of Neolithic and Bronze Age burial mounds surround the henge, including the wonderfully named Plumcake Mound. Finally, six miles to the northeast on the Bay of Skaill on Mainland's west coast, **Skara Brae** is Britain's earliest known Neolithic village. People occupied Skara Brae between 3100BC–2500BC, though the earliest community may have been a few centuries earlier. Its abandonment preceded a further occupation. Today's site comprises an interpretation centre with artefacts such as dice and jewellery from excavations, a reconstruction of a Neolithic house and a path from where you can look down into the remains of eight houses. They have several features in common: a roofed passageway allowing entry into a single room with stone furniture; beds to the side, a central hearth and a dresser. The residents used deer skins and other methods to make it more comfortable. In House 1 you can also see stone tanks embedded in the sand, which the families used for preparing fish bait.

The discovery of Skara Brae's remains after a storm in 1850 was down to William Graham Watt, the 7th Laird of Breckness and owner of nearby **Skaill House** (HH ✎ skaillhouse.co.uk). The house and surrounding lands were farmed by Norse settlers and later belonged to the bishops of these islands, since when 12 generations of lairds have lived here. The austere grey exterior belies a charming house, whose contents show that many of the lairds enjoyed distinguished service records. Look out for the Russian flag on the staircase which the 11th Laird obtained while serving with the White Russians in 1919, and the enormous tiger skin in the drawing room which the current laird's grandfather brought back from India. Visitors, staff and the current laird claim to have sensed ghosts. Maybe that's no surprise given the number of skeletons here; 15 were found under gravel in front of the east porch, with carbon dating indicating they were Norse.

DAY 2 On the eastern side of Mainland, the capital Kirkwall has a history of habitation dating back to the Iron Age. Norse settlers arrived in the 10th century and today's main street follows roughly where the shoreline was at that time.

↑ Skara Brae. (Louie Lea/S) ← Skaill House. (Pecold/S)

↑ The Italian Chapel. (Paula Fisher/S)

Kirkwall remained an important trading and political centre under the Vikings and for the Scottish nobles who ruled during the late Middle Ages. More recently Orkney's strategic position between the North Sea and the Atlantic brought trade but also conflict, as Britain's naval fleet used Mainland as a base in both World Wars. There are several reminders of Kirkwall's medieval past in and around Broad Street, with the most substantial example being **St Magnus Cathedral** (⊘ stmagnus. org). Magnus was Earl of Orkney in the early 12th century in partnership with his cousin, who had him killed after a dispute. Magnus' nephew Rognvald built the cathedral in his honour, and the bones of both men are now within the walls of the choir. The use of red and yellow sandstone gives the exterior a pleasing appearance, especially in the early evening sun. The cathedral's interior features decorated headstones lining the walls, metal rings in the pillars supporting the tower, which local tradition says that Oliver Cromwell's soldiers used to tether their horses, and the brass bell from HMS *Royal Oak*, a battleship sunk in nearby Scapa Flow in 1939. The south side of the chapel contains a memorial to John Rae, an Orcadian explorer who worked for the Hudson's Bay Company and discovered the Northwest Passage. Across the road stand the remains of the **Bishop's and Earl's Palaces** (HS). This ensemble started life as a 12th-century residence for the Bishops of Orkney; almost half a millennium later it fell into the hands of the 2nd Earl of Orkney, Patrick Stewart, who added a Renaissance residence. Stewart was unpopular with his people, having a reputation for cruelty, and his eventual fate was indictment and beheading for treason. The Bishop's Palace was a two-storey building in its earliest form. Alternating red and yellow stonework

ESSENTIALS

GETTING THERE & AROUND Loganair (⊘ loganair.co.uk) operates flights to Kirkwall from Glasgow, Edinburgh, Aberdeen, Inverness and Shetland. Northlink Ferries (⊘ northlinkferries.co.uk) runs vehicle ferries between Shetland, Aberdeen and Kirkwall and between Scrabster in Caithness and Stromness, while Pentland Ferries (⊘ pentlandferries. co.uk) does likewise between Gill's Bay near John o' Groats and St Margaret's Hope on South Ronaldsay. While the public transport network is good, the most flexible way to travel on Mainland is probably by car (try ⊘ orkneycarhire.co.uk); nothing is more than an hour away from anywhere else.

STAYING The north wing of **Skaill House** (⊘ skaillhouse.co.uk) contains two self-catering holiday apartments. There are many other options, particularly in the seaport of Stromness and Kirkwall. Ten minutes from Kirkwall airport, **St Ola Hotel** (⊘ stolahotel. co.uk) offers old-school charm, an excellent breakfast and – if you get either of the rooms at the front – unbeatable harbour views.

is visible around the windows of the basement's west wall, resembling St Magnus Cathedral. A major redevelopment in the 1550s saw the building of a four-storey round tower, which Stewart adapted into quarters for his bodyguard. The Earl's Palace must have been attractive, if the chequered corbelling on the upper floor and in the great hall fireplace, and the oriel windows in the great hall, are any guide. There are plenty of gun holes, suggesting that security and privacy was at least as important as comfort to Patrick Stewart. Eight miles south of Kirkwall, across a bridge on tiny Lamb Holm outside the village of St Mary's, the **Italian Chapel** is a moving reminder of the presence of Italian prisoners of war on Orkney during World War II. The men, captured in North Africa, were here to work on the Churchill Barriers, a series of concrete causeways to block German attacks on the strategically important Scapa Flow. A sympathetic camp commandant granted the use of two Nissen huts for a chapel, which a team of artistically gifted prisoners redesigned using plasterboard, concrete, painted glass and other materials which they obtained secondhand, such as wood from a wrecked ship for the tabernacle. The interior was painted to replicate brick walls, carved stone, vaulted ceilings and buttresses. The altarpiece representation of the Madonna and Child took inspiration from a 19th-century Italian original *Madonna of the Olives*. The Orcadians cared for the chapel after the end of the war, restoring it in the 1960s with the help of the lead artist who visited from his home in Italy. Don't forget to look at the Barriers; they're one of four causeways in the archipelago, with the others linking Mainland to the island of South Ronaldsay via Burray and to Glimps Holm.

EATING Kirkwall's options include **The Real Food Café and Restaurant** (⊘ judithglue.com) inside the Judith Glue souvenir shop, and the **Daily Scoop** (⬛ thedailyscooporkney) ice cream parlour and café, both on Broad Street. The **Storehouse** (⊘ thestorehouserestaurantwithrooms.co.uk) is a renovated herring and pork curing store on Bridge Street Wynd where the confit duck with rhubarb ketchup is a knockout starter. In Stromness, drop into the **Pier Bistro and Takeaway** (⬛ Thepierbistro) next to the arts centre for a coffee and an apple flapjack.

TIME TO SPARE? Opposite St Magnus Cathedral, the **Orkney Museum** (⊘ orkney. gov.uk) provides an overview of the islands' history from prehistoric times to the present day, in a building which used to house cathedral clergy. Highlights include finds from a burial of a boat with three bodies off the island of Sanday. The **Stromness Museum** (⊘ stromnessmuseum.co.uk) covers, among other things, Orkney's role in World War I and the scuttling of the German fleet at Scapa Flow in 1919. Don't miss the **Skara Brae Buddo**, a rare Neolithic figurine; 'buddo' is a gender neutral Orcadian term of endearment.

DEPENDENCIES

51 ISLE OF MAN

THREE-LEGGED KINGDOM

This beautiful island of 221 square miles, which the anthem *Ellan Vannin* celebrates as 'green hills by the sea', lies between England, Scotland and Ireland. Although geographically it lies at the centre of the British Isles, as a self-governing Crown dependency it is not part of the United Kingdom. The Isle's Celtic inhabitants didn't succumb to conquest by Romans or Anglo-Saxons, but 9th-century Norse raiders settled in significant numbers as the island became part of the Viking kingdom of Mann and the Isles. Later, it was a bargaining chip in wars between England and Scotland. Henry IV granted the Isle of Man to Sir John Stanley, then the Dukes of Atholl acquired it in 1765. The Victorians left their mark with engineering projects and the arrival of modern tourism, which the 20th century cemented with the annual Tourist Trophy (TT) motor races. The national symbol of a triskelion, three armoured legs with golden spurs, is appropriate, summing up the Isle's military past, the perpetual motion of its engineering and motoring heritage – and its quirky charm.

↑ The Great Laxey Wheel. (tr3gin/S)

THE ITINERARY

DAY 1: From Douglas, the capital, travel eight miles up the eastern coast to the village of Laxey and **Great Laxey Wheel** (MNH; MNH sites offer free admission to NT and EH members), the world's largest surviving working waterwheel. This red and white monument to industry, which has a diameter of over 72ft, was built in 1854 to pump water from the Glen Mooar part of the Great Laxey Mines industrial complex. The deposits of lead and, in particular, zinc ore were the prize for this project; at one point, this mine produced more zinc than every other mine in Britain combined. Today you can get up close with some of the equipment, enjoy a panoramic view from the top of the Wheel and even walk a short stretch of adit (a tunnel cut into the rock face). In summer, two replica steam engines run along a restored section of track, echoing the journeys of the locomotives which hauled ore out of the mines. A replica small waterwheel in the centre of Laxey, where workers crushed and sorted the ore, is another reminder of the Wheel's glory days. Ten miles further up the eastern coast is the small town of Ramsey, the site of many conflicts. Robert the Bruce landed here in 1313 on his way to capture Castle Rushen in the south, enemy prisoners were interred here in World War II, and 1960s pirate radio station Radio Caroline based itself in Ramsey Bay for four years. **Ramsey Heritage Centre** (**f**), next to the railway station, provides further information on the town's history. In the town centre, cross the Victorian Swing Bridge to **Mooragh Park**, once a 200-acre swamp but now endowed with a boating lake, bowls, gardens, tennis courts and two cafés. A mile west out of central Ramsey is **Milntown** (HH, RHS ⏧ milntown.org), the island's oldest surviving estate. The house's dramatic white Strawberry Hill Gothic exterior, a 19th-century addition, belies the fact there has been a dwelling on the site for half a millennium. It was the ancestral home of the Christian family, whose original surname, McCrysten, hints at Scandinavian origins. Many of the family were Deemsters, the Isle's term for senior judges, and some held leading political positions. Branches of the family lived elsewhere on the island; Fletcher Christian met William Bligh when both lived in Douglas and the rest was… mutiny (on the *Bounty*). The estate was latterly owned by Sir Clive Edwards; now it's run by a charitable trust and the house is open for tours. The fumed oak bookcases in the library are full of bound copies of *Autocar*, in which Sir Clive's various cars appeared; he took part in motoring events on the island and on the mainland, including the London to Brighton run. There's some incidental social history, too, in the dining room: its 1970s flock wallpaper was sub-standard because it was made during the era of the three-day week and the manufacturing process needed a reliable electric current. Surrounding the house 15 acres of grounds include woodland, a walled garden and a kitchen garden, the latter providing ingredients for an excellent café in the conservatory. On Ramsey's northern outskirts, the beautifully preserved **Grove Museum of Victorian Life** (MNH) tells the story of the Gibb family, merchants from Liverpool, and their summer retreat which later became their permanent home.

DAY 2: On the western coast, almost directly opposite Laxey, is the town of Peel, strategically vital in medieval days, later a centre for fishing, trading and shipbuilding. It also has modern motoring pedigree, as you'll find in the **Manx Transport Heritage Museum** (⏧ manxmuseums.com). This little beauty is inside an old brickworks office which was scheduled for demolition (ironically, to create parking spaces), before volunteers stepped in to save the day. There are details and original prototypes for racing car parts, scale models of railway stock and trains and transport-related photos, maps and memorabilia from around the island. But the star is an original P50 car, 54in long and 39in wide, designed and made in Peel in 1964 and one of just 50 made in all. This was the world's smallest production car; it has three gears, no reverse and a top speed of 37mph – but buckets of charm. A few doors down, the **House of Manannan** (MNH) recounts Isle of Man stories going back over 2,000 years. The eponymous Manannan, who appears on screen, is the island's mythological sea god, capable of shrouding it in mist to defend it from enemies. Impressive reconstructions and interactive displays bring to life, among other things, the house of a Manx Celtic chieftain (c500BC to CAD500), a Viking longhouse, the Viking longship *Odin's Raven*, Peel's quayside in 1891 and a kipper smokehouse.

Facing the museum and the House across a small causeway is St Patrick's Isle and **Peel Castle** (MNH); according to legend, St Patrick came ashore here, bringing Christianity to the island. A community of monks lived here before Vikings built a fort under the rule of the wonderfully named Magnus Barelegs, King of Mann. After centuries of disputes between the Church and the Isle's rulers, the Lords of Mann, the castle was abandoned by the 18th century. But the remains of St Patrick's Church and the Round Tower (10th and 11th centuries) are still here, as is the crypt of the 13th-century Cathedral of St German. The top of the Gatehouse Tower offers great views of Peel. You may or may not see the Moddey Dhoo, the ghost of a black dog said to haunt the place. A couple of miles east of Peel, pause to remember the Vikings' greatest legacy to the Isle: parliamentary government, as embodied in **Tynwald Hill** at St John's. *Tynwald* is

↑ Peel Castle. (Powerofflowers/S)

a Viking word, based on the Norwegian *Thing vollr*. The Manx parliament and people meet here annually (nowadays on 5 July) to hear the proclamation of new laws. This national gathering and the constitution date back to the time of the

ESSENTIALS

GETTING THERE & AROUND The island's airport at Ronaldsway, less than half an hour from Douglas, takes direct flights from London City, Gatwick, Liverpool, Manchester, Birmingham and Dublin, with connections from other British airports (⌀ loganair.co.uk & ⌀ easyjet.com). The Steam Packet Company (⌀ steam-packet. com) operates ferry services from Heysham in Lancashire, Liverpool, Birkenhead, Dublin and Belfast. Some Irish Sea cruises also stop at Douglas. For getting around, the Bus Vannin network (⌀ iombusandrail.im) includes buses and three heritage rail lines: the Isle of Man Steam Railway, the Manx Electric Railway, and the Snaefell Mountain Railway which takes you over 2,000ft to the Isle's highest point. And for travel with a difference, jump on the Douglas Bay Horse Tramway (⌀ douglashorsetramway.im) for a jaunt along Douglas's seafront.

STAYING Many of the Isle's hotels and B&Bs are in Victorian townhouses, especially in Douglas. **The Devonian** (⌀ thedevonian.co.uk) in central Douglas is an excellent example, with comfortable accommodation and hearty breakfasts (we enjoyed a Manx kipper with a poached egg). For self-catering, try the cottages clustered around **Langness Lighthouse**

↑ The Old House of Keys. (Borka Kiss/S)

Manx Kings, the last of whom died in 1265. According to the earliest written account, the King of Mann sat on top of the hill, facing east, holding his sword, point upwards, in front of him. Beside him were his barons, with the Deemsters and high officers before him. The terraces below were for the 24 Keys (members of the Manx parliament), the clergy, squires and yeomen, with the commons on the ground below. The manmade hill, 12ft high, is said to have been built in the 13th century, using soil from each of the island's 17 ancient parishes. Nearby is St John's chapel, which served as a courthouse and church. Continue 10 miles south to the island's ancient capital, Castletown, and two more historic sites. First is **Castle Rushen** (MNH), a well-preserved medieval castle. It originated in the Norse period, with the fortification of a strategic site by the Norse kings, and was developed between the 13th and 17th centuries by the Kings and Lords of Mann. It's been a royal residence, a mint and a prison. You can ascend steep spiral stairs for panoramic views or admire the reconstructions: the lord's private dining hall has a table set for a medieval banquet. Roast peacock, anyone? The **Old House of Keys** (MNH), meanwhile, has been restored to its appearance in 1866, when the representatives, or Keys, who sat there passed a law to move from self-selection to popular elections. You can join in debates on various motions with a costumed 'secretary' and virtual representatives. (The Isle was sometimes ahead of the UK: women with property gained the vote here in 1881, almost 40 years before the UK.)

(⊘ isle-of-man-holiday.com) at the island's southeastern tip, or one of three apartments on the **Milntown Estate** (⊘ milntown.org).

EATING For lunch or afternoon tea, we recommend the café at **Ballacregga Corn Mill** (◉ ballacregga), next door to the Great Laxey Wheel. If you're self-catering, try a kipper or two from **Moore's Traditional Curers** (⊘ manxkippers.com), and take a 30-minute tour of the facility. For dinner, the many seafood options include **The Boatyard** in Peel (⊘ theboatyardpeel.com).

TIME TO SPARE? Manx National Heritage's other sites include **The Manx Museum** (AF) in Douglas, for an overview of the Isle's history, the Cistercian **Rushen Abbey** in Ballasalla, Castletown's **Nautical Museum**, featuring *Peggy* (1789), the oldest complete vessel on the UK National Register of Historic Ships, and **Cregneash** in the southwest, an authentic 19th- and 20th-century farming community. Transport-themed attractions include the **Isle of Man Motor Museum** (⊘ isleofmanmotormuseum.com) and **Jurby Transport Museum** (⊘ jtmiom.im) in Jurby on the northwest coast, and the **Port Erin Steam Railway Museum** (⊘ manxmuseums.com) on the island's southwestern tip.

52 JERSEY

ISLAND AT WAR

Nine times a day on the hour, on the corner of King Street and New Street in Jersey's capital, St Helier, a humorous ritual unfolds. Figurines revolve into view below the Rivoli jewellers' shop clock, accompanied by music: a pinstriped man and a businesswoman to the tune of 'Who Wants to be a Millionaire?'; a Jersey cow to 'Old Macdonald had a Farm'; and a boy and girl with a bucket and spade to 'I do Like to be Beside the Seaside'. This routine recognises the importance of finance, agriculture and tourism to the island: St Helier's banking buildings tower overhead, Jersey Royal potatoes are on every menu and tourists pound every pavement. Jersey's popularity reflects its status as the largest and best known of the Channel Islands, 85 miles south of England's coast and 14 miles from France. The island has also had to repel many invasions; the reminders of these conflicts, particularly the German occupation during World War II, form the basis of this itinerary.

THE ITINERARY

DAY 1 Start in central St Helier at the **Jersey Museum & Art Gallery** (AF, JH). The museum reveals some surprising facts: Guernsey and Alderney split off from the continental landmass before Jersey, with one side-effect being that they don't have toads and moles while Jersey does. Christianity, both from Britain and from continental Europe, began to exert influence in early medieval times,

↑ Mont Orgueil, above Gorey harbour. (Gary Le Feuvre/S)

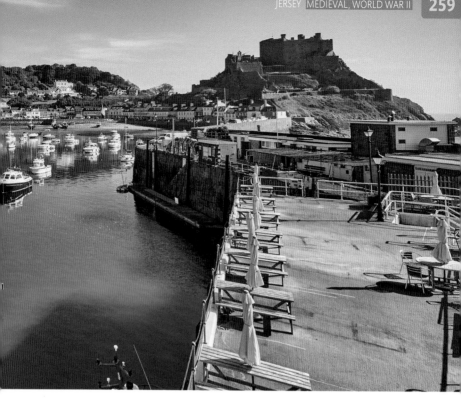

before the islands came under the control of the Vikings and then the dukes of Normandy, of whom William the Conqueror was the seventh. England lost control of Normandy to Philippe II of France in 1204, but the Channel Islands remained loyal to the Duke of Normandy – then King John – and have retained their allegiance to British monarchs ever since. Jersey is now a self-governing Crown dependency, with Guernsey, Alderney and Sark in a separate bailiwick (legal and administrative region). The museum covers Jersey's social, legal, economic and political development, its role on the front line of various Anglo-French conflicts and its language, Jèrriais (Jersey Norman French), which a few thousand islanders still speak. It also includes a restored house from which the Ginestet family absconded in 1869 when their bank stopped an auction of the house and its contents intended to pay off the family debts. You can follow the story via imaginative displays in the form of auction notices and videos of actors recreating the family arguments which led to their escape to France and a new life. From the museum, walk right to pass the **Liberation Square Sculpture** commemorating the end of the German occupation on 9 May 1945. The Prince of Wales unveiled this work 50 years after liberation; it shows a group of islanders holding the Union flag at the centre of a fountain, with 12 water jets, one for each of the island's parishes. From nearby Liberation Station, the 13 bus will take you to two significant historical sites in the east of Jersey. Standing above the charming village of Gorey and its harbour, **Mont Orgueil** (AF, JH) has millennia of pedigree as a site for defensive structures going back at least to the Iron Age and possibly earlier. Following the events of 1204, Jersey was on the front line of potential conflicts between England and France, hence the need for a castle, which was complete by 1212. It repelled a series of French attacks until, in 1461 during the Wars of the Roses (page 17), Henry VI's wife Margaret of Anjou gave up the Channel Islands in return for French aid for her husband's cause; English forces recaptured the castle seven years later. Walking around this impressive structure today, you will also see a number of art installations portraying aspects of medieval and Tudor life. Brian Fell's *Tree of Succession* in the Medieval Hall shows the complex inter-relationships between the French and English royal families; in the Southeast Tower are 12 prayer nuts (devotional objects) created by Steve Manthorp. Another, more gruesome highlight is the large sculpture of a medieval soldier which demonstrates the many ways in which he could die in battle. Two miles west of Gorey at **La Hougue Bie** (JH) is a Neolithic passage grave dating back 6,000 years. This was a tomb and a place of ritual and ceremony. You have to bend double to move along the passage itself, towards the oval main chamber, two rectangular side chambers, a platform and a 'terminal cell' at the end. At sunrise on the equinox, the sun's rays could shine through to the back of the cell, which may have been an area for the exclusive use of the spiritual leader. Medieval Christian missionaries built a chapel on top of the mound within which the passage grave lies. Today, a small museum houses archaeological and geological artefacts from Jersey including flint tools made by the first islanders. Also in the grounds, a battalion command bunker built by the Germans during World War II is now a moving memorial to the prisoners they forced to work for them, displaying heartrending quotations from those who were there at the time.

DAY 2 The 8 or 28 bus from Liberation Station takes you four miles west to the **Jersey War Tunnels** (⊘ jerseywartunnels.com), an exhibition about the German occupation of 1940–45 set in an underground tunnel complex which the Germans built using slave labour from Russia, Poland, Spain and France. The German plan was to store munitions and provide safe cover for the occupying forces, with the addition of a hospital and operating theatre in 1943 when an Allied invasion seemed imminent. In the event, the Allies bypassed the Channel Islands, so all the work on these tunnels and other fortifications was for nothing. The exhibition makes difficult viewing and reading. There are tales of privations and escape attempts; mannequins of Germans and islanders, with signs asking what you would do in the same situation; and stories of islanders who took

↑ Jersey Museum & Art Gallery. (Chris Lawrence Travel/S) → La Hougue Bie. (Johncw41/S)

↑ Exhibits at the Jersey War Tunnels. (Allard One/S)

differing paths, such as Louisa Gold who hid an escaped Russian slave and died in a concentration camp as a result, or Alexandriene Baudains, an informer for the Germans who was deported to England in 1946. Les Vautier's recollection of the crowds hearing the announcement of liberation on 9 May 1945 is simple and moving: 'I think every man, woman and child cried.' Taking the 28 bus back as far as Bel Royal, change on to the 22 to St Ouen's Bay on the west coast to find the **Channel Islands Military Museum**. This is also set in a German-built construction, a concrete bunker from which a crew of 12 would have manned a gun in the event of an Allied landing on the beach. The contents form part of one man's extraordinary collection of military and other memorabilia from the occupation years, including official proclamations and newspaper articles. Our favourite items were two examples of subtle subversion: a collection of four drawings of a pig which fold to reveal a picture of Hitler, and the board game 'Occupation'

ESSENTIALS

GETTING THERE & AROUND Jersey Airport (⊘ blueislands.com), five miles west of St Helier, has direct connections with various English and Scottish airports; the nearest is Southampton, a 40-minute flight away. Condor Ferries (⊘ condorferries.co.uk) operates high-speed catamaran trips to the island from Poole in Dorset. For travel around Jersey, Liberty Bus (⊘ libertybus.je) runs an efficient network of routes, mostly circular, with Liberation Station as the fulcrum.

STAYING St Helier's **Pomme d'Or** (⊘ seymourhotels.com) offers an excellent location, facing Liberation Square, and a rich history. It opened for business in 1837, Victor Hugo was among its guests, and German Naval Headquarters used it as their base between 1940 and 1945. The raising of the Union flag on its balcony marked the island's liberation.

EATING By Liberty Wharf near the bus station, **Meat and Eat** (⊘ meatandeat.info) serves a generous seafood platter, and the king prawn curry includes some of those ubiquitous Jersey Royals. There's a fine view of St Helier from across St Aubin's Bay in the port of that name, as you sample tagliolini with truffle in **Sorrento** (⊘ sorrento.je). While visiting the Military Museum, try the sea bass in the café at **Jersey Pearl** (⊘ jerseypearl.com), a family-run business which buys direct from pearl farmers.

TIME TO SPARE? Take a trip on *Charming Betty* or *Charming Nancy*, Jersey Heritage's amphibious vehicles, from St Helier across the short causeway to the islet of **Elizabeth Castle** (AF, JH). Helier was a 6th-century Christian from what we now call Belgium, who came to the islet for solitude. Legend says that, after his murder by sea rovers in 555AD, Helier picked up his own severed head and carried it for 200yds; a gruesome route to

which parodies a Monopoly board but with occupation-related instructions for each square ('EXTRA BREAD RATION, GO FORWARD 5'). Return to St Helier to find, in four historic warehouses by the harbour, the **Maritime Museum and Occupation Tapestry** (JH). The museum presents a highly interactive exploration of Jersey people's relationship with the sea, including fishermen, chefs, sailors and tourists. The tapestry, unveiled for the 50th anniversary of liberation in 1995, depicts life and hardship under military rule and was created from the memories and stories of people who experienced it first-hand. Islanders created 12 panels, one for each parish of Jersey, with an additional new panel about the victims of the Nazis, acts of resistance and showing how the island has marked liberation over the years. For each of the original panels, a touchpad provides links to eyewitness memories, comments from the embroiderers and points of interest on the artwork.

canonisation. A millennium later, Elizabeth Castle succeeded Mont Orgueil as Jersey's main point of defence against invasions, with Sir Walter Raleigh being the new castle's first governor. Back in St Helier, **16 New Street** (NT) is a charming Georgian house which has, in its time, housed a gentlemen's club, the Jersey YMCA and a curtain and blind manufacturing and repair workshop. Four miles north of town, in the northeastern district of Trinity, **Jersey Zoo** (⊘durrell.org) continues the conservation work of its founder Gerald Durrell (1925–95). It has reintroduced, among other species, golden lion tamarins to Brazil and pink pigeons to Mauritius. The animals' comfort is the priority and it's a privilege to watch the gossiping of the flamingos or the tree-swinging grace of Sumatran orangutans. A small museum profiles Durrell's life and work. A treat if you're nostalgic for the days of steam, the **Pallot Steam, Motor & General Museum** (⊘pallotmuseum.co.uk), a couple of miles west of the zoo, houses a wonderful variety of cars, fire engines, organs and even one of Clive Sinclair's C5s.

↑ Elizabeth Castle. (Emel Malms/S)

INDEX

Entries in **bold** are major entries.

INDEX OF PERIODS OF HISTORY

INDEX OF ADVERTISERS

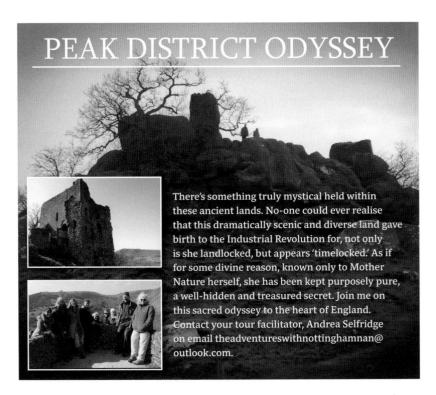

PEAK DISTRICT ODYSSEY

There's something truly mystical held within these ancient lands. No-one could ever realise that this dramatically scenic and diverse land gave birth to the Industrial Revolution for, not only is she landlocked, but appears 'timelocked.' As if for some divine reason, known only to Mother Nature herself, she has been kept purposely pure, a well-hidden and treasured secret. Join me on this sacred odyssey to the heart of England. Contact your tour facilitator, Andrea Selfridge on email theadventureswithnottinghamnan@ outlook.com.

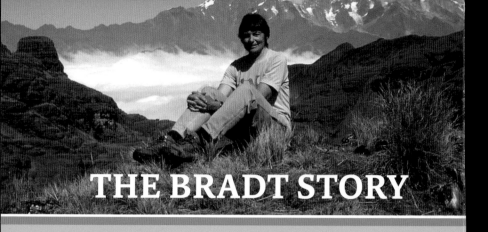

THE BRADT STORY

In the beginning

It all began in 1974 on an Amazon river barge. During an 18-month trip through South America, two adventurous young backpackers – Hilary Bradt and her then husband, George – decided to write about the hiking trails they had discovered through the Andes. *Backpacking Along Ancient Ways in Peru and Bolivia* included the very first descriptions of the Inca Trail. It was the start of a colourful journey to becoming one of the best-loved travel publishers in the world; you can read the full story on our website (bradtguides. com/ourstory).

Getting there first

Hilary quickly gained a reputation for being a true travel pioneer, and in the 1980s she started to focus on guides to places overlooked by other publishers. The Bradt Guides list became a roll call of guidebook 'firsts'. We published the first guide to Madagascar, followed by Mauritius, Czechoslovakia and Vietnam. The 1990s saw the beginning of our extensive coverage of Africa: Tanzania, Uganda, South Africa, and Eritrea. Later, post-conflict guides became a feature: Rwanda, Mozambique, Angola, and Sierra Leone, as well as the first standalone guides to the Baltic States following the fall of the Iron Curtain, and the first post-war guides to Bosnia, Kosovo and Albania.

Comprehensive – and with a conscience

Today, we are the world's largest independently owned travel publisher, with more than 200 titles. However, our ethos remains unchanged. Hilary is still keenly involved, and **we still get there first**: two-thirds of Bradt guides have no direct competition.

But we don't just get there first. Our guides are also known for being **more comprehensive** than any other series. We avoid templates and tick-lists. Each guide is a one-of-a-kind expression of an expert author's interests, knowledge and enthusiasm for telling it how it really is.

And a commitment to wildlife, conservation and respect for local communities has always been at the heart of our books. Bradt Guides was **championing sustainable travel** before any other guidebook publisher. We even have a series dedicated to Slow Travel in the UK, award-winning books that explore the country with a passion and depth you'll find nowhere else.

Thank you!

We can only do what we do because of the support of readers like you – people who value less-obvious experiences, less-visited places and a more thoughtful approach to travel. Those who, like us, take travel seriously.

Bradt GUIDES

TRAVEL TAKEN SERIOUSLY